The
Crack
in the
Universe

Jean-Claude Bourret

The
Crack
in the
Universe

*What you have not been told
about Flying Saucers*

Translated from the French by

Gordon Creighton

JERSEY
NEVILLE SPEARMAN LTD

Original French title: *La Nouvelle Vague des Soucoupes Volantes*
(Editions France-Empire, Paris, 1974)

First published in Great Britain by Neville Spearman (Jersey) Ltd
PO Box 75, Normandy House, St Helier, Jersey, Channel Islands

Distributed by Neville Spearman Ltd
The Priory Gate, Friars Street, Sudbury, Suffolk

© Neville Spearman (Jersey) Ltd

ISBN 85978 029 5

Printed in Great Britain by
Biddles Ltd, Guildford, Surrey

For Caroline

CONTENTS

PART THREE
Opinions of the Scientists Broadcast on *France-Inter*

PART FOUR
Opinions of Scientists that were not Broadcast on *France-Inter*

FOREWORD

For the past thirty years a general cover-up operation has been conducted on the subject of the so-called 'Flying Saucers', with varying degrees of success. In the United States, despite the quite extraordinary lengths to which the CIA and the Air Force were frequently prepared to go in slandering and ridiculing the witnesses of UFO phenomena and in breaking lives and reputations, the fact remains that a Gallup Poll two or three years ago indicated that no less than fifteen million Americans claimed to have seen a UFO and that 51% of the American people believed the 'saucers' to be real. So the massive campaign of officially inspired 'debunking' (the term actually used in the CIA directive of 1954) would not appear to have been particularly successful in the USA.

Here in Britain it has perhaps been another story. Quieter and more subtle techniques of ridicule and denigration, plus, no doubt, the occasional discreet telephone call to the newspaper that has offended by printing a serious looking UFO report, have yielded far better results than the CIA's methods. We may be very sure that, in 1977, the proportion of the British population who suspect that there may after all be something behind the UFO stories cannot be anywhere near as high as 51%.

This book arose out of the widespread public response to a series of no less than thirty-nine or forty discussions and interviews conducted by one of France's leading radio reporters, Jean-Claude Bourret, on the *France-Inter* channel in January, February and March of 1974, and it is one of the extraordinarily few good books on UFOs — out of the several hundreds that have appeared so far in various languages. Indeed, in one respect it might head the entire list, since it contains what no other book before it has ever contained, namely the admission, by a serving Minister of Defence, that UFOs exist and that his government has long been taking them seriously and has had a department secretly studying them for over twenty years. (Just as the British Government has!)

I will outline briefly various other reasons why the appearance of such a book is of major importance.

In the first place, France — as is well known to all who study these matters — already holds a pre-eminent position in the world-wide field of UFO research. Despite the deeply ingrained French attachment to Cartesianism and the well known predilections of the French for logic, reason, clarity, realism, and commonsense, it is an astonishing fact that, so far, in no other country have so many well educated, trained minds consented to apply themselves seriously to a study of the evidence for the existence of this new phenomenon of which mankind is gradually becoming aware — assuredly one of the most weird and, by any standards, utterly illogical and nonsensical phenomena with which, in all probability, our species has ever been confronted. French UFO research is a model of excellence and careful scientific analysis and documentation. Their two case journals, *Lumières dans la Nuit* and *Phénomènes Spatiaux*, are first class.

Secondly, this book is important because it contains a remarkably comprehensive collection of thoughtful opinions gathered from scholars and scientists, including many of the respected authorities who have devoted years of study to the UFO problem and who alone can therefore rightly claim to be experts in this domain. Interspersed among the interviews and discussions with these people is a series of chapters giving a good sample of well authenticated, detailed cases involving landings, near-landings and contacts with, or sightings of, some of the various types of beings reported to be associated with the mysterious craft. Those who read the specialist literature of 'Ufology' will already be familiar with some of these cases, but to the English-speaking public I am sure that they will come as a very great surprise indeed. And it must be borne in mind that the few cases given here are only the tip of the proverbial iceberg, a tiny proportion of the evidence now available from every part of the globe but far too voluminous for treatment in one book, or indeed even in two or three books.

Those whose appetite is whetted and who wish to know more can only hope to do so by consulting the specialized literature. So far as Britain and British and English-speaking readers in general are concerned, this means *Flying Saucer Review*, now in its twenty-second year of existence and admirably edited since 1964 by Charles Bowen. The *Review*, or *FSR* as it is called, has readers all over the world, including the USSR, where Soviet astronomers and members of the Soviet Academy of Sciences take a surprising number of copies of each issue — surprising that is, if you bear in mind that UFOs 'do not exist'.

Thirdly, Jean-Claude Bourret's book is important because it proffers a balanced view of what is a disturbing but unclear and tangled situation. Unlike so many of the other UFO books that we have seen, it gives us no saccharine platitudes about 'Elder Brethren from the Cosmos' who wish us well and are here simply to get us off the hook. (Would that more of the evidence pointed that way!) Unfortunately, the overall picture, as we know it at present, contains too many features that are conducive to far more sombre avenues of speculation. That there does seem to be some evidence for the existence, among the aliens, of a 'benevolent' faction, or maybe factions, most researchers will admit. But any sort of blanket assumptions of kindly intentions on the part of alien and unknown beings could prove terribly costly and dangerous. The UFO creatures — or some of them — may constitute the greatest threat that our human species has ever had to face. For we have already accumulated plenty of evidence to show that there are alien beings endowed with great powers of telepathic control and mental manipulation — in other words, beings capable of nothing less than the downright *brainwashing* and *programming* of humans. If this can be done to individuals, maybe it can also be done to governments and to whole nations. How long such a situation may have prevailed here we have of course no way of knowing. But, if one takes a look at human history, one may perhaps conclude that it has been going on for a long time, and it may help to explain the desperate plight in which mankind now finds itself.

Inevitably, in any discussion such as this, enormous questions impose themselves upon us, involving the whole vast problem of the origin and nature and destiny of mankind, and of our place both on the ladder of terrestrial evolution and in the Cosmos at large. It has to be admitted that these are matters that few individuals of our species are yet prepared or able to contemplate.

Another count on which this book is of capital importance relates to the scientific nature of some of its revelations. The British public has been consistently informed that UFOs *'have never been tracked on radar.'* Precisely why our authorities should be so sensitive about this particular issue of radar may be thought somewhat puzzling, as I shall show. Be that as it may, there is abundant indication that somebody in the Air Force and the Security departments in Whitehall regards this business of radar sightings of UFOs as a particularly hot potato. Many British television viewers will not have forgotten a disgracefully dishonest and 'slanted' programme on UFOs which was shown in February 1972, and in the course of which we were regaled with the

3

spectacle of an RAF officer who had been introduced into the programme for the special purpose of assuring us that any talk of UFOs being captured on radar was quite ridiculous, all such anomalies having been explained away long ago as 'temperature inversions', and so on.

In this book the reader will see however that Monsieur Robert Galley, French Minister of Defence in February 1974, has confirmed that such radar 'sightings' of UFOs do exist. And they will also see in this book the statement from one of France's top scientists, Dr Claude Poher, Chief of a department in the CNES (France's National Centre for Space Studies) *who says that in fact about 10% of the cases on file are radar cases.*

The spectacle of British officialdom clinging so tenaciously to its policy of denying all radar UFO sightings may moreover be thought to be even more odd when one reflects that, so long ago as 15 December 1967 (more than four years before our notorious TV programme) *Soviet Russia had already admitted publicly that they had radar sightings of UFOs.* For, on the date in question (but seemingly only in its first edition — maybe the editor received a phone call?) a respected and authoritative London newspaper, the *Daily Telegraph*, carried the following *Reuter* report:

RUSSIANS SEE FLYING SAUCERS LIKE PEARLS

Moscow, Thursday. Soviet astrophysicists believe most flying saucers are enormous, pearly bodies with centres like spheres. Because the objects apparently have the ability to absorb electromagnetic waves they can become practically invisible.

The newspaper *Sovetskaya Latviya,* referring to a recent sighting of a 'flying saucer' over Liepaja, Latvia, quoted the head of a space-tracking station as saying that red-to-blue colour changes which appeared in the unidentified flying objects apparently depended on their altitude.

Radar sightings of 'flying saucers' had demonstrated that some were in fact solid bodies and not simply optical illusions, the official said. Generally, they appeared on radar screens as perfect circles, and could not have been artificial satellites or meteorological equipment.

—*Reuter*

I come now to yet a further reason why British readers

should find in Jean-Claude Bourret's book considerable food for thought.

As one would have expected, the startling interview granted by the French Minister of Defence immediately received wide coverage in the French press, much of it under big headlines, and in the press of neighbouring European countries, as well as in various other countries all around the world. While we do not have on file at *FSR* a complete record of this French and European coverage, I possess clippings from many of the French papers of the following day, including *France-Soir*, *Le Parisien Libéré*, *L'Aurore*, and *Le Figaro*. We know that there were many more French papers that carried it and that we did not see. We know furthermore — we have Monsieur Bourret's statement in this book — that his historic, epoch-making interview with the Minister went round the world. He tells us that he received in due course German, Spanish, Swiss, Italian, Brazilian, and American newspapers in which the interview had been given a prominent place.

Note that Monsieur Bourret makes no reference to 'British newspapers'. For the simple reason that there were none! So far as I can ascertain, the French Minister's statement was given the full silence treatment throughout the British media. There was not one word about it anywhere, in any British newspaper or in any radio or television programme. This total blackout has been maintained until the present day. Only Flying Saucer Review *has given its readers here and abroad a full report on the Minister's statement.*

While it is true that the British often seem to take pride in their insularity, and in their ignorance of anything that goes on to the east of Calais, I do not find it possible to believe that this national trait accounts for the silence.

In 1974 Bantam Books in the USA published an important new paperback about recent UFO landings and encounters in that country. This was *Beyond Earth: Man's Contact with UFOs*, by the Harvard graduate and former Fulbright scholar Ralph Blum and his wife, Judy Blum. A British paperback edition (Corgi) followed later in the same year. In January 1975, during a visit to Britain, Mr Blum secured a number of TV and radio interviews. Before one of these interviews, he was discussing with me the important happenings that had taken place in UFO research since his previous visit here, and I took the opportunity to brief him on the French Minister's statement and the British policy of silence, and suggested that he make sure to get in some mention of it in those interviews that were still to come.

5

The next of the interviews was with the BBC (*Radio Four*) on the following morning. Among the one or two other people in the studio with Mr Blum there was one of the BBC's top scientific correspondents, and I thought it was rather obvious (as I have noticed on a number of similar occasions) that these other folk seemed to be doing all the talking, so that the guest speaker was finding it difficult to get a word in edgeways. The interview contained nothing about the French Minister's statement. At least, nothing was broadcast.

A few weeks later I wrote to the BBC's science correspondent, and mentioned the silence about the French Minister's statement, which I said I felt was surely important enough to deserve a mention. In his reply to me, dated (appropriately enough, I thought) 1 April 1975 — *April Fool's Day* — the science correspondent informed me that the French Minister's revelations could not possibly have been discussed with Mr Blum, for the very simple reason that the interview with the latter had been in January 1975, whereas the French Minister's statement had not been made until a month later — *in February 1975*. (Whereas of course it had in fact been almost one whole year previously, namely in February 1974.)

By that time I had perceived that I was wasting both my time and my postage money. If you can't win, then you can't win.

We come now to the last of my reasons for thinking that Jean-Claude Bourret's book deserves our careful attention. I refer to the curious affair of the stolen tapes. No less than three of the pilfered tapes (those containing the thoughts of the former consultant to the US Air Force on UFOs, Dr J. Allen Hynek; of Condon Committee member Dr David Saunders; and of myself) contained ideas revolving around the possibility that the origin of at least some — or maybe indeed all — of the so-called 'flying saucers' might not be extraterrestrial at all, as had so readily been assumed by so many folk, and that if we hoped to find a solution to the enigma it might be more profitable for us to seek a 'different' sort of source for them — in a sense a source that might be 'right here' ... or very close to hand. ...

Jean-Claude Bourret had broadcast all his selected UFO and occupant cases (twenty-two of them) as well as the opinions of ten investigators and scientists, before the theft of the tapes took place. Of these last-mentioned ten authorities, interesting as all their views may have been, almost all had kept to the popular assumptions about 'extraterrestrials'. Dr

Jacques Vallée however had discussed a possible 'manipulation of Time and Space' for he too has his doubts about the popular assumptions.

Now, was it fortuitous, we may again ask, that the break-in occurred when it did at Monsieur Bourret's office in the Maison de la Radio in Paris, and that our particular tapes were 'liberated' in this fashion? I venture to think that it was not.

So far as we know, the mystery of the pilfered tapes has never been solved. Here is a translation of the letter which Monsieur Bourret subsequently sent me about it. The reader may perhaps agree that, like so much else in the UFO business, this letter provides food for thought.

France-Inter
Bureau 3431
Maison de la Radio
75016 PARIS

10 May 1974

My dear Mr Creighton,

There has occurred here a scarcely believable happening, which I authorize you to publish in your excellent *Review*. My office at the ORTF has been broken into, and the recordings of various people (yourself included) have been stolen.

The accounts of Messrs Gill, Baird, and Russell were broadcast on *France-Inter* on Thursday, 14 February, at 8.30 p.m. The interview which you yourself had very kindly given to Henri Di Donna was due to be broadcast on some date after Monday, 11 March — that is to say, in the *second part* of the Programme, which was reserved for the views of the scientists and specialists on the UFO Problem.

Unfortunately however, on Monday, 18 March, a mysterious burglar carried off all the tapes which were still waiting to be broadcast. That this was an act of deliberate malevolence is beyond question. In the metal press where these taped recordings had been stacked, there were two piles side by side: those interviews that had already gone out, and those that were still to be broadcast. *Only this second pile was taken.*

Consequently, they carried off not only your interview, but also the interviews that had been given by Dr Hynek, Dr David Saunders, the astronomer Pierre Kohler, Cardinal Daniélou, and other scientific notabilities, particularly Swiss and Belgian scientists. Who did this, and why? That is the question.

However, as it turned out, by a surprising chance, and almost as though I had had a presentiment, I had already asked my secretary to make a transcript of your interview as soon as we had received it. So I still have the written text of what you said to Henri Di Donna. The only interviews that we had in fact transcribed in this fashion were yours and those of Dr Hynek and Dr Saunders. If you will now give me your authorization I shall be very happy to publish your interview in the book which thousands of our radio listeners have been demanding from me ever since this series of programmes went out, making a considerable impact in the world, and particularly so after the exclusive statements made to me by Monsieur Robert Galley, the Minister of Defence. (*It is certain that there are phenomena which are unexplained.*)

I hope you will forgive me for not having advised you immediately after the theft of the tapes, but I was anxious at the time not to give too much publicity to the affair, hoping that in this way our enquiries would be facilitated.

Unfortunately however the thief has not been identified and is still at large.

Yours very cordially,
Jean-Claude Bourret

Those who are inclined to share my own view, which is that in the so-called 'UFO Phenomenon' we are probably coming face to face with some of those forces that are described in the religions as 'Angelic' and 'Demonic' respectively, may be interested if I include a few words here about Cardinal Jean Daniélou, one of those whose taped interviews vanished. No transcript of his talk was made, and I do not know what clear opinions, if any, he had upon the subject of the UFOs. But it is worth noting that, on 20 May 1974, just a few weeks after the conclusion of the *France-Inter* series of broadcasts on UFOs, this eminent Cardinal of the Church, a man noted for his great classical scholarship, his integrity, and his courage, (he was considered by those in the know to be *papabile* — i.e. likely to be a candidate for the Papacy one day) died in Paris, seemingly of a heart attack, and allegedly in altogether strange and embarrassing circumstances. He was the author, so I gather, of a book about

8

the existence of a Hierarchy of Angels and Higher Beings in the Cosmos (I have not yet managed to see a copy of it) so possibly his views on the UFOs might indeed have been of more than usual interest. Perhaps his death, and the ensuing campaign throughout France to discredit and dishonour him, his name, and his writings, are also not fortuitous.

This is perhaps the moment to record another incident, this time not a tragic one but an amusing one. When he heard about the statement concerning the reality of the UFO Phenomenon which had been made on the national radio by his Minister of Defence, the late President Pompidou, at that date in office, delivered himself of a piece of pithy and characteristic French comment which I refrain from quoting verbatim here (although we know, on very good authority, precisely what he said.) Shall we paraphrase it in English as: *'We've already enough — on our hands, without you needing to bring in the question of flying saucers!)*

(Note that the French President apparently did not suggest that the saucers do not exist, but merely that talk of them was embarrassing.)

And indeed we are left with a question mark in our mind as to precisely why it was that Monsieur Galley should have got out of line by making such an extraordinary public admission? I have speculated at some length about the possible reasons for this and have come to the conclusion that it probably is closely related to France's obsessive determination since the end of World War II to go her own way whenever and wherever possible (as shown for example in de Gaulle's behaviour towards NATO and her go-it-alone atomic policy) and to express her independence of alleged 'Yankee imperialism' even if at times this involved betraying us all into the hands of Russian imperialism. If the USA was so anxious to clamp down on all talk about UFOs and to make everyone else clamp down on it too, then perhaps it is understandable that a French Minister might have eagerly grasped the opportunity to affirm that France speaks for herself in all things — even about UFOs.

As for the two Super-powers, the USA and USSR, there is plenty of evidence to suggest that, despite their global rivalry, there may at least be one solitary subject on which both their regimes (KGB hand-in-hand with CIA!) see entirely eye-to-eye and that is on the need for collusion in suppressing popular interest in UFOs. Once again, it cannot be fortuitous that, after several years during the 1960s when the UFO Problem was beginning to be discussed remarkably freely in the Soviet press and in their scientific and popular-scientific journals, the USSR Academy of Sciences should have suddenly silenced all discussion of such matters, and for good, with one article in *Pravda* or *Izvestiya*. And this sudden turn-about more or less coincided with the publication, early in 1970, of the notorious Condon Report, the work of a group of American scientists whose Chairman, as was quite quickly discovered, *had actually been briefed from the outset that their job was to come up with a negative answer and to rule that there was no evidence that UFOs existed!*

The position today seems consequently to be that, however much they may differ on other issues, the American and Soviet Governments remain united in their determination to damp down all interest in the UFOs and their activities, and the British are content to tag along in the wake of the Big Two. As for France, where Robert Galley is no longer the Minister for Defence, we have seen some signs of an attempt in official circles there to discount and nullify in the public mind the effects of his unwelcome revelations, but it is probable that the reality of the craft and their alien occupants of several different species is still accepted by a far larger proportion of the French public than is the case here in Britain. In this respect then the position in France resembles that in the USA.

As the human species and sub-species find themselves more and more closely beset by a host of intractable difficulties which could conceivably foreshadow our early departure from the scene, it becomes easier to perceive that maybe we men are not the masters here after all; that we have no real control over events on this planet; *and that our governments very likely know who does exercise that control.* If we will but think back to all the talk about the 'Space Age', and about 'Space Travel' that we heard and read ten or fifteen years ago, we will note that those voices are mostly silent now. Can it be that, in his hubristic venturings into realms which are not his for the taking, poor Homo Sap, as he has chosen to dub himself, has already collected some sort of a rap over the knuckles? Was Charles Fort on the right track when he mused: *'I guess we're property'?*

The question is: *whose?*

Gordon Creighton
Flying Saucer Review
FSR Publications Ltd.
West Malling
Maidstone
Kent

Postscript: I am aware that, during his pre-election campaign, President Carter revealed that he himself had had a UFO sighting, and said that, should he become President, he would have all the records thrown open for public scrutiny. I will only say that I'll believe that when I see it happen, and that I already have on my files a photostat of a letter which Mr Gerald Ford once wrote to a lady in the days when he was a mere Senator. In this letter Senator Ford dwelt in much the same terms as Mr Carter has done, and emphasised his intention to do all in his power to see that the truth be told. But after he had become President of the United States we heard no more of that kind of talk. Where UFOs are concerned accession to high office seems to have a powerful deterrent effect, so that those who once waxed eloquent promptly fall silent. So I beg leave to doubt whether we shall hear any more about UFOs from President Carter.

G.C.

INTRODUCTION

*'Just between ourselves, eh, this business about flying sau-
cers is a load of old rubbish, isn't it?'*

I have been asked this question hundreds of times. How
could a 'serious' journalist be interested in the 'little green
men'? Just for the sake of creating a sensation?

No. In order to do my job: to inform. I admit that prior to
the affair at Turin on 30 November 1973 the 'saucers' and I
went our separate ways. But on that day, while I was broad-
casting, I was handed the famous AFP (French Press Agency) telegram which first triggered off my curiosity. The
AFP is one of the four big international press agencies.
There is no need for me to emphasise their seriousness and reliability. Well now, on the evening in question, the AFP correspondent in Turin reported what seemed to me to be a totally
unbelievable story. A 'saucer' had passed through the sky
over Turin. It had been followed on radar. Pilots had seen it.
One of the pilots had even pursued it in his aircraft! Yes, the
story was indeed unbelievable. At once I wanted to get to the
bottom of it. It is wonderful being a journalist on *France-Inter*; powerful resources are at one's instant disposal. I alerted
our Rome bureau. Gerard Dupagny went after the story. You
will find his report, among others, in this UFO dossier.

It was the investigation of the Turin story that convinced
me of the reality of the UFOs, and it has encouraged me to
take the matter further. *'Yes, indeed, this business of the
"saucers" is quite true.'* Dupagny told me over the telephone
after he had completed his lengthy investigation. His words
tally well with the only answer that, since then, I have ever
given to the sceptics: namely that I don't know of a single person who has investigated the UFO business seriously and
who is still in the camp of the 'antis'. And, believe me, I have
tried to find them!

What I have found highly amusing since then is the hostil-
ity of the official scientists of the 'anti' faction. I use the term
'official scientists', for those whom I have contacted are generally the mouthpieces of science for the audio-visual media.
I recall a conversation I once had with one of them. He said:

'Monsieur, the saucers don't exist. And for a very simple

reason. Read the official American Condon Report. The Americans spent a fortune, and in the end all it boiled down to was a bunch of tales about fellows who had slept with female Martians!'

That's all that a scientist knew, in 1974, about the UFOs in general and the Condon Report in particular.

So let me now say a few words about the Condon Report — that famous report of nearly a thousand pages, which everybody talks about, but nobody has read.

First of all, we must go back to 1952. During that year, in the United States, the U.S. Air Force found itself having to cope with an ever-increasing number of UFO sightings. On July 26, 1952 eight luminous blobs appear on the radar-scopes of the airport at Washington D.C. A technical error? False echoes? No. for the Air Force radar at Andrews A.F. Base confirm the blobs. The objects are flying in an incredible fashion, at 500 km.p.h., and then suddenly at 10,500 km.p.h.

Fighter planes take off: the objects vanish. The fighters land: the objects reappear. Ground observers see the UFOs, and confirm the radar readings. The fighter planes take off again. The objects flee. Civilian airline pilots on regular routes later confirm that they saw the 'lights' flash by, vainly pursued by the fighters. This year of 1952 will be studded with many more incidents of the same kind. And the American press is full of the UFOs. A commission of experts are appointed after the alert at Washington. In January 1953, this commission gives its explanation, and concludes that the UFOs are natural phenomena. But in the corridors behind the scenes the C.I.A. has been playing its role with the commission of experts. The American secret services have done a little 'coaxing' of the scientists, in order to reassure a public opinion in which 'saucer hysteria' is starting to develop.

Why? Because:

1. The UFO phenomenon is incomprehensible.
2. It presents no danger to the national defence of the United States. The UFOs have attacked neither towns nor military units of the armed forces of the USA.
3. The Americans are positive that it is not a secret Russian weapon.
4. In these circumstances, it is dangerous to mobilize the military *telex* operators for the purpose of transmit-

14

ting UFO sighting reports, or to mobilize radar personnel and pilots, who have other and more 'terrestrial' defence tasks to perform.

Whence the official directives to defuse the UFO business. From the Under-Secretary for Air the instruction goes forth: reduce to the minimum the number of reports of sightings of weird and unwonted things. Two private investigation groups are closed down. President Eisenhower himself puts what he hopes will be the final full-stop to the questions asked by the journalists when he declares:

'The saucers exist only in the imagination of those who see them.'

But there is worse to come. With each wave of UFO sightings, the hoaxes, diversely motivated, begin to appear. A restaurant proprietor kills two monkeys, shaves them, paints them green, and calls in the press: *'See — I've killed two extraterrestrials.'* Obviously the fraud won't stand up for more than 24 hours or so, but the harm is already done. Today, in 1974, there is still talk of the 'little green men'. And graver still was the Adamski affair — a notorious hoax. Adamski claimed to have met extraterrestrials who emerged from a saucer. Later, he published his recollections of the 'historic meeting'. When, recently, on *France-Inter*, Claude Poher recalled that Adamski was a 'merry joker', I promptly received fifty indignant letters! As for the celebrated saucer photographed by Adamski's 'witnesses', it was the lid of a dish with the nipple of a baby's feeding-bottle mounted on top. Its 'landing-gear'? Three ping-pong balls sliced in half. That's as good as the famous 'poster' put on sale by a French private investigation group. It shows a 'saucer' hurtling through our skies. Pierre Guérin, who headed the investigation of this case, found what the 'saucer' was. A hubcap from a *Peugeot 404*, launched by hand into the Corsican sky.

The whole history of the 'saucers' is strewn with serious eyewitness accounts side by side with hoaxes. Whence the natural revulsion felt by a scientific mind only superficially informed about the problem.

In 1953 an official attempt was made to finish off the UFOs once and for all time by the publication of a scientific 'report'. But, unfortunately for the conclusions arrived at by the commission, the 'natural phenomena' came back again in strength in 1954. And, moreover, throughout the entire world. In the USA a new private organization was about to come into being, in compensation as it were for the authoritarian suppression of the two former ones. The new body, N.I.C.A.P. (National Investigations Committee on Aerial Phenomena) was launched in 1956. Its principal members were officers of the Air Force and a former C.I.A. official who was holding a very high post in the latter just before his retirement from it. The U.S. Air Force's consultant, Dr Hynek, began calling, from 1963 onwards, for a genuine scientific enquiry. He appealed again in 1965, and then again in 1966, in the very responsible international journal *Science Magazine*. Meanwhile the UFOs, which presumably don't care a button about petty quarrels among scientists, continued to navigate the skies.

On 27 August 1966, the officer in command of the North Dakota strategic intercontinental missile base was in a state of panic. All his communications with the outside world were severed. And yet there is a triple security system to ensure that the base's liaison with the outside is always maintained. The explanation: the base's radar had just detected a UFO at a height of 200 metres overhead. Suddenly the UFO shot away upwards at lightning speed, and the radar men lost trace of it at an altitude of 27 kilometres. Then the contact with the outside was instantly restored.

Once again confronted with the UFO problem, which this time had disturbed the U.S. National Defence authorities, the Air Force called for further investigation. A group of scientists, under the direction of the physicist Edward Condon, would endeavour, so it was now announced, to find out everything, and consequently to tell everything, about the UFOs. And this was the famous Condon Committee. Physicists, astrophysicists, meteorologists, psychologists, most of them belonging to the University of Colorado, totalling sixty in all, set to work. The U.S. Air Force at first envisaged an outlay of $300,000 for them. In the end they spent more than $500,000 on them. And for what result? For reports on 'sexual intercourse with female Martians', as the eminent French scientist put it? No. Let us be serious. The entire work of the Condon Committee was in fact reduced to zero through the revelation by two of its members that its objective was to liquidate the UFO phenomenon by selecting solely those cases that could be rationally explained. The conclusions of this faked investigation would however carry great weight thanks to the calibre of the participants. The two scientists who had leaked the facts were of course instantly expelled from the Committee. But already the full 'value' of the famous Condon Report could be measured.

In the first place, this document only studies a hundred or so sightings. Of those hundred cases, one solitary one was of a landing — and that too a doubtful one. Now what appears to be the truly interesting thing about the UFO phenomenon is the landing cases, whether or not humanoids are seen. In such cases you can indeed no longer talk of 'natural but unidentified light phenomena'. The Condon Committee studiously eliminated the whole of the 1500 landing cases known up to that date — all of them landings upon the soil of the United States. Dr. Hynek in due course refused to sign the Committee's Report when it was presented to the Government in 1968. Shortly after that the U.S. Air Force terminated its contract with Hynek.

Nevertheless the Condon Report is accepted by the American Academy of Sciences.

The supreme dishonesty of this unreadable and watered-down report of a thousand pages is its summary on the front end-paper, at the beginning of the book. Everybody has read the summary, but nobody has read the Report. The summary concludes that UFOs do not exist, while inside the Report itself one finds that 20 per cent of the cases, even though carefully selected, cannot be explained naturally. But more than that; the Condon Report contains some UFO photos that are judged to be authentic! It is true that they were taken by a sheriff, who, moreover, was not the sole witness. How's that for the 'sexual intercourse with the female Martians' and for the reliability of certain scientists? So much, anyway, for the Condon Report. Since then the UFO business has been in the hands of the American Secret Service. And what about other countries? What about the U.S.S.R. or France?

Here again we are back once more in the realm of the absurd. On 18 October 1967 the Permanent Cosmonautical Commission of the U.S.S.R. was set up in Moscow. Its aim: to study the growing number of UFO reports. Eighteen scientists are on it, and with them there is one cosmonaut. The president of the Commission is Air Force General Porfiry Stolyarov, a general of severe mien, but who nevertheless later enthralled the Russian public by showing on the State Television UFO photos taken by Soviet military and civilian pilots.

On 1 December 1967 the magazine *Sputnik* offered its readers a number of especially trustworthy eyewitness accounts of UFOs. In particular, one by an astronomer. And in 1968 another Soviet magazine, *Zhizn'*, (*Life*) published a further article on the UFOs. It was an appeal to all the scientists of

17

the world to collaborate in resolving the UFO problem.

Two months later came the final clampdown on the saucers. The President of the Academy of Sciences of the U.S.S.R. published an official statement: the flying saucers don't exist. They are hoaxes or wrongly interpreted natural phenomena. Exit the Soviet 'saucers'. And when, later, I asked our Moscow correspondent, Daniel Saint-Hamond, to investigate, he found plenty of Soviet scientists who were *pro* the saucers, but he could not get permission to interview them.

In France, the Deuxième Bureau of the Army has taken the UFOs seriously since 1950. In 1952 there was a radio station in Saigon, directed by a colonel, which was listening for them. A member of this French Commission told me in confidence at the time that they thought the UFOs were a Soviet secret weapon. A UFO did fly over Indochina in 1952. We sent up fighters after it, but by the time they were in the air it had disappeared.

When Monsieur Robert Galley, at that time the Minister for Defence (Ministre des Armées) received me in his office, he had an impressive series of sighting reports and files. The sightings were listed year by year, covering 25 years. But he also had the work done by Claude Poher, one of the rare French scientists who, on his own and without financial support, has been studying the phenomenon. You will read his conclusions in this book. I shall long remember my interview with the Minister. My appointment with him was for 5.30 p.m. on Tuesday, 19 February 1974. I expected him to give me a quarter of an hour of his time. But Robert Galley, who has always had a good contact with the press, for he is an open-natured man, kept me for four hours. During the recording of the taped interview, you can hear the clocks striking 8.00 p.m. The discussion was indeed lively. Around the table, in the vast ministerial office with its discreet gold wainscotting, there were also René Favre, technical adviser to the Minister, and Mlle. de Saint-Seine — whose brother had himself seen a UFO. After three hours of hypotheses and ardent discussion, Robert Galley granted me the first interview given by a Minister of Defence in France on the UFO question. An Interview that will go down in history, as several scientists, among them Aimé Michel, have said to me in letters.

The interview was broadcast on Thursday, 21 February 1974, at 8.30 p.m., on the *France-Inter* programme. Next day it had large front-page headlines in *France-Soir* and *Le Parisien Libéré*, and there were also important articles about it in *L'Aurore*, *Le Figaro*, and all the big provincial papers. Thus the 'saucers' were once again to be the subject of a debate between the 'fors' and the 'againsts'.

You are now holding in your hands a book which can make your mind up for you. It is a transcription of the thirty-nine broadcasts put out on *France-Inter*. Part One gives the investigations by the reporters of the French Radio and Television Organization (*ORTF*) and here I would like to thank them all for their valuable help. Part Two gives the opinions of scientists, of those scientists who have genuinely looked into the problem, and not those who say that the Condon Report is about stories 'of sleeping with female Martians'. Here then are the thirty-nine reports from *France-Inter*, together with some other statements and opinions from scientists which were not broadcast in the series, partly because we had not time to put them all out, *and partly because some of the tape-recordings were stolen from me.*

If this book could induce any official body, the C.N.E.S. (French National Council for Scientific Research) for example, to decide to grant funds so that researchers can begin a serious enquiry — the first serious enquiry in the whole world — I should of course be delighted.

France, so often in the lead in various technical fields, would bring honour to herself by taking such an initiative.

PART ONE

*Sighting Reports and Investigations
Broadcast on* **France-Inter**

EXCLUSIVE: AN ASTRONOMER SPEAKS

For this first report — here comes a shock. The anti-UFO brigade, amongst other arguments, advance this one: The UFOs don't exist, because astronomers, whose job it is to watch the skies, have never seen any. Untrue! In France, just as in other countries, there are astronomers who have seen them. Like this astronomer whom I interviewed in his observatory, somewhere in France. He desires to remain anonymous for the time being. A professional astronomer, he has seen UFOs: he says so.

●

—Yes, I've seen them, but not from observatories, which, incidentally, has always surprised me.
—*Can you describe what you saw and when you saw it?*
—The first sighting goes back to June 1960. Furthermore, I have brought with me here documents in which I have written down my successive sightings. So it is a record that is thirteen years old. For the first sighting, owing to the panic I experienced that day, I forgot to note down the precise date, but I do know that it was in June of 1960. That day, at about 9.30 p.m., I was preparing to make some obervations of satellites and also of Jupiter. I have always had a great interest in these satellite phenomena. Suddenly I saw four oblong objects appear in the sky, with a central condensation of magnitude of from 2.5 to 3, and surrounded by diffuse haloes. The objects moved in two directions; first they appeared near Altair, which at that time was fairly low on the horizon. The four objects flew from the east towards the west. Then they moved up towards the zenith and came to the level of the star Vega, which was almost at the zenith. Finally the objects flew off towards the south-west, very suddenly.
—*Do you mean that the objects which you saw did not change direction in a curve? That they made a definite angular turn?*
—That is so. It was a completely angular turn and, what is more, their formation was changing all the time. What I mean is that they were in a slightly staggered formation; but their relative distances from each other kept changing all

the time, and it seemed entirely at random, and with an absence of inertia that was quite astonishing.

—*Now, you who are accustomed to seeing shooting stars, satellites, balls of plasma, ball-lightning, and so on, are you absolutely positive about this? Were they indeed objects that could not be said to have any natural explanation?*

—Yes, I am quite positive. As you say, I am used to seeing astronomical phenomena; but what I saw resembled nothing — absolutely nothing — that we know on Earth. Our physics cannot explain what I saw; it really was extraordinary. The objects were elliptical in shape, and the angle made by the major axis of the ellipse with the direction in which they were going was about 45°. One detail struck me particularly: when they suddenly changed direction to the south-west, the angle to the trajectory remained constant, that is to say, the axis of the objects was changed to the same extent. The angle remained constant despite the change of direction. It was a remarkable phenomenon. It enabled me to eliminate one interpretation which in those days used to be given to phenomena of these kinds, for at that date I did not believe at all in the existence of such objects. There was much talk of light-beams from the headlamps of cars, moving around in the sky rather like the lights of aircraft, on a thin layer of cloud at very great altitudes. Now, on the evening in question, the sky was very clear, though one would have had to admit that there was a thin layer of cloud on which beams of light could have produced a diffuse patch. But the single fact that the major axis of the ellipse turned when they changed direction ruled out any such explanation. What I saw is inexplicable.

—*And your second sighting?*

—The second sighting was on 10 September 1960, at about the same time: 9.30 p.m. On this occasion I saw five objects, identical with the earlier ones, but this time travelling from south to north. I noted that their movement was very much faster. The duration of the sighting was very short — about four seconds. Their formation was the same, and it varied in the same way. There was no shadow of doubt about it: those objects were identical with the ones I had seen earlier. That is why, on this second occasion, I was able to note the details more precisely. Indeed, in the newspaper next morning, I noticed a report by an observer in Lyons. He had seen the same five objects, moving very fast from south to north. According to his chronometer he saw them one minute later than I. He said he could guarantee that the time shown was exact. I made a simple calculation, and worked out that the objects had travelled 100 kms. in one minute. That gave 6,000 kms.p.h. Knowing their apparent speed, as per my calculations, I was able to deduce their diameter and altitude. I found that the objects were 100-150 metres in diameter, moving at 1-2 km. per second, at an altitude of 20-30 kms. After that I had my third sighting. This time I simply noticed something at the edge of my field of vision, travelling perceptibly from north to south, as I was not looking in that direction at all. And I had the impression that it was an object of the same nature as the previous ones, but of course I am not absolutely certain.

—*In the light of these three sightings, can you try to describe these luminous discs?*

—Yes. Well, they have an extraordinary resemblance to what is called an elliptical galaxy. Namely an object whose edges are diffused without being completely hazy, with the brightness lessening progressively towards the edges. It was elliptical with a ratio between the greater and the lesser side of about 1.5 to 2. The appearance was indeed of a somewhat hazy object with a central condensation occupying about one third of the exterior dimension. The central condensation was the most marked in its intensity. The brightness and luminosity of the objects had nothing particularly spectacular about them. The objects were far from being brilliant, not in the least glittering, and, to sum up, I should say that they were not something that could be noticed very easily, especially from a town.

—*And no noise?*

—No, absolutely no noise, no trail, nothing at all.

—*What proof is there that you were not the victim of an illusion?*

—Well, simply that my father participated in the first sighting at the same time that I did. He saw the four objects coming from the east. His aim had in fact been to look at Jupiter and its satellites with me. So he was just getting ready to look at them, as I was. He saw the objects approaching from the east at the same moment as I did. He was just as flabbergasted as I was, and I shall always remember how he shouted : 'What's that!'

Edmond Campagnac is a graduate of the famed French Ecole Polytechnique. He is an eyewitness. Not a lone one either, since in fact the whole city of Tananarive, capital of Madagascar, also observed the passage of two unidentified flying objects. Impressed by what he had seen, Edmond Campagnac later became the president of G.E.P.A., the French Group for the Study of Aerial Phenomena. He has given Euloge Boissonnade an account of what he observed:

●

—It was a Monday in August 1954. The time was 5.45 p.m. People were just coming out of their offices. We were gathered together in front of the Air France offices on the Avenue de la Liberation, in the centre of Tananarive, waiting for the evening post. Suddenly a friend of mine pointed to a great luminous green ball in the sky, the colour of an electric spark, which was coming down almost vertically, just like a small meteorite. Its light then vanished behind the mountains, and everyone thought it was a meteorite that had just fallen. A few minutes later however several persons pointed out another light, also green. This time, instead of falling, it was travelling horizontally, and flying over the hills near the Queen's Palace. Its apparent size was smaller, and its speed was of course less than that of the light seen earlier in vertical descent.

—*Were you able at that moment to make out any details?*

—At first we saw a sort of green ball, and it was quite amazing. It came down to roof-height, and then went along above the Avenue de la Libération, on the other side of it from where we were standing. When this green light came level with us, we realized that it was the result of an optical effect. In actual fact it was a sort of green lens, still of the colour of an 'electric-green luminous gas', which was travelling along and, about thirty metres or so behind it, there followed an elongated metallic cigar. Its surface reflected the sunlight, and we could see that it was indeed something metallic. From behind it were coming reddish-orange flames. That cigar must have been 40-50 metres in length; its speed could have been around 300-400 k.p.h., that is to say the speed of an aircraft like the *Constellations* that used to pass over Tananarive in those days.

A curious thing was that everything had fallen completely silent. Everybody who was out of doors — and they were very numerous — was dumbfounded by the phenomenon. Everything occurred in complete silence. And another curious phenomenon which spectators also witnessed was that when the object was over a block of flats or a shop, the electric lights all went out, and when it had gone by they came on again.

—And then?

—The craft flew over the city and went away towards the airport; then it flew off towards the west, and one of the places it passed over was a park with zebu cattle, where there were about a hundred of these animals. Although the zebus are quite used to aircraft flying low over their field when coming in to land at Tananarive Airport, they were so panic-stricken by the two UFOs that they stampeded and broke down the park fences, and the Army and Police had to be called in to help round the animals up.

—Can you, as a graduate of the Ecole Polytechnique, explain the phenomenon you saw?

—It has been established that these objects are frequently linked with electromagnetic phenomena which affect electrical currents and also affect internal combustion engines. Often cases have been observed in which cars have been stopped and where human beings and animals have shown disturbed behaviour. I have had the opportunity to read reports from the *Gendarmerie Nationale*: there have been cases where craft on the ground have paralyzed people up to a certain distance from them, when the individuals tried to approach the machines. For several years now I have been studying these phenomena, which have always fascinated me. I don't think they can be of terrestrial origin — not unless there exists somewhere some civilization on our own globe which has maintained its existence in some marvellously secret place.

—Does that mean, then, that they are beings who come from elsewhere?

—Yes, I think that, on that score, if the Earth were the only place that was inhabited in the whole Universe, I would be setting myself some other problems to think about.

THE CAR UNDER SURVEILLANCE FROM THE SKY

Monsiur Villeneuve de Janti is not likely to forget his experience. It was also in 1954, the year which saw the great UFO wave over France. Afterwards Monsieur de Janti related his adventure to the UFO review *Phénomènes Spatiaux*, who published it in their issue No. 15. For *France-Inter* he tells his story once more.

●

—It happened in 1954. I was driving my car along the route nationale 307, outside Rheims, and on the way towards Masagran. I was alone. Suddenly I saw, through my windscreen, a luminous beam of an electric-blue colour, like the light of a cine projector. It gave me such a turn that I almost hit a tree, for it happened just on a bend in the road. I should explain that as I was leaving Rheims I had passed a convoy of military vehicles. My first thought was that perhaps a helicopter had flown over me.

—*Was that because the beam of light struck your car vertically?*

—No. The first beam of light appeared horizontally, so that I got the visual impact of it through the windscreen, right in the eyes.

—*So you might have thought that it was maybe a car coming towards you from the other direction?*

—Yes, but the source of the light appeared to be higher up than the lights of an oncoming car would have been. Anyway, I drove on for a bit, and then I pulled up to see what was going on. When I started up the engine again, the car was enveloped in another beam of light, this time coming vertically. I was, in a word, 'spotlighted', like an artist on a stage. This beam of light was coherent, by which I mean to say that its edges were parallel. Later on I thought it might have been a laser beam. This beam came on three times in succession. Every time that I started up the car it came on again. Each time I pulled up, it went out.

—*Do you mean to say that each time you stopped, you got out of the car and looked around, and saw nothing?*

—Precisely. In the end I parked the car at the side of the road: I thought to myself, I must get to the bottom of this. So I stopped, got out, and lit a cigarette. At that moment, I saw a shining object at the side of the road. It was not a disc, but a geometrical ring. That is to say, it was a luminous band between two circles, the centre being dark. The luminosity of it was not very strong. It reminded me somewhat of a luminous dial, like the dial of a watch for example.

—*And the diameter?*

—The diameter, according to the people who are competent in these matters, might have been estimated at about 40 metres.

—*At what height was this object?*

—About 100 metres from the ground.

—*What happened next?*

—I watched this object, which had me really puzzled, as you may well imagine. After a few minutes, I was the target of another beam of light, of the same colour as the previous one, but coming from the edge of the ring. It was directed right at me. So it hit the ground at an angle. After a few minutes the disc then changed colour, shifting towards a reddish-orange. At that moment I heard a noise which might be compared with the sound of an electric motor. But I must put it more precisely, and say that it was like an electric motor which was racing a bit, and then changing and going slower. Then I saw appear, beneath the object, a lot of sparks or tiny flames of many colours. Shortly after that, the sound of the engine died away and the craft took off. I'll never forget how that thing went, for from a stationary position, it changed to a staggering speed, seemingly without any gradual acceleration. The machine left a red trail behind it, which quickly dispersed. Then I saw little flames, shooting out and falling from it, but not reaching the ground. I went over to take a look at the field beside the road, over which it had been. I found no marks there, either of any object that might have landed there, nor any burn marks of any sort.

—*Did you have no trouble with your engine?*

—In sightings of this kind it has indeed often been noticed that car engines stop, the headlights go out, and aircraft experience disturbances to their instruments. I noticed nothing like that however. The only thing I must emphasise is that I myself suffered quite a shock. When I arrived back home, where I was heading, they asked what was the matter with me. It seems I was in a decidedly excited state.

—*Did you meet anybody else at the time of the sighting?*

—Two cars passed, coming from the other direction on route

nationale 307, after Masagran. (This road runs from Rheims to Luxemburg.) The drivers did not stop.

—*So, when the ring was in the sky, and you caught sight of it for the first time, it was motionless. Was there any noise from it?*

—Absolutely none.

—*Silent?*

—It was completely silent and motionless. I did not observe the rocking motion that has been noticed in many cases where discs have been seen hanging stationary above the ground.

—*What was the lapse of time between your seeing the first beam of light and the final disappearance of the ring in the sky?*

—About an hour. If you will permit me, Monsiur Bourret, I would like to emphasise one thing, which seems to me to be important: prior to this incident, I had always thought this question of saucers or UFOs belonged to the realm of hoax. I was therefore inevitably against the whole idea. But this incident has convinced me.

—*Did you think that people who said they had seen UFOs were mentally deranged?*

—Yes. At any rate, some of them — those who in my view wanted to draw attention to themselves by saying they had seen various types of machines performing various manoeuvres that were absolutely out of the ordinary.

—*I imagine that you are now convinced that UFOs exist?*

—Completely. In any case it is a question which now interests me very much. To revert to my sighting, I can affirm that it was no helicopter, or sonde balloon, or any kind of known machine — or at any rate none known to me.

THE 'SAUCER' PHOTOGRAPHED FROM THE FRENCH *CONCORDE*

Our UFO dossier at France-Inter had only been open for three days when an extraordinary story came through on the teleprinters. Concorde had photographed a saucer! All the illustrated papers had it in big headlines, with the famous photo.

We were to learn later that it was in fact a small cloud caused by the impact of a meteorite on the upper layers of the atmosphere. But it is interesting to re-read what was said about it at the time, in order to understand the double necessity which we have for displaying a cautious attitude towards all sensational reports, and of following up everything with a searching enquiry.

I will recall the affair for you in a few words. On 30 June 1973 Concorde was flying over Africa at 2,300 km.p.h. They were observing, from over Africa, the longest eclipse of the sun to occur in this century; several automatic cameras on the plane took thousands of pictures. But one of the technicians was also taking photos with his own camera. When one of these photos was being examined later, the expert from the French National Council for Scientific Research (C.N.R.S.) who was looking at it could not believe his eyes. It showed what one would have said was an enormous flying saucer. Three months were to elapse while the evidence was being checked: analyses, counter-analyses, hypotheses: the mystery could not be explained in any rational fashion. This extraordinary picture has, up till now, only been seen by one journalist, my colleague Georges Fabre of the ORTF (French TV and Radio) office in Toulouse.

●

—*Well now, Georges Fabre — about this photo, What does it show?*
—What is so extraordinary is in fact to see three different things on the same picture. You see, bottom left, the wing of *Concorde*, taken with a wide angle lens. You see, far off, the

31

shadow of the eclipse of the Sun, taken over Chad, because the supersonic aircraft was at that moment at an altitude of 17,000 metres and travelling at 2,300 km.p.h. High up on the right, and so in the black of the stratosphere, you see a small bright patch. A patch which, when you examine the image carefully, has the shape of what we commonly call a UFO. This photo and the patch have been enlarged. The enlargement shows an extremely bright object at its centre, for the gelatine of the film has literally been burned.* The bottom of the machine is green. There is some red at the top, and there is a storey. Above the oval shape of the lower part there is a storey, which is also black and red. The global shape of the craft is certainly the shape of the UFOs, as thousands of eyewitnesses have described them since 1947. There is no doubt about that. The disturbing fact remains however that, having analyzed the picture, the scientists assure us that this object must have been at least 200 metres in diameter. You can hardly imagine a terrestrial craft of dimensions like that.

—You have examined this photo. Have you genuinely the impression that it is of an unidentified flying object, a UFO?

—Like you, I have read an enormous number of books about this subject, and about everything that has been written *on* it, and I have even seen drawings made, not by laymen, but by scientists. It is indeed (and you can look at the photo yourself tomorrow) the shape of a UFO: there is no doubt about that. Even Monsieur Turcat, the *Concorde* pilot, who is an expert and remains very discreet — and who incidentally did not see the object when he was airborne — has admitted, without sticking his neck out too far, that it is disturbing and that it will be necessary to study it further in order to know precisely what it was.

TESTIMONY OF ONE OF THE SCIENTISTS WHO STUDIED THE FILM

—Two things remain very important for the interpretation of this picture. First of all, you have to decide the altitude of the phenomenon. By examining the image, you can tell that the object is at a higher altitude than *Concorde*. You can also, on the basis of simple reasoning, by studying the way in which the object appears in the photo, arrive at a smaller

---

* This is true on the copy of the original document which Georges Fabre saw, but it is not true of the original negative itself. In actual fact, the degree of brightness of the patch is that of a rather darkish object, normally illuminated by the Sun.

estimated measurement than 200 metres. For, in fact, while the picture was being snapped, *Concorde* travelled about ten metres. From this you can deduce, on the basis of an image of this size, that the minimum size of the object, had it of course been stationary, is at least 200 m. diameter. On the basis of the angular dimension which can be determined on the image of the object, you can say that the phenomenon was at least 20 kilometres distant — probably more. But clearly the object was not necessarily stationary; it could easily have been following the aircraft, and under these conditions all the parameters would then be different.

—*In that case the object, following the aircraft, would have been smaller than that?*

—Yes, undoubtedly.

—*I believe that this photo has been the subject of a serious study, and that all the possible interpretations have been examined. Have the following possibilities been thought of: a cloud (which would seem pretty extraordinary, at 17,000 metres); an optical effect; a meteorite; a sonde balloon, for example?*

—Yes, of course, we have considered pretty well every explanation possible for this photograph. In the first place, you can explain it in terms of a fault of photographic origin, but on the evidence it has not been possible to show that it was an image on the gelatine. We have also considered the possibility that it might have been of an optical nature, or it might have been a reflection in the port-hole, a reflection between the object and the porthole, or a reflection from the wing of the aircraft itself.

We have examined this hypothesis too, after looking at all the photographs. We thought too about atmospheric effects, very often cited in this sort of observation, such as the phenomena of atmospheric refraction sometimes termed mirages. We have eliminated all these hypotheses too.

As regards meteorological phenomena, such as those due to condensation, or even the formation of a small cloud, the fact that the sighting was made in the stratosphere, at 17,000 metres, and that the object itself was estimated to be at 18,000 metres, makes the cloud explanation highly improbable. The least one can say is that we do not at present have much information about phenomena which it might be possible to observe at that altitude in the Earth's atmosphere. We are left therefore with the most plausible suppositions: a satellite; the head of a rocket; or any of the objects involved in the recovery of a rocket head; likewise weather balloons; sonde balloons, etc. At the present moment most of those are ruled out. Firstly, owing to the estimated size of the object; secondly, because no balloons or rockets had been launched over the Chad Republic. In the circumstances, we must simply classify this sighting among all those which pertain to what have been dubbed 'unidentified objects.'*

A second scientist testifies about the UFOs: Claude Poher, chief of the Space Probe Division in the C.N.E.S. (French National Centre for Space Studies). Monsieur Poher has also studied the photograph.

—We must accept the evidence, and prepare for ever more frequent confrontations with the UFOs. Not because they are becoming more numerous, but because mankind is growing more and more aware of them and is capable of facing this phenomenon scientifically and calmly.

—How, we asked, had Monsieur Poher, a scientist, a rocket specialist, arrived at his belief in the certainty of the existence of the UFOs? It was assuredly not in any case due to the Concorde photo, which had merely confirmed his opinion. Monsieur Poher has in actual fact been convinced for several years. How did this come about?

—Well, I arrived at this conclusion because I had started out by saying to myself that UFOs were not possible. I wanted to prove for myself, by scientific methods, that it was not true. But unfortunately, after studying the UFOs for four years, I came to the opposite conclusion. The eyewitness accounts are in fact extremely coherent, and you find, in the statistical studies made on a great many of the accounts, certain phenomena that are not present in the accounts themselves. The phenomena in question only appear when the statistics are fed into the computer. My conclusion is that these eyewitness accounts are extremely coherent. And it is very probable that the witnesses did indeed see these objects crossing the sky.
—*Can you be more precise as regards these revelations which appear only after study on the computer?*
—Ah, well, it is something very specialized! You can say two

---

* The author of this statement is an astrophysicist. He has used the word *object* in its enlarged sense. (For an astrophysicist a nebula or a cloud is an *object*.) It is quite clear that the journalist however took the word *object* in its usual sense of something of solid construction. Hence the confusion which is at the root of this affair.

things. The first is that these things obey the laws of optics. The clearer the sky is, the more sightings there are. Exactly, just as it is more probable that you will see an aircraft flying at a distance when the sky is clearer. And that is something that is not contained in the eyewitness accounts. Other phenomena of the same kind also appear. When the witnesses say: 'I saw something go over; it was raining', they do not know that, statistically, there will be ten times fewer other witnesses when it is raining that when the weather is fine.

—*Monsieur Poher, how long have you been interested in the UFOs?*

—Going on for about four years now.

—*How many cases have you studied?*

—Oh, I have studied personally several hundreds. In fact I have read thousands of sighting reports by eyewitnesses. That takes a lot of time.

—*And you are in communication, I believe, with other scientists at the international level?*

—Yes, many foreign scientists have also been studying this problem. In France, we exchange our impressions, our reports, so as to try to make a little progress in the subject.

—*To how many countries does your network of contacts extend?*

—Basically, to the countries where French and English are spoken, as I can only use these two languages.

—*Is it your conclusion that UFOs have been seen in every country in the world?*

—Yes, I am absolutely certain of it. Every country in the world is involved. Of course, in order for an eyewitness to make himself known, he has to be able to communicate. Thus, the countries which have lots of newspapers, radios, chains of television stations, etc., are better placed in this respect. But even in those regions of the world where there are absolutely no communications at all, you will find natives, for example, who have observed phenomena of precisely the same kind.

THE *CONCORDE* SAUCER:
REJECTED BY THE COMPUTER

At the time of our discussion on the previous day, I had not seen the famous photo of the giant saucer. As soon as it appeared on the TV screen, I exclaimed: 'But that's no saucer, it's a cloud'. Indeed, you can make out, quite clearly, gaseous protuberances on the pseudo-UFO photograph. We had in fact been a bit over-hasty in this affair; nevertheless we were also the first to state the true facts of the case when two eminent scientists joined us in our round-table discussion, Pierre Guérin, astrophysicist, Principal Research Officer with the C.N.R.S. (French National Council for Scientific Research), and Claude Poher, Head of the Space Probe Division of the National Centre for Space Studies.

●

—I have known about this photo for several months, as they were good enough to pass it to me for my information, and I did not personally attach any great importance to it. Moreover I have recently carried out on the photo the usual tests that apply to sightings of this kind. And the information system of the computer refused to accept it as a UFO sighting, since there are other possible explanations in this sort of sighting, such as you will not find with better photos.
— *You said, Claude Poher, that the computer rejected this photo. Could you please be a bit more precise on this?*
—It is rather complicated. In fact a certain number of tests enabled us to verify, in a purely impersonal fashion, that the sighting could not be explained in any plausible manner. These tests are quite independent of any passion that one might personally feel for *Concorde*, for the eclipse, or for the team of scientists. These tests are purely mathematical. The results are calculated in terms of the chances there are of our being able to explain the phenomenon or not being able to explain it. The computer refused to digest this test in the list of sightings, considering its strangeness and credibility ratings as not first class.
— *So the computer has rejected this photo, affirming, as it*

were, that this is no UFO?

—Not at all. It rejected the operation because the criteria that enable it to select out UFOs were not fulfilled. In particular, it is not at all impossible that light may have got into the camera, either before or after the photo was taken. We have no visual confirmation of the phenomenon at the moment when it was photographed such as would enable us to affirm that the object and the background were photographed at the same time. And then again, the quality of the photograph (its value as testimony) is itself very weak in relation to the total documentation that we already possess on the subject of UFOs.

—*Pierre Guérin is with us here in the studio in Paris. Pierre Guérin, you too have seen the photo — in exceptionally good conditions for examining it. What do you think?*

—Yes, I have seen the original negative. I have also seen copies, because it was I who made them in the first place and sent them to Poher in Toulouse, so that he might verify whether or not there had been any rocket launchings or any of the classic phenomena capable of accounting for this image on the film. The result of Poher's enquiries was that no rocket, no parachute — a parachute opens at a lower level than that — can explain the phenomenon. And then again, from the astronomical point of view, I can state categorically that (contrary to what was said at the Nice Observatory) no planet could account for the phenomenon, because the apparent diameter of the image was much too big for it to have resembled any planet. That is how the matter stood, and, like Monsieur Poher I had reached the very firm conclusion that this photo did not necessarily have to be of a UFO and that is why — and I have said this time and time again — I was absolutely opposed to the idea of this photo being put out on the television and being taken seriously by people. Some journalists happened purely by chance to get hold of it. The mistake they made was to take any notice of it, and to question the man who took it, or one of the friends of the man, in order to wring from him statements which have snowballed, to the great regret of the parties concerned. They found themselves in a totally impossible situation yesterday morning, as though they had said the photo was of a UFO, when *nobody* either at the Astrophysical Institute or among the astronomers, had said any such thing.

To sum up, then, we cannot even say any longer that it was an object. And I must tell you frankly that neither Poher nor I were in any way responsible for this photo being published.

—And what do you say, Claude Poher?

—I share Guérin's view entirely, and I can tell him that I too had no hand in it. A team of reporters were making a study of the Kohoutec Comet, and discovered, through certain rumours, that this photograph existed, and this is how the whole affair has been blown up to vast dimensions. The fact is that of course folk ought not to make so much out of this sort of thing. The emotion has got to be taken out of the debate about the UFOs.

—This seems to me to be a very serious matter, precisely at this moment when France-Inter *is beginning on its scientific dossier on the problem of the UFOs. All those who have not studied this problem — and Heaven knows there are plenty of them — and who have no opinion about it (either that the UFOs exist or that they don't exist) will certainly have every right to say: just look at these UFO stories — the UFOs don't exist. Or, if they do believe in the existence of UFOs, they will find themselves in a difficult situation.*

—Why, yes — absolutely so.

THE UFO THAT LIKED TRACTORS

Colonel Pierre Berton, is a very likeable officer. He expresses himself with ease and precision. He is frank and open. For this reason he takes an interest — in a private capacity — in the UFO phenomenon. He is one of the G.E.P.A. investigators. They asked him to enquire into the La Chapelle affair, which took place in the Département of Lot-et-Garonne. It was at 1.00 a.m. in the early hours of 14 November 1971.

●

—I went to see the officer of the Gendarmerie at Marmande, who thereafter accompanied me to the site, together with the commandant of the local Gendarmerie Brigade. Both of them told me that the farmer who had seen the flying object was a serious fellow, reliable, a good citizen, and of perfectly sound mind. This was, therefore, a good indication.

So we went to see Monsieur Angelo Cellot, who runs a farm. He related to us the following facts.

On the evening of 13 November, after dinner, at about 9.00 p.m., being a bit behind with his work, Monsieur Cellot decided to go and plough a field of four hectares or so. This big field lies beside a small local road. It is all sloping. At the bottom end it is bounded by a small brook, and at the top by the road, and by hedges on each side. So he started ploughing at about 9.00 p.m., and he carried on working till about one o'clock in the morning. By that time he had almost finished the field. As he was going to and fro along his furrows, he arrived at the top end of the field where the road is, and as he made his turn and began to face down towards the bottom of the field again (about two kilometres across) he perceived a light. He told me he thought it was a neighbour who, like himself, was doing some night-ploughing. But in fact when he reached the other end of the furrow, at the bottom of the field, and he was once more making his turn, he realized that the light wasn't on the ground at all as he had assumed, but in the air. He thought he saw lights, like headlamps, shining down vertically and, on one of the sides, a small red light. He thought it must be an aeroplane or a helicopter. Owing to the noise made by his tractor, he did not pay too much attention to it. Incidentally, I must point out that his tractor is fitted with headlights at both front and rear. This enables him to keep an eye on his ploughshares. And a swivel-lamp also provides against trouble. So he set off once more up the slope of the field and then, all of a sudden it seemed as if it were broad daylight. He looked around. And he observed, we will not say an 'object', but lights, with no well defined contours, right overhead. He could see all around him just as if it were in the middle of the day.

—*How high were the lights?*

—Monsieur Cellot thought they were at about fifty metres.

—*Was there any sound?*

—He heard no sound, but, as I have just said, the sound of his own tractor would have blotted out any other sound for him. It was at the top end of the field, near the houses of the village, that he had the unpleasant surprise of seeing this machine, with its lights, coming straight down, right over him. Not having been frightened up till that moment, he had thought it was an aeroplane or a helicopter, he now panicked suddenly at the sight of this machine coming lower and lower. He left his tractor with the engine still running and the lights on. He ran towards his brother's house, a few hundred metres distant. When he had covered some thirty or forty metres in a fast dash despite his Wellington boots, he turned round, and saw five lights, seemingly parallel. These lights had descended to about ten metres above his tractor, still as visible to him as in broad daylight, and the lights were now stationary. Still with no sound. The only noise he could hear was the tractor engine. He now stopped, for his first thought in running away was to go and get help and also another witness. But a few seconds later the machine began to rise again.

—*How did he describe this machine to you?*

—There were four or five lights, according to Monsieur Cellot, who, seeing the machine rising again, recovered his nerve sufficiently to start gradually moving back towards the spot as the machine rose. It went up to about fifty metres or so, and began to move away along the same flight path by which it had come. By now he was back at his tractor. He switched off the engine and the lights, and still heard absolutely no sound coming from the object. He detected no odour and no effects upon himself. The UFO, which had continued to climb, was by now over the little stream lower down the field. Then, while he stood there watching, it suddenly accelerated in staggering fashion and was gone in a few fractions of a second.

Was Monsieur Cellot the victim of a hallucination? Colonel Berton went on with his investigation. Now, it so happened that, fifteen kilometres from there, someone else also saw a flying object that night.

—This person told me that his sighting was much more blurred, for the object was not vertically above the point from which he saw it. This second eyewitness was also a peasant. He too was engaged in night-work, in a little village on a hilltop from which one can see for a long distance. He told me that he saw something bright, without being able to tell very clearly what it was, owing to trees which were in the way. Then he went up to his father's house in the village on the top of the hill, and to his surprise beheld a machine which was moving about, sailing to and fro several times, quite distinctly, above the horizon.
—*So in a way this is a confirmation of the account given by the first eyewitness, Monsieur Cellot?*
—Yes indeed it confirms the first account.
—*What is your personal impression, Colonel. Were those folk just spinning yarns?*
—Oh no, not at all. Those peasants saw something. I am not a scientist. I do not know much about these questions, but I am not in the habit of attributing importance to stories that are devoid of much detail. Monsieur Cellot has told his story several times, to the Press, to the Gendarmerie, and to an investigator, who, incidentally, made a tape-recording of his statement. Each time he told it with the same precise details. Monsieur Cellot is a reliable man. So he did not tell a parroted tale. He was the witness to an extraordinary event, which he has reconstituted to the best of his ability.

THE SQUARE UFO AT BOLAZEC

On 16 January, Monsieur Eugène Coquil, a carpenter of honourable reputation, was driving home in his car from Callac. The night was fine. It was 4.00 o'clock in the morning. The witness describes his adventure to René Pleïbert, a journalist in the Brest office of French Radio and Television (ORTF).

●

—*You live near Morlaix at present?*
—Yes, five kilometres from Morlaix.
—*That was eight years ago when it happened. How old were you then?*
—Twenty-three.
—*You weren't married?*
—Not yet.
—*Now you are a married man, and father of a family?*
—Yes, I have two children.—*What is your occupation?*
—Carpenter.
—*Does this event, which dates back eight years, still remain vivid in your memory?*
—Yes, I remember it as if it were yesterday.
—*You were in your car?*
—Yes, a *Dauphine*.
—*Where were you going?*
—I was going home. It was about 4.00 o'clock in the morning. It was in the hills on the border between the Départements of Côtes-du-Nord and Finistère. I had taken the Callac road, leading to the road to Bolazec. I was one kilometre from the town. I was driving along peacefully, and suddenly I saw a light in a field.
—*What was your first thought?*
—A tractor with engine trouble. It was a kilometre or so from me, so all I could see was some lights ...
—*And then?*
—I came to the cross roads. I took the Bolazec road. When I had done about four hundred metres or so, I said to myself: 'you must stop and see what it is.' I got out of the car. It was bright moonlight. Bright as in broad daylight. [In fact the moon had only just risen, it was very low on the horizon, and

42

the witness could have mistaken the glow from the UFO for moonlight.] I took a few steps into the little field. And suddenly I saw a light coming from a machine which was travelling up the slope.

—*What colour was the light?*

—I couldn't define the colour all that well. But light was coming from its four corners — a very visible light. It was like the rear lights of a *Peugeot 404*.

—*Do you no longer remember the colour of the lights?*

—No. But it was like neon tube lights. In my opinion, 'they' no doubt were using it to guide them.

—*Did you see anything else besides these lights?*

—Yes. It seemed to me that there were portholes and that they were changing colour.

—*Where?*

—About half-way up the side of the machine.

—*You saw straight away of course that it wasn't a tractor?* (A laugh from Monsieur Coquil).

—Yes, that's for sure!

—*What did this machine look like?*

—It was at least as big as two cars.

—*Did the machine come towards you?*

—No. Towards my car. I had left the car at the side of the road, with all my lights on. You could have said the machine was heading towards my car to see what it was. I myself was at least a hundred metres from the car.

—*Then what did you do?*

—I went back towards the car too! I kept turning round to look at the machine, wondering to myself: what on earth is it? It was moving along quite slowly, maybe at five or six kilometres per hour, or maybe ten, shall we say, but no more than that.

—*Did it make any noise?*

—No, none at all.

—*What was the shape of the machine?*

—It was square. It was about 3½ metres by 3½ metres. And about 1 metre 30 centimetres high.

—*Did you go at once to your car?*

—Indeed yes. For I didn't want to remain there!

—*Were you worried?*

—Oh, certainly I was worried ...

—*What happened when you reached the car?*

—Well then, as I say, I was returning to the car, looking back all the time to watch the machine but not stopping. And we both got to the car at about the same time, more or less. I got into the car. I shut the door. I peered out through the windscreen. And saw the object right above me.

—*At what height?*

—Not even three metres!

—*Could you perhaps have touched it?*

—Pretty well. It was about as high up as a ceiling, say about two-and-a-half or three metres or so.

—*Did you have any urge to touch it?*

(Monsieur Coquil laughs).

—Oh no, no, no! How could I have done? I was inside the car, and even if I had wanted to, I wouldn't have been able.

—*What did you really want to do?*

—To get away.

—*And that is what you did?*

—No, not at first, because I couldn't.

—*Why not?*

—Because I stalled the engine three or four times.

—*Due to emotion?*

—Well, yes, I suppose so.

—*It wasn't the car itself?*

—No, no. It was me!

—*Were you scared?*

—Oh, yes!

—*And what was the machine doing during all this time?*

—I watched it land, four or five metres from me. It was just the width of the road. It came down very softly. In fact it didn't actually quite land. It remained at less than fifty centimetres from the ground — at the height of the top of the grass.

—*And then?*

—Well, all this time I was still trying to start up the engine, but too panic-striken to succeed. After the machine had landed, I still remained there for half-a-minute or so before I managed to start up. Then I just went. I looked in my driving mirror and could still see the thing there. It was about fifty metres in a straight line from there to the bend in the road. . . .

—*And so you got home. Did you speak about it at once to anybody?*

—No. I was afraid of being taken for a madman. I didn't even mention it the next day. It was only on the Monday morning, two days later, when I spoke about it to a baker from Carré. He told the Town Hall. That's how the business became known. But I hadn't intended to talk about it.

—*Did you go back to the spot next day, when it was light?*

—No. I had no desire to go and look. I was still uneasy.

—*Was an investigation started?*

—Yes, the Gendarmes and the press. A brigade of Gendarmes was sent over from Quimper.

—*Were you told the results of that enquiry?*

—No. Never.

—*But on that astonishing night, when you were back home after having seen the machine, what was in your mind?*

—Well, I didn't know at all. I was so upset....

—*But did you imagine all the same that it was something quite extraordinary?*

—Oh yes! That wasn't a helicopter or an aeroplane; it made no noise....

—*Did you have the idea that it was a machine from another world?*

—I wasn't reading any novels at the time, and I didn't have any ideas about anything like that.

—*Had you ever heard people talking about flying saucers?* Vaguely — on the television. But it didn't interest me.

—*That night, you suddenly came face to face with this phenomenon: you could even have touched it?*

—Yes, surely.

—*So you weren't dreaming?*

—Oh no, not in the least!

—*You hadn't just come from a party?*

—No. And incidentally I have a witness, my wife. At the time, we were engaged. We had spent the day and part of that evening together. I had left her at half-past-three. I had been at her house, with her and my future 'in-laws', chatting for four hours beside the fire. And we hadn't even drunk a glass. Everyone who saw me that day at Bolazec has confirmed that I was in a perfectly normal state.

—*And what do you think about your adventure now?*

—People are telling me all sorts of things now. Lots of other witnesses have seen machines. I simply hope that one day we'll know the answer....

Shortly before this interview with the first-hand witness, I had met one of the G.E.P.A. investigators who had also interrogated this witness, at the time of the occurrence. It has been interesting to compare the account given by the witness himself and that given by the investigator. It has enabled me to confirm that, down to the smallest detail, Monsieur Gestin of G.E.P.A. gave a faithful report of the facts. That is important, because the scientists depend partly on reports of this sort when they have not the time to go themselves and make an investigation on the spot.

—On 16 January 1966, Monsieur Eugène Coquil, a carpenter, is returning by car from Callac. It is four o'clock in the morning. The night is very fine. Arriving near his home village, he perceives, in a hollow in a field, near a clump of bushes, a very vivid red light. Astonished, he thinks that, despite the late hour of the night, it must assuredly be a tractor that has broken down. Arriving at a point level with the light, he leaves his car and walks towards the light. After going some 200 metres or so, he sees a machine coming up the field at a height of three metres off the ground. Obviously, Monsieur Coquil is surprised. He told me that the light from the machine was so bright that he could have driven without using his own carlights at all.

The machine comes up as far as his car, which is standing with its lights still on. It is at this point that Monsieur Coquil is seized by panic. He asks himself what can possibly be happening, and what this machine is. He makes a dash for his car, where he has a shotgun (every peasant is a bit of a poacher on the side.) Obviously, however, by the time he gets to the car he is no longer thinking of his shotgun as a means of defence. He is thinking of flight. For, just as he reaches the car, the machine, a sort of dark mass of about the size of two *Dauphine* cars and about 1.20 m. high, comes and takes up position between his vehicle and the telephone lines flanking the road. The machine remains there stationary, without a sound, emitting from its corners a very harsh red light, similar, he says, to the rear lights of a *Peugeot 404*. He quickly gets into his car. He stalls the engine several times, so great is his fear, and he has only one thought: to get away from there as quickly as possible. At the precise moment when he moves off, the machine too moves, and now takes up a position on the other side of the road, about ten metres from him and just off the ground, at the height of the tops of the fairly tall grass growing there. He is so frightened that he finally 'gets away on his hub-caps' as the French saying puts it.

—*Were any marks found at the spot where the machine had been?*

—I put this question to Monsieur Coquil, who replied that it had snowed on the following day, and that he had not gone out there to look. I went there myself, a month after the incident, but it was too late to find anything.

—*Did he tell the Gendarmerie about it?*

—It was the secretary at the Town Hall who was the first to know of the incident, and who informed the Gendarmerie. The gendarmes questioned Monsieur Coquil. After that, everybody knew about it. I would like to emphasise that Monsieur Coquil is a responsible sort of man. He is not trying to draw attention to himself by telling this story.

THE AFFAIR AT TURIN

Here now is the famous case at the International Airport at Turin, in Italy. It occurred on 30 November 1973. This is a case in which it is difficult to speak of 'collective hysteria': the UFO was seen by two professional pilots, and a third pilot chased it on orders received over his intercom. The airport's radar detected it. Scores of eyewitnesses saw it, even inside the airport itself. Gérard Dupagny, *France-Inter*'s correspondent in Rome, spoke to Captain Mezzelani first.

●

—About seven minutes before the termination of Flight No. 325 of our *Alitalia* machine, the control-tower informed me that an unknown object, emitting a very big light, was on my flight path. I looked around the sky, and so did my second pilot, but we saw nothing. We were then flying at about 2,000 metres. At two minutes from landing time, and at an altitude of 300 metres, we suddenly saw a very big light over Turin. This light was of a bluish-white colour.
—*Did it change colour?*
—No. I can't say how far off the light was. However, I think it was at about 15° to 20° above the horizon. This light was very large, and was certainly nothing known. So far as I am concerned, it could not have been either a satellite or a star, or even a balloon. I had never seen anything like it.
—*Was the weather fine? Were there no magnetic storms around?*
—No. None at all. The instruments indicated nothing abnormal, and the sky was clear. Turin control-tower had told me that they could see the UFO on their radar screens. They said they could see something approximately the size of a *DC-8* or a *Boeing 707*. I can't estimate the size of the thing. All I saw was a light, very big and very bright.
—*And what about your instruments on board? Did you notice any effects?*
—No. Absolutely nothing. Everything was normal. After landing, we went to the Terminal and we could still see the light. By then it was smaller. I think it must have moved, going off towards the south-west. At the Terminal, the captain of another *Alitalia* flight, No. 043, confirmed that he too had seen a very big light over Turin. And finally another pilot, in

a *Piper*, had a very good view of the light and tried to follow it, with the help of the radar.

—*Did the Turin Airport radar have the object on their radarscopes for long?*

—Yes. They watched it for a long time, and they confirmed that it was of the size of a *DC-8*. On the other hand, I was told nothing about the speed of the object. The radar specialists have told me that it was not moving on a straight course or in curves, but as it were in a zigzag.

—*Did the passengers in your plane see the object?*

—No. I didn't say anything to them, but I don't think they saw anything.

—*You have had many hours of flying. Is this the first time that you have seen a phenomenon of this nature?*

—Yes, it's the first time of this kind.

—*Well, Captain, what is your opinion about it?*

—At the time, I did not think about it. Reflecting on it now, I don't reject the hypothesis that it was a flying saucer.

The second report — an exceptional piece of testimony — comes from Riccardo Marano, a pilot. He is surely one of the very few who can boast that they have pursued a UFO on orders received over their radio!

Here is his statement:

—Along with pilots of other aircraft, I was waiting for permission to land at the Airport. I heard the Control Tower warning an aircraft, which was just about to land, that an unknown flying object was at about 1,200 metres not far from where we were due to touch down.

—*So the Turin Airport radar people told you of the presence of this object?*

—Yes. A controller in the Tower warned us. The radar had got an object on their screens. Then I requested permission to contact the Airport with a view to changing my course and getting near the object so as to see what it was. I received permission. The radar gave me the course to take for approaching the object. As I was nearing it, the radar people told me it was moving. and was heading for the Val Suza. So I changed course. But suddenly the radar told me that they had lost it from their screens. I searched the sky, to see if I could spot it with the naked eye. Just at that moment, another aircraft, which had just taken off, told me that the object was behind me, at 3,600 metres. I was then at about 3,000 metres. I immediately started to turn, and saw ahead of me an object which looked like an intensely luminous, very white sphere. Its light kept fading and then increasing again; it never went out. Only its brightness varied. The object was at a slightly higher altitude than my own aircraft, so I started to climb to the same height so as to get near it. While I was climbing I had the clear impression (my controls confirmed this) that the object was rising and falling in front of me. Taking advantage of a moment when it was below me, I dived, accelerating to over 400 km. per hour. But I could not catch up with the object, for it drew further and further away from me, putting on speed as I put on speed. The machine made off towards the south, and I tried for several minutes to follow it. Then, owing to my short radius of action, I had to turn back towards the Turin Airport.

—*How long did your pursuit last?*

—From the moment when I first saw the object till the moment that I got near to it: seven or eight minutes. The alert was given at 7.00 p.m., and you could say that the apparition in the sky over Turin lasted some 15-20 minutes.

—*What was the colour of the object?*

—An intensely white colour, like the light of a neon tube.

—*Are you equally sure that the object changed speed?*

—Yes, it changed speed. By how much? I couldn't say. What is certain however is that its speed was greater than mine, as I wasn't able to catch up with it.

—*Could it have been a sonde balloon?*

—I rule that out absolutely — for a sonde balloon can't move at over 400 km.p.h.

—*Could it have been an ultra-secret military prototype?*

—That I cannot say. It was an object which was probably piloted, for it moved about in all directions. The manoeuvres it performed gave me that impression. But I couldn't swear to it.

The third account of the Turin affair is from a technician at the Turin Airport. He has preferred to remain anonymous. What he is going to tell us is of capital importance: the radar too detected the UFO.

—A very powerful white light was stationary in the sky at about 1,000 metres over Turin Airport on 30 November 1973.

—*Did you see the object moving about in the sky?*

—No. But many of my colleagues saw it, and followed its movements. I returned to my office, and heard the conversation between the pilots of the three airborne planes and the Control Tower.

—How long did the object remain over the Turin Airport?
—About forty-five minutes.
—Did the object change colour?
—I only saw it as white. I followed on the radio the conversations of the pilots who saw another colour.
—What colour was that?
—Blue, I think.
—What was your impression when you saw this 'thing' in the sky?
—I don't know. I don't think it was a normal aircraft. Perhaps a prototype?
—Did the radarscope register the presence of the object?
—Yes. The radar operators saw it on their instruments. Here there are no instruments adapted for that, but I heard that the people in the Control Tower could see it clearly on their radarscopes. It was as big as a four-engined jet plane.

Finally, we come now to the last of the reports on the affair of 30 November 1973 over Turin, by Franco Contin. Signor Contin is an amateur photographer. On the evening in question, 30 November, but earlier, he had taken photographs of a 'star', the behaviour and shape of which were truly peculiar.

—I was walking along, and I saw an object which resembled a star. It was 5.00 p.m. The sky was very clear, and I saw this star — extremely bright. I looked at it, and I was surprised, for it began to move about. It looked like a slightly misshapen luminous globe.
—What colour was it?
—It was white at first, and then suddenly turned to a deep orange. It was following a vertical course. At times it made zigzag movements. Twice I saw it make step-like movements.
—Was its speed regular, or did it vary?
—The object altered speed. It moved slowly, or at high speed.
—Was the machine piloted?
—I think it was steered.
—Do you believe in the extraterrestrials?
—Yes.
—Did you hear any sound of an engine?
—No. The machine was silent.
—Could it have been a sonde balloon?
—No. I have seen sonde balloons in the air; they do indeed make circuitous movements, but never at 90° angles.
—Was it moving faster than a jet aircraft?

—Yes, I think so.

—*Is it true that several days later some Italian fighter planes came and patrolled over the Val de Suza?*

—Yes, formations of fighters did patrol there.

—*For how long did you observe this object?*

—For a total of some 15-20 minutes.

—*The first time you saw this object you were with your fiancee, and you went home to get your camera in order to take these fantastic pictures which the papers have now published?*—Yes, that's right. I only managed to get one photo at first, because the object then disappeared from sight. Then I went up on the mountain and took the other eight photos.

—*Were you impressed?*

—Only when I had developed the pictures.

—*On these photos, one genuinely has the impression that one is looking at an enormous flying saucer, oval in shape and very luminous. Could it in actual fact have been a saucer?*

—Everything that the photos show indicates that one might well believe so.

THE WHITE GLOBES AND THE ITALIAN FARMER'S WIFE

To round off this Italian section Gérard Dupagny, our Rome correspondent, went to see another witness. This case has no connection with the Turin affair. But it concerns a piece of testimony which, when we compare it with several others, acquires significance. First, if we compare it with the testimony of Monsieur de Janti, when he is describing the peculiar 'noise' produced by the UFO. And secondly, with the account from the beach at Carteret, in the Département of Manche. This latter story is given further on. But here is the account of the Italian farmer's wife:

●

—It was when the TV programme was ending. Suddenly the light went out. A few moments later, it came on again. I waited about five minutes, without doing anything. Then I went and started up my washing machine. Meanwhile, I could hear a noise like a low-flying aeroplane. Like an aeroplane circling round and round without going away. There was also a very high wind at the time; it was blowing hard, and as the aeroplane continued, I went to open the window. I looked out, and was most surprised at what I saw. The sky was not natural. There were two light beams in the sky, luminous bands, one of them of a violet colour and the other one reddish-orange. In between these two beams, over there, quite near, behind a little hill, there was a very bright light. Then I called my daughter to come and look at the sky, and she came and stayed with me and watched. After a very short while, I suddenly caught sight of a light — a very white light — in the middle of the trees. Then still another light appeared, and then another. They were all in line. Behind the house there is a small tree-covered hill; I saw these three lights just above those trees. After they had 'lit up', others immediately appeared. Then everything went red, a dark red, and this 'thing' at once rose into the air. My daughter and I just stood there looking at this unbelievable sight.
—*And so this 'thing' of which you speak rose up vertically?*
—Yes. And while this 'thing' was rising vertically, we saw in

the sky, very low down, something else that is very hard to describe. It was like a disc, something round and red in colour, the same red which had appeared in the middle of the lights and — it is very difficult to explain this — this thing appeared to pulsate at least three times. Then it moved backwards three times. We stood there watching it and we were dumbfounded. The phenomenon was more than strange! Then I told my daughter to go and call some friends upstairs. And then I went upstairs with her too. I asked them to open their window, but when we went out on to the balcony there was no longer anything there.

—*How long had the phenomenon lasted?*
—From the moment I first opened the window to the time when I saw nothing more, six or seven minutes.
—*And during all that time was the noise still going on?*
—The noise of the aeroplane?
—*Yes.*
—No. From the moment that I opened my window, the noise had stopped. But while the object was completely red there was a noise. A truly indescribable noise. . . .
—*Could you try, all the same, to tell me what it was like?*
—It was a noise that I can scarcely describe. It was a noise rather like the noise the television set makes when it is turned on and when there is a frequency whistle. However, the whistle was not continuous, but came and went. . . .
—*Were you frightened?*
—No. We were too surprised for that. We remained there as though stunned at the sight of the thing. We had never seen anything like it. My daughter, who was at the window with me, saw the disc move off at high speed. It disappeared behind the clouds — almost behind the moon. Then she saw what seemed like a very bright beam of light come from the moon, and that was all.
—*And all this at a very high speed?*
—Yes. At an incredible speed.

A UFO ON THE FISHING NETS!

There were the two of them. Father and son. Two fishermen who, early in the morning, like fishermen the world over, went to pull in their nets. This happened on the beach at Carteret, some 30 kilometres from Cherbourg, in December 1973. It will be a long time before they forget that night.

Charles Mélingue, our correspondent at Cherbourg, conducted the investigation for us. He found one of the fishermen: the son. The father was away for some time at sea. Here is the son's story:

●

—We got to our fishing lines, which had been set for several days. We got there at about 5.30 a.m. A big light appeared, at sea level.

—*Was the light on the water or on the beach?*

—It was on the beach. We went on down. The light did not move. At first we thought it was the light of a car. But a car has two headlights, and we saw only the one. We thought too that maybe it was some smugglers, and so we didn't dare to go on down to the beach. Then my father said: Come on, we'll go down there all the same.' So we went down. My father went to his lines, and I was walking over to mine when I saw that the light was right in the middle of them. I quickly went and got Father, for I wasn't feeling at all happy about it. I asked him to come over, explaining that this light was right bang in the middle of my nets. We went towards them, shining our torches straight ahead. We got nearer. The light still did not budge. Then we decided to quit, and not to come back till daybreak. We put out our torches and went back to our scooters. Before we left we saw the yellow light go out. Then a greenish-blue light appeared, above the ground. After that we saw nothing more.

—*Did you see the light moving about among your nets?*

—Yes, it moved about, with a beam which swept the beach. It reached the dunes in a few seconds.

—*Did you see any marks on the sand afterwards?*

—We came back at dawn, with my brother-in-law, but found no trace of anything on my lines. We also looked about, further afield, but without finding the slightest trace. By the way, we thought that was very odd too.

—*Was the object standing on the ground or was it hanging in the air?*

—We had the impression that it was standing on the ground, because the light was at ground-level.

—*Did you hear any suspicious noises?*

—No noise at all, not even when the object departed.

—*And you yourselves felt nothing? No after-effects, no disturbance?*

—No.

—*Were you frightened?*

—Yes, very frightened.

—*And now, do you go back to the beach all the same to take in your fishing lines?*

—Yes, I've been back. But my father hasn't wanted to come since that extraordinary night. . . .

ere is one of the best photos taken during the new UFO wave of 1974. Didier B—,
hom I have interrogated personally, was studying the sky with his telescope. He is
n amateur astronomer. Suddenly six luminous balls came skimming over the hill tops.
e took five pictures, of which this is the best. The photo has already been published
y *Paris-Match*. He took it at Saint-Vallier-de-Thiey in the Maritime Alps at 8.45 p.m.,
rench Standard Time, on 7 January 1974. As the eyewitness told me: 'Seen through
y telescope at enlargement 150, they looked like regularly shaped yellow discs, but
ith no details visible. The diameter of the object I estimated at one minute of arc.
hey were about 15 kms. distant from me. The six luminous balls were approaching
owly over the hills, but to the naked eye their movement was not perceptible. You
uld only begin to see it clearly at enlargement 36 on my telescope. I had some
fficulty in taking the photos as a strong *Mistral* wind (a powerful cold wind from
e N.W.) was blowing. All the same, I managed to get five pictures, with two good
es, thanks to my 115/900 telescope.'

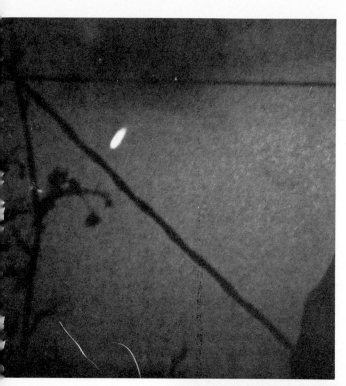

Top. A still from a [...]
of film exposed at 9.0[...]
on 8 December 19[...]
Crosnes, 20 kms. [...]
Paris, by Monsieur R[...]
L—. This film was s[...]
on French Telev[...]
Channel 1, on 4 Feb[...]
1974 in the programm[...]
Grands Reporters.

Below. The same p[...]
enlarged 350 times. A[...]
be observed, there [...]
trail, and there is a [...]
area in the luminous[...]

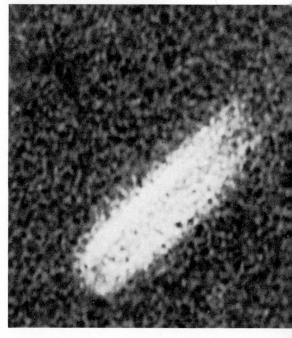

AFTER TURIN AIRPORT —
GENEVA AIRPORT

One might think that the UFOs are interested in aircraft. After the Turin affair, came the one at Geneva. Again an airport was overflown. You might almost say was 'spied on', if prudence in interpretation were not an absolute rule. But the behaviour of this UFO, described by a meteorological observer in the Geneva International Airport, is disturbing all the same. It was on 14 May, 1969. Monsieur de Sarzens tells us his story:

●

—I was just ending my night duty. It was exactly 34 minutes after midnight. I stepped outside to take my temperature readings, and was surprised to see, at a distance of some 800 metres or so from me, at an altitude of some 700 metres or so towards the north-east, a luminous object.

—*How are you able to be so precise?*

—I know the area very well. There was also an aircraft coming in, just shortly before I made the sighting. The runway was still lit up, and the approach as well, so I had pretty precise reference points for gauging how far off the object was. For the height, I took as my reference the 'ceiling', that is to say the clouds. It was a compact 'ceiling' of stratocumulus at 900 metres, and this luminous object, shaped like a perfect ellipse, was at about 200 metres below the cloud layer. This luminous object, orange in colour, with the centre part brighter, was stationary, perfectly motionless beneath the layer of clouds. I had the time to fetch a pair of excellent binoculars (unfortunately I had neither a telescope nor a camera — I do have both now!) and with the binoculars I watched it for 25 minutes. It was visible in the sky for a total of 34 minutes. What interested me was to see if I could make out anything solid inside the luminous glow. But I could see nothing.

—*Not even with the binoculars?*—No. With the binoculars I could see a light in the form of a perfect ellipse. The circumference was not diffuse at all. It was exactly as though the object was made of white-hot metal.

—*Was the object absolutely stationary?*

—Absolutely. I estimated its minimum diameter as about ten metres and its thickness as about three-and-a-half metres. One feature puzzled me: at moments there were breaks in the luminosity, lasting maybe about 1/500th of a second or so. Abrupt breaks.

—*Like a blinking light?*

—Yes, like a blinking light, that is to say about the time it takes an eye to blink. The object gave the impression that it was there, just by chance, to observe the comings and goings of the aircraft, but I can't say how long it had been there. Suddenly the intensity of the light increased. Then it moved off very slowly, for about 300 metres, still under the cloud layer. Then it tilted a few degrees and accelerated, and rose up into the clouds. That was the moment I had been waiting for. I got a very good view of the stratocumulus clouds parting around the sort of luminous hull, though I didn't actually observe any metallic structure.

—*In your view, what did it prove?*

—In my opinion, the object was 'intelligent'. It wasn't there for nothing. It was beneath the clouds, clearly visible: it did not interfere with the approach flights of the incoming aircraft. I also got the impression that its position beneath the cloud layer was strategic and that, if disturbed, it could take cover.

—*All this presupposes that it was observing, and that it was controlled by intelligent beings.*

—I am not going so far as to say 'intelligent beings', but let us say 'something intelligent'. Having been in my job for several years, I must state at once that there can be no question of its having been a patch of cloud lit by a luminous source on the ground or anything like that. ...

—*Obviously you are used to observing?*

—Yes. For sure.

—*And when it went, did it move fast?*

—Not at first, when it began to move horizontally. I had plenty of time to watch it. It was a very beautiful sight. It was just the intensity of its *brightness* that increased at first. But then later, when it tilted in order to go up into the cloud layer, it accelerated, but its speed was still not very great.

—*Are there any other witnesses of the phenomenon?*

—No, there were no other witnesses to my knowledge. I was the only one.

58

We have no correspondent of *France-Inter* in Nepal. However, Henri Di Donna, our permanent special representative in London, made an indirect investigation there of a case on our behalf. He met two witnesses in England whose accounts tallied. Valuable testimony. The two witnesses are teachers. Here is the account of the first of them, Mr Stephen Gill:

●

—At about 8.00 p.m. on 18 April 1972, at one end of a lake in a valley in Nepal, we had just been bathing when, off towards the west, I noticed something like a number of dots grouped very close together, just like migrating birds. I at once asked my companion if he could see the migrating birds, but by then they had vanished. A few minutes later, however, the birds were back again there in the sky. And then suddenly the spots concentrated together into the shape of a veritable flying saucer. Then the object slowly started to move. Most astonished, we watched it. The object had now assumed a very indistinct shape. It looked like a small smoke ring, and lasted for about thirty or forty seconds. Then suddenly, before our eyes, in the sky, we saw an extraordinary phenomenon. Lots of groups of dots turned into saucers, and then into a smoke ring. This phenomenon lasted almost half an hour. The saucer-shaped objects moved at an unbelievable speed. We felt that we were witnessing something that was beyond all probability. I am sure that it had to do with what are called 'unidentified flying objects'.

Roger Baird, the second teacher, confirmed the story:

—I had the same impression as my companion. It was just like groups of bees coming together. This impression lasted about four seconds. Then we saw the dots joining up. There were about eight or nine saucers. Several of them moved about irrationally in the sky, like a flying ballet. I had the impression that the objects were being controlled by a superior force. We had a camera with us. There was only one exposure left in it. Steve told me when to press the button. Between the moment he said 'Now!', and my pressing the button, the saucers started to vanish, till there was nothing left but rings of smoke. I think myself that 'they' had detected our presence. The smoke rings disappeared too a few seconds later. The photograph we took has been examined by specialists. It was not faked. Our story has been published in the British magazine which is the world authority on the subject, *Flying Saucer Review*.*

After Nepal let us now return to Great Britain, to Mr Anthony Russell. Mr Russell had a lot of luck. Not only did he see a UFO, but he saw it at the precise moment when he was trying out a new camera with a telephoto lens.

—In November 1965 I was living at Streatham, on the outskirts of London. Being a very keen photographer, I was in my sitting-room and was trying out my new camera at one of the windows. I was focussing it on a church and, in particular, on the cockerel on the lightning conductor on top of the spire. When I take a photo, I keep both eyes open. I was focussing with one eye, when, with the other eye, I saw an object come to a halt in the sky. I swung my camera round on to the machine, for it had the traditional shape of a flying saucer. I took one picture, and then I put the telephoto lens on to the camera. At that moment the object started to drop gently, swaying from side to side like a dead leaf. The weather was very fine and clear, and the machine was red. It remained stationary for about ten seconds after the falling leaf movement. Then it began to move and to change shape, as it would, if seen from different angles. Then, in a flash, the object was moving again, and vanished at an extraordinary speed. Experts have examined my photos. They say categorically: 'these photos are not faked.' They were transparencies. My photos have been published all over the world, and my story too.**

—*Do you believe in flying saucers?*
—Before, no! Frankly, I didn't! I thought it was all nonsense. But now I am certain that flying saucers exist, for I have seen one with my own eyes and I have photographed it.

---

* *Flying Saucer Review*, published six times yearly by FSR Publications Ltd., West Malling, Maidstone, Kent, England. G.C.
**Full reports, with three of the photographs and detailed analyses of them, were published in *Flying Saucer Review*, Volume 13, No.1 and No.2 (1967), both of which issues are now out of print. G.C.

We are still in England. But on 14 July of 1934. In those days nobody yet talked about 'flying saucers'. This expression dates only from 1947 when, over the State of Washington, USA, a pilot sees some discs which he describes, to the journalists who have come to interview him, as 'like saucers'. In the present case, the witness who tells this story for *France-Inter* is himself a Frenchman. His name is Paul Faiveley:

●

—One evening, having sat up reading longer than usual, I found, just as I was going to bed, that my wallet was missing. This was annoying, as it contained all the money I had for my visit to England. So I went outside. It was about 11.30p.m. The sky was clear and the stars were shining. Going to the swimming-pool, I walked towards the bathing-hut I had used that afternoon. Groping around in the darkness, I found my wallet. I was happy and, my mind now at rest, I was about to return to the house. There was a slight rise in the ground before you came to the level area where the house stood. And beyond that was the road.

When I was about half-way up the slope, I had the impression that everything was getting light, and soon this impression was a certainty, for everything was brightly lit up. I saw my own shadow in front of me getting shorter and shorter. I began to feel a little uneasy, as I knew that there was nothing behind me that could be the cause of the light — no road, no house. Yet it went on getting lighter and lighter. I turned round to see where the light was coming from, and saw a disc — a perfectly circular disc — of a vivid white colour, yet which it was impossible to look straight at with the naked eye. I saw it at an angle as, say, you might see a plate at a distance of four metres. I remember asking out loud, several times: 'What's that!'

When this thing caught my eye, it was still moving. After two or three seconds from the moment when I had first seen it, it came to a halt, more or less right above where I was. After about two minutes or so, the machine, which lit up the whole countryside around, developed a blue fringe around it, like a halo, concentric to the dazzling white circle. After about a minute the blue itself faded out, while the disc remained a dazzling white, just as it had been when I first saw it. Then its light slowly started to fade. It turned a dull white, and from dull white it imperceptibly turned to yellow, and then on through orange and then to red. Then the disc started to move. It was going at a certain speed and then, all of a sudden, came a fantastic acceleration. And it vanished in a few seconds. At that time nobody had ever heard talk of such phenomena. Now they have a name for it: flying saucers. In 1934 this term did not exist. It was only concocted in 1947, in the course of a conversation between a pilot and some journalists. They were asking him: 'What was it you saw?' and 'How did it look?' 'Like a flying saucer', replied the pilot. The expression was born.*

When I got back indoors, I woke up an English companion, to tell him what had happened. He replied: 'How totally absurd! That story won't hold water! Let me sleep!'

—*Are you therefore certain that you saw a UFO?*

—Oh yes. For me there is no doubt about it. I realize that folk may be sceptical about my story, but all the same, believe me, it was true!

—*What is so extraordinary is that you remember all those details so well forty years afterwards.*

—Yes, it is remarkable. I knew from the moment I saw that object, and after it had disappeared, that I would remember it all my life.

---

* As we now know, there is a little more to it than that, and the term is in fact nearly a hundred years old! For we have a photostat from the archives of the American provincial newspaper *Dennison Daily News* (Dennison, Texas) showing that their issue for 25 January 1878 contained the account, under the heading 'A Strange Phenomenon', of how, on the previous day, 24 January 1878, a local farmer named John Martin, described as 'a gentleman of undoubted veracity', had seen a dark flying object travelling 'at a wonderful speed' over his property six miles north of Dallas. He told the newspaper that when it was right overhead it looked '*about the size of a large saucer*'. The photostat of the newspaper's report was given to *Flying Saucer Review* some years ago by Dr J. Allen Hynek, for over 22 years the official Astronomical Consultant to the United States Air Force on UFOs, and now Director of the Center for UFO Studies, 924 Chicago Avenue, Evanston, Illinois 60202, USA. G.C.

THE UFO AS BIG AS A HOUSE

This witness is an educated woman. She studied at the 'Beaux Arts'. She has never told anybody else about her sighting. Now, for the first time, she speaks. But she desires to remain anonymous, as Madame C.—.

Interviewed by André Darcheville, Mme. C— remembers perfectly, eighteen years afterwards, that terrible night in September 1956. She was in a car. Her friend, an Air Force pilot, was at the wheel. Here is Mme. C—'s story:

●

—It happened in September 1956. I was a student, and so enjoyed the benefit of long vacations. I had been with my family for three months. It was at the time of the new moon — so new that you don't see it at all and the sky remains completely black. I'll tell you afterward, why this detail struck me, and why it has remained in my memory.

—*Where was it precisely?*

—I was at a farm called *La Ferme de Plaisance*, on the outskirts of the village of Serdon, in the Loiret, on the road from Argent-sur-Saulne to Serdon. I was returning home with one of my friends.

He was in the French Naval Air Arm at the time, and had just rounded off a trip around the world aboard the aircraft-carrier *Jeanne d'Arc* with a course of training in carrier-landing, in the USA. He was spending his vacation leave with me, in the little village I mentioned. We had been to dinner with some other friends, and had promised to be home early. However, we did not get away until about midnight. We were a ten-minute drive from Serdon. When we reached the big chestnut tree opposite the *La Plaisance* farm, the engine sputtered and we stopped. Behind the chestnut tree there was a small wood, and a field of maize. My friend, who was driving, got out. He found that everything was normal with the engine. Then he suddenly looked up and shouted, 'Hurry! There's something around us.' We tumbled into the ditch, near the field of maize, and hid there. He forced me to hide, but I hadn't seen anything up till that moment. Then I raised my head. I have to admit that I am very short-sighted, and my evidence may not be as accurate as it would have been had I been possessed of keen vision. On the other hand my friend, being a sailor and an airman, had excellent eyesight. He told me these details, which I remember perfectly, despite it's being so long ago — for it all made a great impression on me.

According to my companion's estimation, an enormous silent mass was stationary about 200 metres above us. When he spoke to me about it afterwards, he said its volume was about that of a house of four or five storeys. It was consequently something immense, visible there in the dark sky. For me the object was something nebulous, but certainly round, and not moving, and it emitted no sound. After about five minutes a light flashed on board the machine. This beam of light did not come straight down like the beam of a projector, but it unrolled like a rope-ladder! It came down quite slowly, yes, just like a rope being uncoiled. Once it had reached the ground you would have said it was just an ordinary beam of light from a lamp. And we had the impression that it was looking for us. That is to say, every time anything stirred, the beam moved towards it. What scared me most, and certainly also made a deep impression on my friend, was that everything illuminated by the beam had its colours changed. This produced, on a larger scale, the same effect that you feel when you pass under the beams of iodine lamps. I have never again seen such a change of colours. The dark trees of the wood stood out beside us against the maize, which has light green leaves and yellow fruit. Every time the beam from the searchlight lit up the maize the colour of the maize became a very harsh blue. At one moment my hand, outside the field of maize, and beneath the leaves, was caught by the beam of the projector, and my hand became a lemon-yellow colour! Those are the two colours — the blue and the yellow — that have remained in my memory and that I shall never forget, colours that I know very well, since at that time I was at the 'Beaux Arts' and I was painting. The sensation was 'inhuman'. I felt a slight tingling in the hand. My companion said: 'Pull your hand back; it's nothing to worry about, it's ozone.' I am merely repeating to you what he said. We stayed there a good hour-and-a-half. The machine remained stationary above us all that time.

— *You didn't leave the maize field?*

—No. We were both too frightened! My fear was increased by the fact that my friend, whom I considered to be absolutely fearless and most knowledgeable about everything in the world, would not have been scared of anything — certainly not of a mere sonde balloon for example.

—*Was the object very bright?*

—No, it was dark. The light came from this sort of beam which was searching for us.

—*Always noiselessly?*

—Without any noise. When we discussed it again, one detail came back. My father, furious when we arrived home an hour-and-a-half late, asked us a long string of questions. He said: 'You say, when anything moved, the beam shifted towards it; so you yourselves did not remain motionless?' Now, there were lots of rabbits and birds around us there, and they did not seem to be affected by what was going on, and they continued to gambol about or to whistle respectively. Thinking about it afterwards, we got the impression that the animals and birds had not perceived the phenomenon.

—*How did the machine depart?*

—Well, you know, we were there watching this machine — and it was terrifying. We had the sensation that we were experiencing something outside the limits of what one can know. A few years previously, I had been through the bombing of Orléans. You have fear of bombs, you have fear of an aeroplane. But that thing had nothing in common with bombs and planes. Those were, alas, something 'human'! Well now, that phenomenon was something completely 'inhuman'. What was it? We had no idea. Then suddenly I had the impression that the 'thing' was moving. The machine rose up vertically; it did a perfect right-angle turn; then it vanished towards the river Loire, in the direction of Les Bordes, a small village on the south side of the river.

—*Still without any sound?*—Without any sound whatsoever. We talked about the 'thing' to my parents. They remarked sarcastically that our 'tales of brigands' did not justify our lateness. They did not believe us. Next morning however my father came down to breakfast quite moved. He said to Mother: 'Don't reprimand them. Their story is definitely true. The dairyman has had the same experience. He saw the machine at Les Bordes, when he was doing his rounds picking up the milk.'

—*Was the milkman immobilized too?*

—Yes. He was delayed for 25 minutes. He dived under his truck, and he swore that he had never been so frightened in his whole life.

—*Did you tell the Gendarmerie or anyone else about your experience?*

—Oh no. I told nobody. You know the sort of reaction you get when you talk of this sort of thing. 'She is completely potty'. Or: 'You've been drinking too much.' In fact they'll say anything.

—*What gave you the idea to talk about it now?*

—Because for some time now certain people seem to have been taking it seriously.

A GIGANTIC CIGAR OVER THE PAS-DE-CALAIS REGION

At 6.00 a.m. on 31 December 1973, Monsieur Lifooghe, a businessman, sets out to make some purchases at the neighbouring market in Haisnes. Monsieur Lifooghe knows the road well. He makes this journey three hundred times a year. Suddenly he sees two headlights. They appear on his right. They are about to cross in front of him. On what road? There is no road at that spot! Euloge Boissonnade, one of France-Inter's reporters, went over the famous stretch of road by car — with Monsieur Lifooghe beside him. ...

•

—I was here, at this place. A hundred metres away, to my right, there were two headlights on the ground, stationary. I drove on. Then, suddenly, the lights moved towards me, and then they turned away abruptly. I saw nothing more. I thought that it was a vehicle that had gone away to the left, along the road I had just passed, but I did not see it. Then, later, I come to this spot, out in the fields, and, at about 100 metres from me, I see a rocket standing on the ground.
—*A rocket?*
—Yes, yes. A rocket. It was lit up. I could see its whole shape; it was just like a rocket. It was about 30 to 50 metres high. As soon as I got there, it began to teeter to and fro. It lit up, that is to say it became more and more luminous.
—*What colour was it?*
—Orange-red, and then later a glowing white. Blinding! The rocket vanished into the sky at an incredible speed. I went on my way, thinking there must be something queer going on. I realized that I had certainly experienced some abnormal event. When I had done my shopping, I came back to the spot, and walked around a bit in the fields to verify whether I really had seen something, or whether I had been the victim of a hallucination. So I looked about in the fields, and I saw footprints. Small footprints! they all converged towards one spot. I followed them, and suddenly I found a basin-shaped depression in the ground. This seemed very suspicious, as the footprints were fresh, and the depression seemed so too,

whereas everything else around about was frozen. I went on looking, and I found more depressions, at the precise spot where I had seen a machine take off.

—*Can you describe the rocket?*

—This second machine. . . .

—*You say 'second machine'?*

—Yes, because the first machine that I saw was beside the road, and disappeared without leaving any trace. So I deduced from this that the first machine had rejoined the rocket.

—*How high was the rocket?*

—About 30 to 50 metres high. That craft had the shape of an artillery projectile, or a cigar with a swelling near the centre.

—*And what were the footprints like?*

—The prints were small, like those of a ten-year-old child, much more delicate than those of a human being. At the spot where these footprints were, the private research group who investigated this case found traces of ionization, whereas there was none anywhere else.

—*What were your feelings when you saw the machine?*

—I felt tremendous astonishment at suddenly seeing a rocket of that size appear beside a road which I was accustomed to use frequently. When I walked forward up the road, I saw the machine take off, and teeter on its base as if it were going to fall on top of me. As it swayed, the craft became luminous. I had the impression that it was on fire. I was dazzled, and the craft had vanished.

When I went back to the place later, I stopped my car on the road, and began to look around in the frozen ploughed field on my left. That is where I saw the footprints. So the beings must have walked about in that field. When I saw the footprints, after a fifteen-minute search, I thought at first that they were the footprints of children who had been there looking for old iron. It is a place where there was fighting during the War of 1914-1918. Sometimes, during the school holidays, children, to make a little pocket-money, go there to look for scrap iron. But the local children, brought up on the farms, would never look in a freshly ploughed field. Moreover the footprints were definitely too small. So I didn't really think that it was children. Then I went over to the other side of the road, and again I saw the little footprints in a spot that was not frozen. I went over to the posts of the fence, and saw a little cavity in the ground, ten centimetres in diameter and four to five centimetres deep. On two spots further away it seemed as though (when the craft swayed or was trying to maintain stability) two other cavities of the same kind had been impressed. There too the specialists, with their counters, found traces of ionization.

—*You speak of footprints. Were they prints of shoes or of bare feet?*

—They were the marks of *shoes*. They had a flat sole with a scarcely detectable heel. The people who study these matters have spoken of '*humanoids*' — consequently of beings resembling us.

Monsieur Lifooghe's story is quite extraordinary. The local Gendarmerie investigated. Here are the conclusions of their Chief, Captain Yves Batard, as given to Euloge Boissonnade:

—*Captain Batard, it was in your District that Monsieur Lifooghe saw, on 31 December last, this mysterious machine which he has just described for us. So you investigated at the spot. You have seen Monsieur Lifooghe. Do you think he is reliable?*

—Monsieur Lifooghe gave us the impression that he had genuinely seen the object. He told us: 'at such and such a place I saw this, and at such and such another place I saw that.' Then, after searching the area, he showed us the marks. And indeed it is a fact that marks were found which do not appear to us to be very ordinary.

—*What form did the marks have?*

—They had the form of little holes, very regular, as though they had been made by something hemispherical where it touched the ground. We measured the distances between these three marks, and we were able to establish that they formed an isosceles triangle with a base of 8.80 metres and the other two sides of 4.70 metres.

—*Did Monsieur Lifooghe mention footprints too?*

—Strictly speaking, we did not find footprints ourselves. The only indications we saw were the regularly shaped holes.

—*Of what did the holes put you in mind?*

—*A priori*, not of anything, because we are not specialists, and we only went over there to take the statement of Monsieur Lifooghe and to make a note of any traces we could record.

—*Monsieur Lifooghe is a local man, and not a practical joker, is he?*

—Monsieur Lifooghe is reported to us to be a trustworthy man.

—When you carried out your investigation was the ground frozen?
—Yes. The ground was frozen and our shoes did not sink into it at all. But we were able to establish that the marks were not frozen, and that the soil did not appear to be frozen at those spots where the marks were.
—Was it light, loose soil?
—Yes, the soil there is relatively light. At any rate so far as the deepest parts of the marks were concerned.
—Did the marks form three small hollows?
—Yes, they were in the form of little hollows, little holes.
—Like grab-marks?
—Well, the holes, or hollows, were ten centimetres wide and had an average depth of four centimetres.
—It is in a field. Couldn't the marks have been made by an agricultural implement?
—We did not have the impression that the marks could have been due to any agricultural machine. However, we did ask the owner of the field whether one of his machines had been over the area at any recent date. His answer was in the negative.

The Gendarmerie Captain thus confirmed what Monsieur Lifooghe had said, except for one detail, which is an important one, namely that the Captain did not see the footprints. There are two different possible explanations for this however. Firstly, it is possible that the snow had melted on the following day. Secondly, a great many idle gapers went to the spot and trampled all over the landing site. Their footprints would thus have been superimposed: footprints of identified humans on top of unidentified humanoids.

CANADA — A UFO AT A HOSPITAL

Dr P. H. M. Edwards is an eminent professor of languages at Victoria University, Vancouver. He is interested in the UFOs and investigates them in a private capacity. Dr Edwards thus investigated personally the astonishing affair of the UFO that 'visited' a hospital. The principal witness is a nurse, whom Dr Edwards met. . . .

●

—I went to see the nurse at the hospital, in a little town on Vancouver Island. The name of the nurse is Miss Timbord. She was aged 51 at the time. She had gone into the room of one of the patients to see how he was, as he was quite seriously ill. The time was 5.00 a.m. She parted the curtains, so as to be able to open the window and let in a little more air. And then she beheld quite a large machine right up against the window. She could have touched it if the window had been open. In the cupola of the machine there were two beings, quite tall, both dressed in a sort of dark-coloured type of ecclesiastical stole, which also covered the face. So she was not able to see their faces, but only their bodies. The two beings were looking in through the window which formed the angle of the building.
—*Which window was that?*
—It was the window of the children's ward. Now, we know that the UFO beings are very interested in children. They often hover around schools: so I think Miss Timbord was telling the truth. Then she began to describe to me the inside of the cupola of the craft. She could see the two beings clearly down as far as the knees. There were two little seats, and a control-panel consisting of luminous dials. Suddenly one of the beings noticed that she was watching him. He touched his companion on the shoulder. Then the companion too turned round, and then he operated some sort of lever or handle, and the disc tilted, as though the two beings wished to show her the inside of the cupola. Moreover, she also gave me a little sketch showing the control-panel, the beings, their very tightly-fitting clothing, and the little seats. She shouted in order to attract the attention of two or three other

nurses. They came running up, and they too saw the machine. It was moving away over the car-park, then it accelerated, slipped between two large pine trees, and vanished.

—*So, Dr Edwards, there is confirmation of the story by the other nurses?*

—That's right, Monsieur.

—*At what distance was the saucer when the other nurses got to the window?*

—It was moving away. It was about thirty metres from the window by then.

—*Are there any other witnesses?*

—Yes. On the previous day, the afternoon of 31 December, a family were out in a sailing boat on Moulin Bay, between Victoria and Duncan. Suddenly a saucer appeared. It was flying low. The family almost abandoned ship because they were all so frightened by the sight of this saucer. Then the UFO climbed away and finally vanished. The UFO was seen again at Duncan at 7.30 next morning. So there was a UFO in the neighbourhood of the town of Duncan for at least two days.

LUCIEN BARNIER: 'I AM UNEASY!'

The declaration by Lucien Barnier on *France-Inter*, on Wednesday 20 February 1974, has had quite a repercussion. *France-Inter*'s own scientific specialist was stating publicly, and for the first time, that his opinion on the subject of UFOs had changed. In 1972 I happened by chance to be discussing 'flying saucers' with him. It was in his home, quite a long way from Paris.

The conversation had veered round to this subject, because we were looking at the sky, across which an artificial satellite was travelling at a good speed. That was all that was needed. At that time I was scarcely interested in UFOs. But I was curious to know Lucien Barnier's opinion on the subject. 'Oh, it's all nonsense!', he said, in substance. His opinion was enough for me. But now, here in the middle of the compilation of our UFO *Dossier*, I was talking — passionately this time — with Lucien Barnier. Here is what he told me, on *France-Inter*:

●

—Yes, what you say is true. I have changed my attitude. Ten years ago, I embarked on a radio investigation on UFOs conducted with a friend of mine, Gilbert Caseneuve. We had gathered together the accounts given in all the UFO books that had appeared up to that date, including those of colleagues in whom I have the greatest confidence. So we went over all the eyewitnesses' stories again. I must say that, of the forty people questioned, thirty-five were of no interest. The majority were simply telling a story to get publicity for themselves. When they said they had seen something, I felt that there was a rational explanation for it. In short, there was no feeling of anything 'extraordinary'. It is true that the evidence of a policeman from Vernon had appealed to me most. This man had investigated two or three strange happenings. His story rang true in a way that troubled me. But I said to myself that since the result was negative in so large a proportion of the cases, why should one give consideration to one solitary account of no great significance?

Chance decreed that shortly after that I met an eyewitness who held an important position in one of the worldwide airline companies. This man really shook me. Firstly, because, being discreet, he sought no publicity — indeed very much to the contrary. I had to urge him quite a bit before he would consent to tell me his story.

Now that I have heard lots of sighting accounts in your radio programmes, his seems quite 'classical'. Everything was finally decided for me one evening, when I was dining in a Montmartre restaurant with Pierre Guérin, an authoritative astrophysicist and a specialist on the planets, especially Saturn. He has a sound international reputation. But nevertheless I did not take seriously his interest in saucers. We had quite a fierce argument about it. He produced proofs and material that I found disturbing. Then chance again decreed that, shortly after that talk with Guérin, the brother of one of my friends should himself have been a witness to some unquestionably extraordinary events. Now, I have great confidence in the opinion of this friend. He too holds an important post in an international company. What struck me forcibly as having changed radically in comparison with the situation fifteen years earlier was *the quality of the witnesses*. They are usually cultured people, that is to say, people who have been taught how important it is to respect the facts. They are not prepared to believe just anybody. They are exacting. They are technicians, engineers, pilots, scientists, in a word, men who reason, men who are logical. And their stories tally with each other!

—*Is this what you found disturbing, and what has made you change your mind?*

—Yes. Absolutely. Look at the Rationalist Union, for example, where, only ten years ago, it was not a good thing to talk about flying saucers. Well, the Rationalist Union have just published a little book devoted to the UFOs. It is honestly presented. In it, astrophysicists explain why they are worried. I admit that I have no ground for clinging to an attitude of negation. I think there is unquestionably a phenomenon here. . . .

EXCLUSIVE: FOR THE FIRST TIME THE MINISTER OF DEFENCE SPEAKS

Here is the interview with Robert Galley, at that date the French Minister of Defence (Ministre des Armées). It was destined to mark an epoch in the history of the UFOs. What Robert Galley said went round the world. I have received German, Brazilian, Spanish, Italian, Swiss, and American newspapers in which this interview has been given a prominent place. As for the specialists on the UFOs, they all quote it. It was an interview which gave the Minister the opportunity to declare: it is certain that there are phenomena which are unexplained.

●

—Monsieur le Ministre, you have granted France-Inter *an interview which will assuredly make history, for I think it is the first time that a Minister for the Armed Forces has consented to speak about the UFO problem. Have you data which enable you to give a reply to the questions which our listeners ask themselves, data about which we would have no knowledge?*
—I don't know about that, because I have spent a comparatively limited amount of time on this subject, though it has always interested me. Consequently I am not in a position to know all that has been said in the course of your programmes, but I do know that certain people in the Ministry are following them assiduously. What I do believe, profoundly, is that we must adopt an extremely open attitude of mind towards these phenomena. A number of advances have been made among the human race by the fact that we have sought to explain the inexplicable. Now, among these aerial phenomena, these visual phenomena (I won't say more than that) which we have grouped together under the term 'UFOs', it is certain that there are things that we do not understand and that are at present relatively inexplicable. I will indeed say that it is undeniable that there are things today that have not been explained or that have been incorrectly explained.
In 1954 a section was set up in the Ministry to study and

gather eyewitness accounts of these apparitions of unidentified objects. I have looked through a certain number of the accounts. These (fifty or so) were in the period up to 1970. One of the earliest of them is an account of personal sightings by Lt. Jean Demery, of No. 107 Air Base at Villacoublay, dated 20 November 1953. They contain reports from the Gendarmerie, a number of sighting reports from pilots, reports from people who are the heads of air establishments, and a lot of material in which the general agreement was quite disturbing — all of it in the course of the year 1954. Consequently, I think that the attitude of mind one must adopt towards these phenomena must remain an open one — that is to say, it is not an attitude which consists of denying *a priori*. Our forebears in past centuries denied the existence of many things that today seem to us perfectly elementary, such as piezzoelectricity, or static electricity, not to mention a certain number of phenomena connected with biology. In fact, the whole development of Science consists in the fact that at a given moment we realize that fifty years ago we knew nothing and understood nothing about the reality of phenomena.

—*Mr Minister, have there been cases in which* Mirage planes have pursued UFOs over France?

—Not, I think, in France, after having gone through numerous reports. But we have had a certain number of radar sightings. In particular, in the 1950s, we had a radar sighting in the Aquitaine region. For ten minutes we had a radar echo that was inexplicable and still remains unexplained. On the other hand, other radar echoes thought at first to be mysterious have been explained by the phenomenon of scatter. But there still remains a small residue. And those sightings are unexplained. Similar phenomena exist in other countries. They are quite well known. There are phenomena in the U.S.A., and there is the recent phenomenon at Turin. But to answer your question precisely, I would say that the number of UFO reports from French military pilots is relatively small compared with what you find in other countries. All the same, there are some that are classified.

—*Are you in touch, Mr Minister, with other international military organizations?*

—No. Since 1970 we have been sending on all sighting reports to the *Groupement d'Etudes des Phénomènes Aériens*, and we are continuing to do so, each time that something extraordinary happens. This refers to sightings by pilots or investigations by the Gendarmerie. Since 1970 the Air Force has in fact held the view that the UFOs represented no sort of threat — and consequently that it was not their task to study these phenomena at the scientific level. We consider that to be the role of the National Centre for Space Studies (C.N.E.S., Centre National d'Etudes Spatiales), where folk like Monsieur Claude Poher are doing work which seems to us to be quite interesting. So we don't have any direct contact. But, I repeat, every time something unusual crops up, we send it to this organization, who, fundamentally, are working on behalf of the whole country.

—*Nevertheless, Mr Minister, unidentified space phenomena in the skies over France are, it would seem, surely of interest to the National Defence?*

—Oh yes, they are of interest to the National Defence, and this is the reason why we are following this question, in order to see whether correlations in it can be established. Personally, I have taken an interest in this phenomenon of the correlations, which Monsieur Poher has explained, between the magnetic field and the passage of unidentified flying objects. Here we have a body of relatively disturbing phenomena which may one day get an explanation which is not due to some specific object, and which may be magnetic phenomena. But, for the time being, we are obliged to admit that there is something that we don't understand. There is also the steady accumulation, absolutely impressive, of visual sightings of luminous phenomena that are sometimes spherical, sometimes ovoid, and which are characterized by extraordinarily rapid movement. All these phenomena are things to which one must pay a certain amount of attention. But I must repeat once more that they do not appear to us in the Air Force to pertain to the Air Defence of the country.

—*If you were asked to make the sightings by military radar available to the scientists, what would be your answer?*

—If anomalies appeared on Air Defence radar screens there would be no reason why we should not pass on these sightings to them. Indeed that is what we are already doing now. And I have here, incidentally, all the sightings that come from both the Air Force and the Gendarmerie, and we send them all on directly to the scientists who are dealing with them.

—*You have spoken of the Gendarmerie, Mr Minister. Now, our listeners on France-Inter have heard, many times, the conclusions reached in investigations conducted by your Gendarmes — spectacular conclusions: when an eyewitness avers that he has seen a flying saucer land and that he has seen small humanoids beside this saucer, the Gendarmes very often conclude that the witnesses are to be trusted and are telling the truth.*

—Well, of course, on that score I shall be infinitely more discreet. But I must say that, if your listeners could see the accumulation of reports, coming in from the Airborne Gendarmerie, the Mobile Gendarmerie, and the Gendarmerie charged with the regional investigation work, which have been retransmitted by us to the National Centre for Space Studies (C.N.E.S.) it is indeed quite disturbing. What I think is that the Gendarmes are reliable folk. When the Gendarmes make a report, they don't do it haphazardly. If there had been only one or two of these reports, one might perhaps imagine that the Gendarmes' good faith had been abused. But I must say that nevertheless there are a great many Gendarmerie reports that are very dissimilar, the ones from the others. All this is of course still pretty fragmentary. To sum up, I think that in this business of the UFOs, we must adopt an extremely open-minded attitude. We must not call in question the good faith of eyewitnesses who are obviously sincere, but at the present moment it would be extremely premature to draw the slightest conclusion from it all.

REPLIES TO THE FIRST QUESTIONS

As the mail piled up, the thousands of letters received by us obliged us to introduce some small degree of disruption into the programme that we had set ourselves. On Friday, 22 February 1974, we asked Pierre Guérin to answer the questions which recurred most frequently in the mail we received. For the present book we have selected the principal replies given by Guérin, who is an astro-physicist and the Chief of Research in the National Centre for Space Research (C.N.R.S.)

●

—*Pierre Guérin: what should one do if one sees a UFO at close range?*
—If the UFO is at close range, it is difficult to give advice. The 'phenomenon' has perhaps in fact chosen to be near the witness. It is obviously desirable that the latter shall observe what happens — if he has enough courage to do so! As for a UFO seen from further away, the ideal thing would be to have a loaded camera ready for use, so as to be able to bring back some pictures. If you photograph a UFO by day there is no problem. At night, however, there is a tendency to over-exposure, in getting shots equal to or better than shots of space-probes, and this results in pictures that are of little use. If there is something shining at night, with a sufficient degree of brightness, you must take an instantaneous photo, just as in broad daylight.

Another question put by young listeners:
—*What does one have to study to become a professional 'ufologist'?*
Pierre Guérin laughs:
—But one doesn't become a professional 'ufologist'. That profession doesn't exist! My emphatic advice to the young folk who put this sort of question to me is: pass your exams, get your degree, and follow some advanced scientific studies. When you have attained a high university level you can then launch out into such difficult sorts of study as this one.
—*Nearly all the eyewitnesses say they have seen saucers at night-time. What is the reason for this?*

—It is quite untrue. So far as the UFOs are concerned. But please don't let us talk about 'flying saucers', I beg you, Jean-Claude Bourrett. ...

—*I am merely reading out the listeners' questions without distorting them!*

—Good! But I wish *France-Inter*'s listeners would use the expression: '*the UFOs*'. For the saucer shape is in any case relatively rare — as compared with other shapes. The thing that characterizes the 'phenomenon' is a certain manner of moving about, a certain sort of luminosity — not the shape. I return now to the question just put: the answer is that the UFOs are not only seen at night. There are just as many sightings by day as by night. In daytime, you often see a structure, and this enables you to say that it is neither an aeroplane, nor a helicopter, nor a sonde balloon, nor a meteor, whereas at night it is often just a point of light in the sky and, unless you are an astronomer, you'd have to be pretty smart really to say what it is. On the other hand, the alleged close-distance UFO landings do have a tendency, according to the statistics, which hold good all over the world, to be observed at about 8.00 p.m. in the evening and 2.00 a.m. in the morning, at a time when the majority of our population are in bed.

—*How is it to be explained that none of these machines have ever broken down?*

—Why do you talk about a 'machine'? The visual appearance is that of machines. From the fact that all the sighting accounts agree that the UFOs defy all the laws of our physics, notably the law of inertia, it is difficult to pin the word 'machine' on to these phenomena. On the other hand, a characteristic feature of the UFO phenomenon is intelligent behaviour. Here we are confronted with the nub of the problem. The word 'machine' must nevertheless not be used, and at once the question about breakdowns becomes a question that cannot be put.

THE HUMANOID IN THE DIVING SUIT

Now we are going to start moving on towards the question of the humanoids, thanks to a number of eye-witnesses whom we have traced and who are willing to confide their fantastic adventures to the microphone of *France-Inter*. So here are Monsieur and Madame Mozin, telling one of our reporters, André Darcheville, about what they saw in November 1954.

●

—I was returning to Maubeuge from Montournère. When I got to the 'Belle Hôtesse' Inn, at the top of the hill, I saw some very bright lights at the side of the road. So far as I was concerned, I thought it was an accident. I was about two kilometres from these huge lights: so I put on speed. I went down the hill very fast, to see the accident. Suddenly, at a distance of a hundred or so metres from the spot, my lights went out. I was doing 120 km.p.h. It was then that I saw the 'little man'.
—*What did he look like?*
—He was like the man in the Michelin advertisements. A big helmet, big gloves, boots, a man of medium height. His silhouette was outlined in a doorway which was about 1.80 in height. Behind the little man, I saw things like controls, rods, and electrical wiring. I should explain that it was all lit up perfectly, with a very white light. You could see as well as in broad daylight. So I went past the machine. Fifty metres further on the lighting in my car came back and my lights were working normally again. A bit further on, I stopped, as I wanted to turn back. At that period I used to carry a revolver in the car, and I said to myself: 'We'll go back and take a good look'. Then my wife started shouting: 'No — I don't want to go back there.' So I drove on. Next day, I was due to go and watch a football match at Rheims. I was the president of the USM team here in Maubeuge. I was to go there with a friend, who was a tobacconist. (He has since died, otherwise he would testify and bear me out.) Before we set off, I said: 'I saw a saucer last night.' He replied: 'It isn't true.' 'All right', I said. 'Since you don't believe me, I'll show you the place on the way to Rheims.' We started out, and when we came to the place in the hollow, we got out. I showed

him the ground. And in fact there were marks there. 'Look, there are three naked footprints, one there, another there, and it's burnt in the middle.' My friend was knocked for six. 'It's true. I've lost' he replied.

—*So you had made a bet with him?*
—Yes, I had bet him a bottle of champagne and a dinner. And I won.
—*Now let us just go back to that fantastic night. What was the shape of the machine that you saw?*
—It had the shape of a cigar three metres in diameter. The doorway in which the chap was outlined was about 1 metre 80 high. There was a space of about fifty centimetres between his head and the top of the door. And I saw the little chap walking. He was just stepping out as we got there. He walked like this: (Monsieur Mozin imitates the gait of a diver.) He was having difficulty in moving about. In my opinion the clothes he was wearing were very heavy. (Monsieur Mozin is here referring to the type of 'diving-suit' worn by the humanoid.)
—*I believe the inside of the UFO was brilliantly lit up, and you had a good view of it?*
—Yes, the inside was exceptionally brightly lit. White, very white, like those chairs over there. (Monsieur Mozin points to two white lacquered kitchen chairs.)
—*How long did you see it for?*
—It all happened very quickly: about fifty seconds.

Here Monsieur Mozin is probably mistaken in his calculations. At 120 km.p.h. the duration of his observation could not have been more than ten seconds. André Darcheville now turns to Madame Mozin, who had been beside her husband in the car.

—*Madame Mozin, what impression did you have?*
—I was frightened. All that I can say is that I was frightened! At the beginning, I thought there had been an accident, a terrible accident, because the lights were so powerful. But when I saw the little man I was terrified. I could not sleep afterwards because of it.
—*And it was you, wasn't it, who saw the little man with the maximum amount of detail, since you were on the right-hand side of the car — that is to say, on the side where the UFO was?*
—Yes, I had a very good view of him. I can still see him if I close my eyes.

THE GENDARMES CHASE A UFO

Tuesday 26 February 1974. Reinforcements of Gendarmerie are despatched to the little village of Montréal, in the Département of Aude. Thrice in one week mysterious lights had been moving about in the fields there. On the previous night, a patrol of Gendarmes had pursued them. After making enquiries, I managed to find one of the two Gendarmes who were on that patrol. He describes his UFO hunt:

●

—We went to the area, together with Monsieur X— who had given the alarm. He led us towards the field where he had seen the phenomenon. When we had gone about 300 or 400 metres, we saw two red circles, like two big headlights.
—*At what altitude?*
—At ground level.
—*In a field?*
—Yes, in a field. The two red circles remained for an instant near the ground and then suddenly rose to a height of 50 or 100 metres. Then they returned to the ground again.
—*At what distance were you from them at that moment?*
—Still around 400 metres or so.
—*Did you have the impression that it was simply a question of a luminous phenomenon, or that there was some sort of structure there?*
—It was simply luminous. All you could see looked like two big car headlights.
—*Any noise?*
—No, it made no noise.
—*Did you find marks on the ground?*
—No, no marks.
—*Then what did you do?*
—After a moment or so we returned to Brigade Headquarters. At a distance of two kilometres from the field where we had seen the lights, we came to a slight rise. From there we had a good view of the phenomenon as the position dominated the whole countryside. We could see one circle about a metre in diameter, and it had indentations, just like the points of a star.

83

—It was still on the ground?
—Yes, still.
—Why didn't you try to get close to it?
—It wasn't easy. We were quite a long way from it, and the phenomenon was happening in the open fields, where there was no access road for getting there. It had been raining. The ground was sodden. We should have got stuck in the mud if we had tried to get there in the Gendarmerie car. On foot, and without Wellington boots, we would have been in a fine state!
—You didn't try to go round the field by another road?
—No. You couldn't have done, because there was no other road. And then, you know, a phenomenon like that, well, you have to see it, don't you?
—Were you scared?
—No, we weren't scared. But a phenomenon like that, well, we just wondered what it was.
—This isn't the first time, is it, that there have been lights of this kind near Montréal?
—No, they were there last Sunday, 17 February, and again on the following Thursday.
—Do you believe in flying saucers?
—Well, I do and I don't.
—Even after what you saw?
—After what I saw, I'd almost believe in them!
—Did you ask for Gendarmerie reinforcements?
—Yes; the reinforcements arrived. They went to the area, but found nothing. No marks. Nothing.
—How many men did you receive as reinforcements?
—Thirty.
—I suppose that, for your sector, this must have been like a mobilisation?
—Yes, it was a mobilisation. It has caused a lot of talk in the region.
—What do the Gendarmerie think about the business?
—We don't think anything: we're there to ascertain the facts and make an investigation, that's all.
—Let us now come back to your sighting of last night. You tell me that you saw what looked like two big red headlights. How far apart were they?
—It varied. The two lights would move apart, and then would come together again.
—So they were two moveable lights?
—Yes, they were moveable. It is impossible to say whether they formed part of a solid body. We only saw the lights.

Such then is the direct evidence of this gendarme. I was also able to talk to the Commandant of the Brigade of Gendarmerie, the Chief-Adjutant responsible for this Brigade at Montréal. This is what he said:

—What they've seen is something rather worrying. An occurrence that is not entirely normal.
—*You are unable to explain it?*
—Well, no! It has been ascertained that there were balls of fire, headlights as it were that lit up. We have six eyewitness accounts regarding the phenomenon, quite apart from the testimony of two of my men. But it is impossible to say what it is.
—*You have reinforced the patrols?*
We are out there every evening now. But yesterday there were too many people there. We had several car-loads of curiosity-seekers and journalists with us. But we haven't given up hope of seeing the phenomenon again.
—*Do you hope all the same to see them again, these famous mystery globes?*
—Yes, for they have been seen three times in a week. There is no reason why it should stop suddenly. We have made all our arrangements. And the journalists too are ready, and even the people of the village. They are taking it in turn to mount guard.
—*Have you radio contact with your cars?*
—Yes. We've got three radio cars.
—*And you are doing this every night?*
—We started last night. We shall continue with it tonight.

The officer responsible for the Gendarmerie Area, Commander Pistre, has taken personal charge of the operations. He has designated one of his officers, Captain Abadie, as responsible for collecting all the reports of similar phenomena that have happened in the Département. Commander Pistre has consented to tell me about the object of his task:

—To begin with, there is one thing I must make clear. We are not taking charge of the affair. We are content to play a controlling role. The Gendarmerie function on rational lines. Somebody reports something abnormal to us: we verify. We may find it is a hoax, or we may find a rational explanation. This is the spirit in which we operate. The facts in this case have been as follows: On Sunday, 17 February, Monsieur

C—, a local vine-grower, saw a luminous phenomenon in a field. He did not attribute any particular importance to it, for he took it to be two tractors working coupled together, but coupled back-to-back. This would mean that there would be two lights at the front and two more lighting the rear. When he had got home, he began to reflect: it was pouring with rain. What would two tractors, or what would poachers for that matter, be doing out in weather like that? On the Thursday following, there was the same phenomenon again, but with a difference. There were only two lights now, and two lights independent of each other. These two lights were moving away from each other and then moving towards each other again, at a distance of a metre or so from the ground. As it had been raining, and as it was already quite late, Monsieur C— was a bit more surprised this time. He returned home, and told his wife and one of his neighbours about it. Now it so happened that the neighbour had seen the same phenomenon. And it was he who suggested that the Gendarmerie be alerted. ...

—*So you went to the spot, in the field. And did you find any marks or footprints, Commander?*

—No marks. However, it had rained the day before, and the ground was muddy, very soft.

—*And that's not the whole of it?*

—No. On the following Sunday, which is to say last Sunday, 24 February 1974, at 10.00 p.m., the phenomenon was repeated, but this time with a few differences, at a spot a few hundred metres from the scene of the initial observations, and right in front of the witness's own farm, the building being vividly illuminated at times. Instead of the 'two tractors' (I say two tractors simply in order to give an idea of size — but obviously it had nothing to do with tractors) the phenomenon this time appears in the form of a simple ball, of the size of a cartwheel.

—*What colour was it?*

—Red, like red-hot iron. With intermittent flashes at the edge, like the twinkling of a star. On the top of the 'ball' the witnesses declare that they saw something which they call 'an antenna', though of course there is nothing to justify our saying that it was an antenna.

—*Did it have a metallic structure?*

—The ball itself — no. As regards the antenna, they claim to have seen a red hemisphere — like a rheostat. The ball was travelling along at one metre off the ground, sometimes slowly, sometimes at 15 or 20 km.p.h., and sometimes at lightning speed. The witness explains that in the latter case the ball seemed to divide into two parts. At any rate, there were two lights moving to a distance of 200-300 metres apart and then coming together again at the speed of lightning.

—*Did the witness and his son try to approach the phenomenon?*

—Yes, the two witnesses approached it, but they did not see any material shape: simply a bright glow.

—*How close did they get to it?*

—They think to 'between 100 and 150 metres from it', but don't seem sure. The phenomenon seemed to come towards them; they got frightened, and it was then that they decided to tell the Gendarmerie. The time was 11.00 p.m. Twenty minutes later, the Gendarmes were on the spot and in fact were able themselves to see the 'ballet of the dancing lights' which by then however had moved further away into the hills.

—*How far have you got with your investigations?*

—Well, we investigated at the spot, but no traces were found. However, I must emphasise this, the ground was heavy, bare, and freshly sown over most of its area. No trace of radioactivity was found either.

—*Did the Gendarmerie carry out the tests for possible traces of radioactivity?*

—No, that was done by the civilian protection authorities of the Département. Let me finish telling you the result of our investigations: no trace then of radioactivity, no sound, no heat effect. That's all. That's all we can say. So it remains difficult to express an opinion. Poachers? Poachers leave traces. The quickset hedges are not damaged. Nothing on the ground — and while we possess no sure data for making judgements about marks left by UFOs, we can be positive on one point, namely that there are no human traces. Of course the whole thing is very, very puzzling for us.

The recording which was broadcast on *France-Inter* by Claude Villiers, Olivier Nanteau, and Monique Desbarbat in the *'Pas de Panique'* programme this Wednesday, 27 February 1974, is an exceptional piece of documentation. Thanks to an investigation conducted by Jean-Paul Guguen of the French Radio and Television station at Poitiers, we have been able to secure the recording in circumstances which I am not at liberty to explain owing to the necessity to preserve the anonymity of the witness. This recording was not made by an O.R.T.F. (French Radio and Television) reporter. It was obtained by a student who had for several years past been interested in UFOs, who made it himself, and kept it at the bottom of a drawer among his personal papers. Two of his friends, a lady teacher of French and her husband, a teacher of music, were camping in the south of France when they were confronted with a UFO and, above all, with a humanoid. For fear of being ridiculed, they consented to tell nobody about it except this friend, the student. They knew that he, at any rate, would believe them — because he was familiar with the subject. Here then is the story told by Madame X—, who at the present time is a teacher of French in a lycée:

●

—It happened at Saint-Jean-du-Gard on Wednesday 9 August 1972, at about half-past-two in the early hours of the morning. We had returned pretty late that night, and were camping at the home of some friends of ours who have a terraced garden. This garden is on the road leading to Nîmes as you leave Saint-Jean-du-Gard. We were on one of the hills bordering the valley. I had stepped outside at about 2.30 a.m. because I could hear the blare of noise from the fete going on in Saint-Jean-du-Gard. Above the town there was a quite bright glow, caused by the illuminations at the fete. But on our side of the valley the sky was quite dark. There were lots of big clouds and absolutely no light at all. All the lights were off in the houses that overlook the valley from the hill-

Top and *bottom*. During the series of broadcasts on *France-Inter*, a young lady came to offer me these photos. She explained: 'I am passionately keen on photography. I go for walks in the countryside with my camera, and this is what I managed to snap in February 1974 in the Forest of Fontainebleau.' A rapid investigation enabled me to satisfy myself that it is a fake, and the lady finally admitted that this was so.

A photo taken at the end of February 1974 near Ajaccio in Corsica. The eyewitnes who was photographing the sunset at the time, suddenly saw a silent, luminous ma move across the sky.

side. So I was enjoying the cool night air when my attention was drawn to a sort of white ball, of the size of an *Isotta Fiat* (an egg-shaped bubble car). It puzzled me. It shone very brightly. I could not understand how the car could be so bright when all around me was dark and there was not a single light anywhere.

It was standing on a little parking-area reserved for the occupants of three or four villas built on the hill. I was looking at this brightly glowing vehicle, trying to grasp why it was so luminous, when I heard footsteps behind me. Weird footsteps, not particularly closely spaced, not all that heavy either, as though a child, walking along at a slow and regular pace, were trampling on dry grass. Hearing these footsteps I turned to my left: and there, three or four metres from me, a form was standing facing me. I don't mean to say 'a being was watching me', because, at that time, I didn't get that impression. The form was about 1 metre 20 cms. in height. It was completely black. A curious point is that the body had about it something of the nature of a parallelepiped*. It seemed to me that the object was made of wood some 30 or 40 centimetres thick. This parallelepiped was surmounted by an egg-shaped form at the place of the head. Two round white discs set at eye-level, two round white discs some 5 centimetres in diameter, alone stood out against the black mass which was turned towards me, motionless. I could see neither feet nor legs (or, let us rather say, whatever it must have used for walking) as they were hidden in the long grass.

I shall never forget the impression I felt — a morbid, unbelievable fear, not a bit natural. It was not coming from me; it seemed to be emitted by this shape that I could see there, as though its intentions were to neutralize me. I had never experienced anything like it before. I felt this sensation for about three seconds or so — which was about how long my vision lasted. The whole of Nature seemed dead, as though frozen, around this 'thing'. I had the impression that this being exercised an extraordinary power over everything around it, whether animate beings or plants. Everything was reduced to the same level, that is to say, and I repeat it, congealed, frozen. And then I was back inside the tent with my husband, Michel. At that time I didn't associate this being with the round, luminous object I had seen in the car-park. Next day however I began to realize that there

* *Translator's note:* parallelepiped: the dictionary definition is 'a solid contained by parallelograms.' G.C.

was a connection between the two. After that short but startling sighting, we had both gone back to sleep. Next morning we did not want to talk about it, but finally we asked the occupants of the neighbouring villas whether they had seen anything abnormal. We were met with total incomprehension. All of them were locked up in their own preconceptions. They tried to rationalize it away, saying: 'what you saw were little bits of gravel shining in the dark, or the lights of the passing motor scooters.' However, I was quite certain that those things had nothing whatever to do with it. But, in the meantime, one of the ladies had been thinking. 'Look', she suddenly said, 'Yes, it's true. Right on the stroke of 2.30 in the early morning I heard footsteps on my terrace.' Her house was only thirty metres from our tent, and a little lower down. But she didn't step out to see the famous prowler. She went back to sleep. All the rest of the people remained sceptical. We were banging our heads against a brick wall.

Such then is the testimony of the teacher of French, Madame X—. Obviously we would never have broadcast such a document had we not been able to trace this lady and her husband. Here too Jean-Paul Guguen pushed on with his enquiries, and he managed to locate the two teachers. Two years later, Madame X— told him precisely the same story. Her account raises a number of questions, which Jean-Paul Guguen put to her.

Here then is his interview with Madame X— and her husband, Michel X—. She repeats her story. Her two accounts show no discrepancy, despite the fact that two years had elapsed between the two tellings. Let us take up her story at the moment when she sees the 'thing', which will enable us to compare the two accounts:

—The tent was behind me. I heard footsteps, and thought my husband had come out or was moving around inside the tent. I did a quarter-turn to my left and there, on the same terrace as the tent, I saw something about five metres from me. Indeed, I can't really say I saw 'something', because I got the clear sensation that whatever it was had life in it. I saw someone — or something — which was looking at me, or was at any rate turned towards me, and which was motionless. Imagine a sugar cube which you have painted black. Then you put an oval head on it. The whole thing not shiny, but a matte black. In the place of the eyes two white discs, very

big. And that's all. No mouth, no nose, no arms. I couldn't see if it had legs, because the rank grass there was quite high. 'He' was about 1 metre 20 centimetres in height.
—*Did you have the impression that he was staring at you?*
—I don't want to say that he was 'staring' at me, because there didn't seem to be any question of 'looking' involved in it. There was simply a head turned towards me, but with a very congealed or frozen attitude. I had the impression that something was happening. That Nature had stopped living.
—*For how long did you, yourself, look at the humanoid?*
—It lasted scarcely fifteen seconds or so. I was scared: I dashed into the tent in one gigantic leap.

The husband, Michel X— confirms for Jean-Paul Guguen:

—I was lying in the tent. All at once I saw my wife appear in the tent in one enormous bound. She said: 'I've seen something terrifying — awful!'. I didn't grasp what she had seen, but I realized she had seen something out of the ordinary.
—*Why didn't you go out?*
—Her face was literally distorted with fear. I just didn't have the courage to go out. I closed the tent fastening from inside. And we waited, listening. . . .
 Madame X— continued:
—When I realized that it was a small humanoid that I had seen, I didn't want to go outside again, as I had read that movements of fear on our part might be wrongly interpreted by them.
—*If I understand you correctly, you were already conditioned by what you had read?*
—No . . . Because I didn't at once think of an extraterrestrial or a flying saucer. I was just very frightened at first, and remained gripped with fear for ten minutes or so. Only then did I start to reflect, and to link it with the round luminous form that I had seen below on the parking-area.
—*Next morning, were you sufficiently curious to go and see if there were any marks there?*
Yes. We checked the spots. To begin with, near the tent, there was grass crushed by treading that didn't have any great significance since it might easily have been done by humans. We looked for any traces down on the parking-area too, but in vain.
 Michel X—:
—When we told our story next morning, a woman, living fifty metres from where we were, recalled that at half-past-

two during the night she had heard footsteps on her terrace. She had very nearly decided to get out of bed and look, thinking it was a prowler. In the end however she went to sleep again.

—*If you saw a humanoid again tomorrow, would you push the experience further? Would you try to enter into contact with it?*

Madame X—:

—Speaking for myself, yes, I would, certainly. . . .

—*Without any fear?*

—The next time — no. Let us say, all the same, that if it were in the same circumstances again, at night, I would perhaps have the same reaction of fear. But if it were in broad daylight and I saw him emerge from a saucer, and come towards me in a much more straightforward and sudden fashion, I would take the meeting further — out of curiosity.

—*Do you think the discovery of these beings brings new data for Science?*

—I don't know whether it is for Science, but rather for every one of us. It helps us to have a more open mind, to enlarge our field of vision and our way of life. We must not forget that it is quite possible that there are other forms of life than ours in the Universe.

REPLIES TO FURTHER QUESTIONS

This is now the end of the fifth week of the UFO broadcasts in the *Pas de Panique* programme on *France-Inter*. We have been inundated with letters and we cannot give individual replies to the thousands of questions put to us. What has struck us forcibly in these letters is their high quality. Many of the letters are from professors, students, high school pupils, doctors, lawyers, mayors, engineers ... I had been expecting to receive many letters from deranged individuals along the lines of: '*I am in contact with Extraterrestrials ...*' But no. Out of four thousand letters received, only two or three patently smack of the psychiatric realm. An extraordinarily tiny percentage. For this reason, every Friday, we are inviting a prominent scientist to give a comprehensive reply to the most frequent of the questions. Today, Friday, 1 March 1974, Dr Claude Poher is the guest of *France-Inter*. An engineer in Electronics, Aeronautics and Radio-Electricity, and with a Doctorate in Astronomy, Dr Poher was responsible, on behalf of the C.N.E.S. (French National Centre for Space Studies) for the only foreign experiment set up aboard the American *Skylab*. At the present time he is Chief of the Space-Probe Rocket Division of the C.N.E.S.

•

—*Claude Poher, what are the different known shapes of UFOs?*
—The statistics show that most of them are circular machines, a few are eggshaped, like rugby footballs, and finally there are a few that are shaped like very big cigars.
—*Never any square shapes?*
—It is very rare.
—*Are there areas where the UFOs appear more frequently than elsewhere?*
—No. Not at all. It seems that the phenomenon is equally distributed over the surface of the Earth.
—*Does anyone have any idea of the method of propulsion of the UFOs?*

—None at all.
—*Do you think the Adamski case was genuine? (Adamski claimed to have met extraterrestrials who had emerged from a saucer.)*
—The Adamski case is a notorious hoax.

I received about fifty letters on the Adamski case. A certain number of the writers are indeed persuaded that Adamski really did meet these extraterrestrials who had come to tell him that the world was hastening to its own destruction unless we changed course rapidly. This type of hoax, which is related to mythomania, turns up regularly in the history of the UFOs. Adamski was the one who was the most successful commercially. At the present time a Sicilian is bombarding several European countries, and notably Switzerland, with his amiable prose outpourings. More recently, a French journalist from Clermont-Ferrand went up in a saucer on six consecutive mornings to listen to the dictation of a number of brochures on the Bible and the near return of the extraterrestrials. In this latter case, which I investigated personally, I came to the conclusion that it too was a hoax. This young journalist spent almost two hours telling me how, when he was strolling about in the cone of a volcano in the Auvergne, he saw a saucer land. (In the Sicilian case it was near the volcano Mt Etna!) A being resembling us had emerged — a being with a white skin but with a greenish tinge to it (an allusion to the 'little green men' whom nobody has ever seen). This entity invited my colleague the young journalist to enter the saucer, so that he might explain the Bible to him! On six mornings running this blithe colleague returned with pencil and paper to take down all that was dictated to him, in excellent French, by the extraterrestrial. A journalist who is invited six mornings running to climb aboard a flying saucer and who doesn't even think to take a single photo ... or to get a colleague (who would be a witness, to boot) to take one for him! 'I didn't think of it', replied my young journalist colleague.

Well then ... he's no colleague of mine!

But let us return now to the questions from listeners to our Dossier on the UFOs, and to Claude Poher's answers to them:

—*Have the Russian or American astronauts seen UFOs from aboard their capsules?*

—We know of a report from American astronauts who say that they saw something which it has not been possible to identify. But that sighting was not very interesting, as it concerned a mere dot scarcely visible in Space.

—*How is the brightness of UFOs to be explained?*

—We know nothing at all about it. One can imagine that it is perhaps a question of the ionisation of the atmosphere, but we aren't sure.

—*Are there electromagnetic phenomena that are created by the passage of the UFOs?*

—Definitely! In 2 per cent of the cases we see a deviation of the magnetic compass and a variation in the magnetic field. We also see engine failures in vehicles when their ignition is electrical.

—*Are there commissions of investigation into UFOs in the world in general and, in France, in particular, are there official commissions?*

—None at the present time, and this, incidentally, is the problem.

Is it correct that a saucer crashed in the desert in New Mexico?

—That story was a hoax.

—*UFO = extraterrestrial craft. Is this a hypothesis that you accept?*

—We just don't know. All the hypotheses that have been put forward are unacceptable in the present state of our Science.

—*One listener, who encloses a clipping from our contemporary* Le Figaro *asks: what is the meaning of the message that was dropped by a saucer and analyzed by the Space Research Centre's computer with the assistance of the S.D.E.C.E.?**

—That too was a hoax.

—*Have many French people seen UFOs?*

—It is thought that about 7 per cent of our population have had sightings.

—*Are the UFOs occupied?*

—Some 5 per cent of the cases involve sightings of occupants. This holds good for all countries.

—*What do the occupants look like?*

—Often they are little men who are about 1 metre 20 in height, but who are never green!

—*When do these UFOs appear?*

* France's MI6. G.C.

—They are often seen at night. Of all sightings, 70 per cent are made at night, and mainly between 8.00 and 10.00 p.m. This is probably a sociological phenomenon.
—*Are the marks left by the UFOs always the same?*
—Yes, approximately.
—*Are the UFOs always silent?*
—In 70 per cent of the cases they are silent when the witness is more than 150 metres from them. At less than this distance very faint sounds are reported, such as humming noises, a soft whistling, etc.
—*Could technicians follow UFOs on radar?*
—Yes. This has already been done in about 10 per cent of the cases.
—*Have witnesses been able to touch flying saucers?*
—It seems that this has happened on one occasion. Not having investigated the case myself, I am obliged to say that it would be well to accept this report with reserve. (The incident took place in Canada; a witness's glove was burned when he touched the saucer, which flew off a few seconds later. The witness suffered discomfort for several weeks.)
—*What do you think about the present wave of sighting reports that we are having? Is there not some degree of psychosis in it?*
—I don't think so. When a detailed analysis is made of these eyewitness accounts, we find that the maximum number of sightings is always in advance, by from four to six weeks, of the greatest number of press articles. We are recording now, at the start of 1974, a wave of sightings which is quite classic. But the 1954 Wave was far more important than this one, for we had up to sixty sightings daily then.

At the *France-Inter* microphone, this Friday, 1 March 1974, Claude Poher is followed by a professional photographer. Jacques Vainstain has been around the world several times with his battery of cameras. Obviously, since it is his profession, he is used to taking difficult photos. Now there is nothing more tricky to photograph than a UFO, especially at night. So I have asked Jacques Vainstain to give some simple advice for those listeners who might have the luck to find themselves confronted with a UFO:

—My first piece of advice may seem silly, but I assure you it is the most important: you must have a camera at hand, and a camera that is loaded.

—That seems obvious, but how many eyewitnesses would have liked to have been able to follow this advice, so as to get the extraordinary sight they have seen fixed on film ...

—Yes, for the witness may be distracted by the fantastic nature of the apparition and forget to take any photos, or may take a whole broadside of shots with an empty camera.

—And what about UFO photos in daytime, Jacques Vainstain?

—Theoretically there is no problem. Photos of a UFO in broad daylight are like the hackneyed snap of the family on holiday. You can get very good pictures of UFOs provided that you take lots of photographs. You must bang away and take as many pictures as you can, use up the film, exhaust all your resources by making all the possible settings that your camera will permit ...

—And next, what about night photos?

—Night-time photographs are a bit more difficult to get, especially for those who have very ordinary cameras. Everything depends on the brightness of the UFO. If its luminosity is low, you must rest the camera, either on a stand, or by propping yourself against a wall or against a tree and holding your breath. This will enable you to observe the trajectory of the object. For sensitive film, that is to say, equal to or superior to 125 ASA, an exposure of three to four seconds ought to be all right. If the UFO is bright, as bright as an electric light bulb, for example, it must be photographed as if by broad daylight. That is to say, take an instantaneous snap. But always, if you have the time, vary the exposure times and the speeds of your shots so as to increase your chances of getting one that is just right.

—And what about developing, Jacques Vainstain?

—Yes, that's very important. You must send it to a good laboratory who, bearing in mind the importance of the film as a piece of documentation, will carry out some control tests on it before the final development. This question of its importance is something that you must obviously tell them about when you are sending the film to them.

THE VALENSOLE AFFAIR: A FARMER
PARALYSED BY A MYSTERIOUS RAY

The Valensole affair is so extraordinary that we had to surround ourselves with the maximum degree of precautions. We had to ask the Gendarmerie. Then we had to ask a magistrate. And then we had to investigate the family background of the witness and interview the witness himself. The incident occurred on the morning of 1 July 1965. First now we have Lt.-Col. Valnet of the Gendarmerie, who, with his men, had conducted the investigations at the time when the events took place.

●

—It happened at a spot two kilometres, as the crow flies, to the northwest of Valensole, which is the centre for the cultivation of lavender in the area, and the chief town of a canton of some two thousand inhabitants in the Département of Alpes de Haute-Provence. The eye-witness? A farmer, Monsieur Masse. Married, two children. He was about 40 years old when the event occurred. He is a down-to-earth sort of man, perfectly healthy in body and mind. I was a Captain at that time, and in command of the company of the Gendarmerie stationed at Digne. The witness agreed to be interrogated and to tell me what had happened.

On 1 July 1965, early in the morning, the witness was in his lavender field. He had been busy hoeing. At about 6.00 o'clock he was taking a break, sitting in the shade of a pile of earth and stones, when he heard a brief whistling sound not far off. He could see nothing from the place where he was. He thought it was a helicopter. Wanting to verify whether or not it had landed in his field of lavender, he made for the direction from which the sound had come. As soon as he had got out from behind the pile of stones, he saw that a machine of weird shape had indeed landed in his field, at about 100 m. from him. He made his way towards it by skirting around a plantation of vines flanking his ground, all the time watching what was going on. He soon realized that the machine, which was standing on legs, was of the shape of a rugby football and of the size of a *Renault Dauphine* car. Beneath the craft there were two beings, who were not men. He got to a point ten metres from them. The beings were squatting on the ground. One had his back to him, while the other was facing towards him. It seemed to him that they were looking at a lavender plant. When he was ten metres from them, the one who was facing him spotted him. Both of them then got up. The one who had had his back to him turned around and faced him, and made a gesture with his right hand. In this hand he was holding an object which he afterwards put into a case that he was wearing on his left side. Instantly the witness was immobilized. He could feel nothing. He was neither numbed nor contracted. He could neither move his head nor make any gesture.

—*How did he describe the beings to you, Colonel?*

—Height about one metre. They had very big heads, much bigger than the head of a man. They were completely bald. No chin. A round hole where our mouth is. Eyes resembling ours, but without eyebrows. Their skin was smooth and of a colour identical with that of Europeans. Their shoulders were scarcely wider than their heads, and the heads were set deep into the shoulders. They had almost no neck. They had arms and legs, but the witness was not able to describe the feet and hands.

—*How were they dressed?*

—The two beings were wearing dark overalls. At their sides they had as it were cases or holsters, quite a small one on the left side, and another, bigger, case, on the right side.

—*What was the attitude of the two beings after the witness had been paralyzed?*

—They talked for a certain length of time, eyeing him the while. They eyes moved, and a sort of gurgling came from their throats.

—*Wasn't the witness frightened?*

—No. He felt no fear. A great feeling of benevolence emanated from the beings.

—*What reason did he give you for that?*

—He felt a sensation of great peace. He was afraid of nothing.

—*Did he have the feeling that this sensation of peace was being suggested to him by the two beings?*

—He thinks that it was indeed suggested by the two beings. I myself have gained the impression that it might have been due to tranquilising rays sent out by the two beings to reassure the witness, and to explain to him they they did not wish him any harm.

—*And the craft, how did he describe it to you?*

—The bottom of the craft was 50 cms. from the ground. On the top it had a transparent dome, as though of plexiglass. After some four minutes or so, the two humanoids climbed in nimbly, using first the right hand and then the left. Once they were aboard, a sliding door closed, from below upwards, automatically it seems, like a roll-top desk.

—*Could the witness still see the beings?*

—Yes, through the dome. Then there was suddenly a muffled sound, while the craft rose about a metre into the air. Then the witness perceived, underneath the craft, a tube, with a glint like steel, which was coming up out of the ground. The six legs of the craft started to turn, without raising any dust, and without producing any smoke. While the two beings sat there in their cabin, facing the witness, the craft began to move backwards, in the direction towards which the beings had their backs, and it climbed away obliquely towards the West.

—*Did the witness manage to follow the trajectory taken by the craft?*

—Yes, for about thirty metres. Then the craft vanished like a flash of lightning.

—*What happened next?*

—The witness still couldn't move, but he could see as far as the hills lying about 10 kilometres off in the direction in which the craft had departed. After about fifteen minutes his paralysis ceased. And he found himself just the same again as he had been before.

—*Then what did he do?*

—He stayed where he was for a few minutes, as it had given him quite a shock. Then he went to look at the spot where the machine had stood. He discovered that the ground where it had landed was soaked with moisture.

—*What did the Gendarmerie find in their investigation of the soil?*

—We observed a shallow depression, 1.20 m. in diameter, and 40 cms. deep. There were four furrows, not very deep, 8 cms. wide and 2 metres long. These furrows formed a cross which had its geometrical centre in the hole.

—*How long after the landing did you arrive on the site?*

—Twenty-four hours afterwards. That is to say, the next day.

—*You said that the ground was soaked by the craft. Had it rained that day?*

—No. Not at all. The ground was soaked by the craft.

—*How long did your investigation last?*

—It lasted several hours, in two phases. The witness did not tell us everything at once. We had to win his confidence. We explained to him that it was something important which would enable us to have a much better understanding of these phenomena which have occurred in France and all over the world.

—*When your investigation was completed, what were your conclusions?*

—I believe what the witness told me.

The conclusions reached in the investigation by Lt. Colonel Valnet of the Gendarmerie are clear: the witness was telling the truth. The witness is a sensible, trustworthy man, and not one to have the wool pulled over his eyes. It is nevertheless interesting to cross-check the Gendarmerie's enquiries by those made two months later by a magistrate, Maître Chautard, who functions in Lyons. He is also a Judge in the Court of Appeal at Lyons.

The enquiry by Maître Chautard:

—I made this investigation — naturally in a strictly private capacity — at the beginning of September 1965. Incidentally, it was at once forwarded to the G.E.P.A. Investigation Group in Paris (*Groupement d'Etudes de Phénomènes Aériens*), of which I am a member.

The object of my investigation was to hear, on the spot, the statements which Monsieur M— had already made to a certain number of people, and in particular to the Gendarmerie at Valensole, about what happened to him on the morning of 1 July 1965. I proposed also to seek all the information I could which might be useful in assessing the degree of credence that it was possible to attach to such surprising statements. I therefore listened to statements by the undermentioned people:

1. The Valensole Gendarmes, Monsieur Azias and Monsieur Santoni, who had conducted the official enquiry.
2. The Commandant of the Company of Gendarmerie of the Alpes de Haute-Provence, Captain Valnet; Captain Valnet had been in charge of the official investigation as it had developed, and he had even interrogated Monsieur Masse personally.
3. I likewise had a talk with Monsieur Richaud, the mayor of Valensole and general counsellor for the Canton, and also with Monsieur Ciapello, the mayor's secretary, and with Mme. Tardieu, the assistant secretary.

4. I met the abbé Gourjon, parish priest of Valensole.
5. Finally, I also had an extremely interesting talk with Monsieur Moisson, the proprietor of the *Café des Sports*, and a friend of Monsieur Masse. Monsieur Moisson was the first person to hear his story.

Outside of Valensole, I was able to meet a technician at the Observatory of Haute-Provence who had also conducted a semi-official enquiry regarding the statements made by Monsieur Masse.

All of these people, unanimously, have vouched for the completely honourable character of Monsieur Masse. He is considered a sober, steady, level-headed, and well-balanced man. Aged 41, married, and father of a family, Monsieur Masse runs a lavender distillery at Valensole. His firm is doing well. His favourite hobbies are hunting and fishing, especially hunting, and he had never taken the slightest interest in flying saucers.

The conversations which I have had with him, with his wife, and with his father and his mother, have confirmed my conviction that he did not invent this story.

I have even had the curious impression that the first person to be incredulous about the affair was, in a certain sense, Monsieur Masse himself, and that it took him a certain amount of time to realize and accept what had happened to him, and to be able to talk about it.

The Statement made to Maître Chautard by Monsieur Masse:

'On 1 July 1965, at about 5.30 in the morning, I was, as it is my usual custom to be, in my field of lavender, situated a little to the north of Valensole and near the road to Oraison. I had not yet started up my tractor, which was parked behind a heap of stones some two metres high. I was just about to start the tractor, and was lighting myself a cigarette, when I heard a whistling noise coming from I didn't know where. Then I stepped out from behind the heap of stones which concealed me, and I saw, about 90 metres from me, a weird-shaped machine which had landed in my field. My first thought was that it must be a helicopter, but I soon realised that it could not be. I was very familiar with these Air Force machines which, whether in difficulties or not, often land in my field or beside it. I never fail each time to go over and have a chat with the pilots who, quite often, are hunters like myself. But since this machine was just like a big rugby ball, as large as a *Dauphine* car, with a cupola on top, and standing on six legs, what on earth could it be? Perhaps, I thought, it might be some experimental craft.

'Anyway, I advanced quietly, empty-handed, across the young lavender plants with which my field is covered. And, near the machine, I perceive two small beings of human appearance, stooped over a head of the lavender.

'Not feeling too concerned, I approach them with the intention of entering into communication with them. And so I get to a point five or six metres from the strange visitors, but they see me, straighten up, and one of them at once aims some sort of tube or "pistol" at me. Then I am instantaneously glued to the spot, unable to make a single movement.

'But I can still see what is going on around me. I have plenty of time to examine the two "little men", with their bodies of the size of an eight-year-old child and their enormous heads, three times as big as the normal human head. I notice the total absence of any hair, the skin, seemingly as smooth as the skin of a baby, and white — at any rate as regards the skin on the face and the head, for the remainder of the body is covered with overalls of a fairly dark grey.

'As regards the face, its proportions and its features are approximately those of a human face, with the exception however of the mouth, which has no lips, and resembles a hole. The two small beings were communicating with each other by means of inarticulate sounds which did not seem to be coming from what passed with them for a mouth. They were looking at me, and must have been making fun of me. Nevertheless their facial expressions were not ill-natured, but very much the reverse. Their total posture did not give me the impression that I was face to face with monsters.

'A few moments later, with a surprising agility, the two visitors returned to their craft, entering it by a sliding door. Then the craft took off towards the west at an angle of about 45° and at an extraordinary speed, the machine emitting a whistling noise just as it had done when it arrived, and leaving a trail behind it. I thought that I was at last going to be able to recover control of myself. But it was not so, and I remained there a further quarter of an hour, totally paralyzed; then the use of my limbs came back to me in stages.'

Monsieur Masse himself speaks. . .

This is the third and final part of our investigation into the extraordinary affair at Valensole. The eyewitness himself, Monsieur Masse, who for nearly ten

years has spent his time in trying to dodge journalists from all over the world, has now been good enough to consent to reply directly to my questions. He is a very pleasant man, manifestly a person of great common-sense. His pleasant manner is matched by that of Mme. Masse, his wife.

—Monsieur Masse, have you had second thoughts about your testimony of 1965?
—Oh, No, never in my life.
—Do you still remember it very well?
—Oh, yes.
—After you had been paralyzed by the two beings, did you sleep more?
—Yes — very much longer.
—How long per night?
—At least ten or twelve hours.
—And how long did you habitually sleep before?
—Five or six hours.
—And then afterwards, did you revert to your normal number of hours?
Yes, I reverted to the normal time.
—How long after you were paralyzed?
—Several months afterwards.
—Ah, several months, all the same?
—Yes, yes.
—When you were paralyzed by the two beings, did you feel that they were not hostile towards you?
—No. Not a bit hostile.
—You felt that?
—Yes.
—How did you feel it? By thought transmission?
—Well, you know . . . I can't explain it to you very well. I just did not 'feel' that they were bad, not in the least.
—Can you describe the two beings for me?
—They weren't very handsome. Very small. . . .
—And of what colour?
—Same as ours.
—They were white?
—Yes.
—How big were they?
—One metre, maybe 1 m. 10 centimetres.
—And their faces were white like ours?
—Yes. But not pretty.
—Did they have big heads?
—Oh-la-la, yes!

—*How big?*
—As big as footballs. Even a bit bigger.
—*And their eyes?*
—You know, I've been asked so many questions. Their eyes must have been like this, or like that, but it is beginning to get a little blurred in my memory. After all, it's nearly ten years ago that it happened.
—*You can't recall any more about it . . .?*
—Not after all this time. . . .
—*But anyway, you are quite positive that it wasn't an illusion?*
—I don't think so. Because the soil was analyzed. And it wasn't me who made the analyses.
—*What was the diameter of the saucer?*
—Not very big, like a small car.
—*Like a* Dauphine?
—Yes, roughly.
—*And the same height?*
—Oh, no. It was higher than a *Dauphine*, as it was standing on sort of feet. . . .
—*How far were you from the saucer?*
—About seven or eight metres at the most.
—*When you got up close to the saucer, what happened?*
—They saw me, and stopped me.
—*Did one of them turn round towards you?*
—Yes, that's right.
—*And what did he do?*
—They paralyzed me, and then later they got into their saucer again. They seemed to have a bit of a discussion together, and then they departed.
—*You say that they had a discussion. What were they saying?*
—Oh, well, it was just a gurgling noise. I couldn't hear anything else.
—*How did they gurgle?*
—As though deep in their throats.
—*How long did they remain there on the ground after they had paralyzed you?*
—Maybe one or two minutes, maybe one minute.
—*What were they doing when you arrived?*
—I can't tell you exactly. They were stooping down, but I don't know what they were doing.
—*After that the saucer departed. Did it make any noise?*
—Yes. A rather dull sound.
—*Has the lavender grown again normally on the spot where the saucer landed?*

—No. It only started to grow again this year, ten years after.
—*It took ten years to grow again?*
—Yes. Even though I planted some there, two or three times, it always remained dead in that circle five or six metres in diameter.
—*But wasn't the circle something natural? Weren't there any other circles in your field of lavender?*
—Oh, no. It was the only circle. ...

At Decize in the Département of Nièvre, UFO sightings are on the increase. We have met two witnesses who are particularly trustworthy: an engineer and a gendarme. On Sunday, 10 February 1974, Monsieur C—, the engineer, has the first sighting:

●

—Coming out of my house early in the morning — it was about 6.00 o'clock — my attention was quickly drawn to a shining object, which by its size and its brightness was in strong contrast with such of the ordinary stars as one can usually observe. Its colour was comparable to that of Venus, and the visible surface of the machine was about ten to fifteen times the visible surface of that planet. The object was stationary at first. At the outset its shape was that of a cigar. Then it began to perform a certain number of evolutions, rising at an angle of 45°, and now assuming the form of a rugby ball. The most remarkable feature, which I was able to see very easily, was the glowing point of light turning quite fast around the object. At other moments, this feature being no longer visible, the brightness of the object varied. The object performed a number of different manoeuvres; it oscillated, it went up vertically, always slowly. The seeing conditions were not ideal: the object was behind a tree and, at one stage, it disappeared behind the trunk of this tree. After I had been watching for an hour, it came out again from behind the tree and could easily be seen. Then it climbed away towards the south at an angle of 45°. One of my neighbours, whom I had called, watched it for about a quarter of an hour. It was also seen by my wife and my daughter, to whom I pointed it out. Clouds eventually hid it from my view towards 7.15 a.m. or thereabouts.

Two days later, another eyewitness account of a sighting in the sky over Decize. This time it is the gendarmes who were the witnesses. Their Brigadier explains the case to *France-Inter*:

—This object was of an apparent size of ten to twenty times

that of the biggest stars.

—*At what distance was it?*

—Quite far, but I can't put a figure to it.

—*Was it really very bright?*

—Yes. It had a most intense luminosity.

—*Coloured?*

—It was a very pale greenish-yellow. There were tremendous fluctuations in its brightness. It was so luminous that I could make out a halo around the machine.

—*Was the machine moving?*

—To all appearance, it was stationary. But when watching it with the binoculars I noticed very small movements. It would rise, and then slowly fall again, but without moving forward. It would change from the horizontal to the vertical, and between these two positions it would be briefly at an oblique angle.

—*What was its shape?*

—I could only make out the shape when using the binoculars. With the naked eye, you could only see a glow. Its shape was variable, but I established it as a big cigar very much inflated in the middle. Finally its luminosity faded out. The machine seemed to be climbing as it moved off. ...

PART TWO

*Accounts and Investigations
not broadcast on France-Inter*

THE GIANTS LAND IN CANADA

This account, like those that follow it, has not been published before. We were not able to use it in the *France-Inter* radio series, for lack of time. We managed to trace the witness, in Canada, after quite a lengthy search and thanks to Jean Cazeau, a Quebec specialist on UFOs. The lady, Mme. L—, lives in Montreal. On 22 September 1969, while out walking, she had the most fantastic encounter of her life. Here is her story as she told it to me:

●

—I was with my son. We were walking along a little road near a wood. We were looking about on all sides, as our dog had disappeared in the course of the walk. Suddenly, near the wood, we saw a bright object on the ground. My son and I stopped in our tracks. We were somewhat frightened, and decided to go and fetch my husband, returning along the route by which we had come. Before doing so however we watched what was going on, for at least two full minutes. There were three men outside the machine and two inside it. Tall, slim men. They were wearing a sort of one-piece garment.
—*What were they doing?*
—They seemed to be looking on the ground for something. What it was, we don't know.
—*Was the shape of the machine of 'human' type?*
—Oh no. It was neither a helicopter nor an aircraft — it was nothing known to Man.
—*After two minutes you turned round to go and fetch your husband?*
—That's right, for I wasn't feeling happy. But when we got back to the spot again, there was no longer anything there. Only a flattened circular area of grass.
—*What was its diameter?*
—About ten metres. There were also a number of broken branches to be seen.
—*At what distance did you observe those beings?*
—From about one hundred and fifty metres at the very maximum: maybe from one hundred metres.
—*And you didn't go closer?*

111

—No, because I was scared. I could see quite well that it was something abnormal.

—*How did you realize that it was something abnormal?*

—It's a place that we know well. For more than ten years we have been going there regularly, and have seen only other people strolling there, never the least sign of any mechanical things or machines, not even a motor-car. The road is entirely unsuitable for traffic. The shape of the machine, the very vivid light inside it, and, above all, the size of the beings, left us in no doubt as to what my son and I were seeing — it wasn't normal.

—*What was the size of the beings?*

—About 2 m. 30 cms., maybe more.

—*And the height of the machine?*

—About 5 metres.

—*Did the beings see you?*

—I don't think so. At least not while we were standing still. When we turned back to fetch my husband it is probable that the beings saw us. In any case they were gone when we returned with my husband.

—*You say you saw two beings inside the craft. How were you able to see them?*

—Around the middle of the craft it seemed as though made of glass. You could see the inside of the cabin.

—*What was the shape of the machine?*

—Oval.

—*Did you see the faces of any of the beings?*

—No, for the three who were outside were bending down; the two others inside the cabin had their backs to us. All we saw was simply their uniform, a type of close-fitting one-piece suit covering their bodies, very tight with no distension.

—*Did you tell the Canadian Police about it?*

—No, because whenever anyone said they had seen a UFO, the papers said — or implied — that he was unbalanced. So we preferred to keep quiet about it.

—*And was there an investigation subsequently?*

—Yes, but by a private Quebec society which concerns itself with UFOs. My son decided to write to them, for the papers were carrying more and more sightings. He asked for my permission to tell the society about our adventure, and I said he could.

—*How long was it after your sighting that the investigators came?*

—In July 1971 — that's to say two years later.

—*Now, Madame L—, let us go back to the day of your sighting. How soon afterwards did you return to the spot?*

112

—About ten minutes later.

—*And what did your husband do?*

—He walked over to near the little wood, to the spot that we indicated to him. He and our son both went over there. I stayed behind, for I was still scared. But he beckoned me to come and shouted: 'Come and see — there are traces of them here.' Then I went forward, and saw the large circle of flattened grass.

—*Were there any footprints?*

—In long grass, it is difficult to say. There were certainly traces of something there, but maybe these were simply marks made by people who had been strolling there.

Mme. B— and her husband wrote to me. They had listened with more than the usual degree of interest to our presentation of this UFO dossier on *France-Inter*, since they themselves had been face to face with the problem. One of my colleagues at the Poitiers station of O.R.T.F. (French Radio & Television), Michel Sorbier, did the investigation. The case had occurred here in France. In 1957, Monsieur and Madame B— were camping, in a caravan, at a place some 30 kilometres from Saint-Etienne. They had just reached an isolated spot when . . .

●

—My husband was overturning a big stone. I was beside him, guiding him.
—*So you were occupied in doing something, and not asleep?*
—We were not asleep, and our minds were certainly on what we were doing. Moreover I have written to Jean-Claude Bourret to say that we were not in the slightest bit 'conditioned', for we did not believe in, and were not thinking about, what you imagine.

Suddenly we were blinded by a sort of searchlight, of an intensity difficult to describe. It was just like a car headlight, but multiplied an incalculable number of times. We found ourselves bathed in light, and had the sensation as though we were being X-rayed, as though we were being 'frisked', as if transparent — yes, in fact, it was just as though the light had pierced us.
—*You are both experienced hunters, and you were armed?*
—Yes. Our guns were in the caravan. My husband is indeed very fond of guns, and we never set out without a rifle or a sporting gun. On the day in question, we had two guns with us.
—*Would you have been capable of using them?*
—We have used them, but never against a saucer! I repeat, however, I did *not* have a gun in my hands.

My husband, who is extremely nimble and alert and clear-headed suddenly shouted: 'A flying saucer'. But I don't know what prompted him to do so.

Just at that moment, the engine of the car stopped. I stepped down from the running-board of the caravan and my husband got out of the truck. Then the searchlight went out, revealing a sort of big ellipse there. I got the impression that it was a sort of big neon tube, round or elliptical, orange-coloured at first, then green later. They were shades of colour that I had not been used to seeing; they didn't appear to me to be 'earthly' colours. The orange was very bright, and at the same time we could hear a slight hissing sound, mingled with a very faint noise like the sound of a sewing machine. This noise was very faint, much quieter than the sound of a car starting up. Then the glow began to move away obliquely, very fast. As the elliptical glow receded, the orange changed to an extremely brilliant green. It was a type of green and a brilliance such as I had never seen. As it got further and further away the green became blurred at the sides. I don't know whether it was because of the altitude, but I had the feeling that its light had gone out rather than that it had moved away. The light went out round the edges, leaving only one large luminous spot. Then that too went out. But it all happened so quickly. . . .

—*How long do you think the occurrence lasted?*
—From the time when the big light took us by surprise, to the final disappearance of the luminous spot, about one-and-a-half minutes.

—*How did your hunting dogs react?*
—When the spot of light had vanished we both remained stupefied for a while. Then my husband asked me if I wanted to go on or to stay. Both of us were trembling. We didn't know what to do. Firstly because we had had the feeling (we were sure that it was a flying saucer) that we had stopped 'them' from landing. Then because, after further reflection, we thought on the contrary that they had in fact already landed, and we had disturbed them. From the way in which it happened, they must have been just leaving and not coming down.

(Monsieur B— joined in here). When I said: 'It's a flying saucer,' I had already seen the side of it, before you had spotted it. . . .

Madame B— continued:
—In the end we decided to stay there and to set up the caravan. My husband unleashed the dogs. They immediately ran off down the hill and up the other side on to a plateau identical with the one we were on, about 500 metres from us. We had decided to spend the night there, without uncoupling the caravan and without using the chocks. We hadn't yet

115

eaten, but we scarcely felt hungry. Our stomachs were still tied in knots. My husband prepared his gun, saying: 'You never know . . .' We were just about to eat, when all five dogs came tearing back, their eyes haggard, their tails between their legs, their hair bristling, slavering, and seemingly utterly terrified. We had never seen them like that before. We knew our dogs well: they aren't afraid of anything. We realized that they must have had a shock, presumably of the same sort as we had. We concluded therefore that during their run they must assuredly have encountered the same experience as we had. Maybe the saucer that we had seen at close range had landed on the other plateau? Or maybe there were other saucers over there? One thing was sure: the dogs had indeed seen something that had had a traumatic effect on them. We could not get them to leave the caravan again all that night. The minute we tried to take them outside they turned vicious. They would have bitten us. They were no longer themselves. Next morning they were normal once more.

—*When you saw the machine the first time, the dogs were shut up. Didn't they react the first time?*

—They were inside the caravan. Besides, when they did go off, they went in a perfectly normal fashion. When we opened the door for them, they dashed out, unquestionably after a hare. From the way in which they were yelping, we realized that they were following a scent. They were dashing ahead normally, up hill and down dale. Then suddenly we couldn't hear them any more. We thought they must have lost the scent. We realized that their wild scamper had been halted by some sudden shock, but by what? They have been quite normal since then, except for old Miro, who can no longer bear thunderstorms. For a long time we have wondered why. We think he suffered some traumatic experience that day, and that he has been unable ever since to stand lightning flashes. We have to shut him up in a locker every time there is a storm, for he goes pretty well mad. He had never done that before. On the contrary, he was a dog who never feared anything.

DO YOU WANT TO COME AND PLAY WITH US?

At 10.30 on the morning of 29 August 1967, at Cussac in the Cantal Département, about twenty kilometres from Saint-Flour, two children are getting ready to pass the day as they have passed all the other days. They are on holiday, and are helping their parents, who run a farm. François and Anne-Marie are looking after the cows. François is thirteen and his sister is nearly ten. The two children are in a field which flanks a little road. Suddenly François notices that, instead of grazing peacefully as usual, the herd of cows are beginning to move away from the road rather nervously — as if they have been disturbed by something. François runs round in front of the cows to make them turn back. Which is all the more necessary, as some of the cows are already into the neighbouring fields. Then suddenly he sees, in the direction from which the cows have just come, and about forty metres distant, behind a screen of trees, a sort of big shining ball, about three metres wide. Silhouetted against the ball are four small dark figures. He and his sister approach them. The two children pause for about a minute on the other side of the road, trying to grasp what it is they are looking at. As the silhouettes are small — about one metre high — François thinks that they are children. He shouts: *'Hi! Do you want to come and play with us?'*

The small beings, who seemed to be seeking something on the ground, raised their heads. Then something unbelievable happened: one after the other, the four little beings flew up into the air, silently. They rose into the air and entered the luminous ball, with their heads downwards, that is to say: head first. Just as the fourth of the little men was about to plunge into the ball, he flew down again to pick up something from the ground which he seemed to have forgotten. Then the ball began to glow more brightly. 'It hurt my eyes', François told the Gendarmes later. The ball began to climb slowly in spirals till it was at a height of about 15 metres. The fourth little being, who in the meantime had picked up the thing on the ground, now caught up with the ball in flight. The ball had now begun to glow more brightly. It started to whistle. This whistling noise was heard by a trustworthy third party: Monsieur D—, the village policeman. The ball then vanished in a few seconds towards the level

117

lands of the Cantal.

Panic-stricken, the two children returned home in a hurry. Their mother wondered what was the matter, and so did their father, who had just come in. Accompanied by the two children, still smitten with fear, he at once went to the place to see what had happened. The children did not want to go with him right to the very spot where the landing had taken place, and they stayed on the road.

The village policeman found no marks on the ground. On the other hand there was a strong and pungent smell there — an odour such as he had never smelt before. He decided to inform the Brigade of Gendarmerie at Neuveglise. The latter arrived shortly before 4.00 p.m., or about five hours after the sighting. The odour was still there. An inexplicable odour, which they compared in their report to the smell of sulphur.

Another important report came from the doctor. After seeing the very luminous object, François, a robust child previously in perfect health, was stricken with an inflammation of the eyes. The doctor subsequently found that the child's eyes were red and were watering, like the eyes of a skier who has been looking at the snow in bright sunlight without protecting himself with sunglasses!

What can we say about such testimony? A hoax is totally excluded. Little peasant children do not leave a herd of cows without a serious reason. Should they by chance do so, then they would find themselves a classic excuse, such as: 'We saw a snake' — or something of the sort. Though these little shepherds, despite their tender years, would anyway have been quite familiar enough with their natural environment to take a stick and kill the intruder. Neither François nor his sister knew anything about UFOs. A concocted story is therefore to be ruled out. Especially as there are already some rudimentary beginnings of proof: namely the odd smell noted by their father and later by the Gendarmes, and the inflammation of François' eyes. I say: the beginnings of proof, since it is *conceivable* that François might have set fire to some sulphur and that he might then have stared at the sun with his eyes wide open to produce the results as reported. But, like the Gendarmes, and like the parents of François and Anne-Marie, I am convinced that they were telling the truth. And what enhances the value of their account is the fact that a precisely similar affair occurred in Brazil. My friend Carlos Marques, a Brazilian journalist who is a specialist in UFO matters, has sent me both the report of the Brazilian Police and the report of his own investigation. Here is this second piece of testimony:

At 9.30 p.m. on 20 December 1971, Manuel Silva e Souza left the Brazilian Air Force Base at Itaperuna. This is a small town in the State of Rio de Janeiro, which makes its living from livestock and from a condensed milk plant, and has four thermal springs. Manuel is a watchman at the Air Force Base. He is 60 years old and the father of a family of 13 children. As he explained later to the Police:

—My attention was suddenly drawn to a light which was coming towards me from the Airfield. An altogether unusual sort of light. I thought it was an aircraft on fire, trying to land. Suddenly the light vanished. I couldn't believe my eyes. I looked around to see whether I hadn't been dreaming. And then I found the light was behind me, standing in a field, near the arrival runway. Then I thought to myself: yes, it is indeed a burning aircraft that has crashed. And I ran towards it. But as I got nearer I saw that the unusual light was quite unlike the glow of flames. It was of a vivid pale blue colour. When I had got to 20 metres from it, I realized that the light was coming from an oval shape. It was very beautiful, but it hurt my eyes. And then I saw the being....

—*What was he like?*

—He was walking about near the dazzling object. He was small. About 90 centimetres in height, or maybe one metre.

—*Did he see you?*

—Yes, he looked at me. Very intently. I was extremely scared, but I looked at him very hard too. I couldn't believe my eyes.

—*And what did he do?*

—A few seconds later, he turned his back towards me. He put his arms out horizontally like this (Manuel makes the gesture). And then — I couldn't believe my eyes — he rose up from the ground without a sound. Without any movement of his own body he returned to his machine, as though drawn up by an invisible force, and he entered it through the top, head first.

—*Do you mean to say that he rose up in the air without making any movement himself?*

—Yes.

—*Did you see only the single occupant?*

—No, there were two others inside. At least two. They were just looking at me, motionless. I was scared. Then a sliding door closed with a faint sound. And the object flew off.

—*Fast?*

—Very slowly to begin with. But at fifty metres from me, it accelerated to an unbelievable speed, and vanished in a second.

—Let us return to the creatures that you saw. How were they dressed?

—They were wearing khaki-coloured uniforms. The material of it seemed very supple but recalled nothing known to me. The beings were wearing, over the uniform, belts of a lighter colour, avocado green. The belts also had very handsome big buckles. On their feet they had little tight high boots. A bit like those worn by boxers.

—And their faces?

—They had faces that resembled ours. But the neck was shorter. I had a good view of them, as they were wearing no masks. Of that I am sure.

The description given by this employee of the Brazilian military authorities is more detailed than that of the children at Cussac, because he got closer to the UFO. But it is not the only report that corroborates the children's story. Senhor Húlvio Brant Aleixo, president of C.I.C.O.A.N.I., a UFO investigation group in Brazil, has a similar report which, after very careful study, he considers authentic. The descriptions of the UFOs and of their occupants vary from account to account. And this makes the phenomenon just that much more difficult to grasp. It is however a significant point to be borne in mind that two small French peasant children and a man of the Brazilian military personnel have described precisely the same thing.

THE MAN WHO WAS KIDNAPPED
BY A SAUCER

Many questions have been put to us, in the letters received, about a case of kidnapping by a saucer. It is said to have occurred in Brazil. Not having investigated this business myself, I can only be sceptical about it, but Carlos Marques, my Brazilian colleague, was able to investigate it for us. Here is his account of this adventure which, incidentally, took place in the same region of Brazil as the last case: near Itaperuna.

●

'On 19 November 1972, Paulo Caetano Silveira, aged 27, a typewriter mechanic, was returning to Itaperuna at the wheel of his car, a *DKW*, together with a friend, Elvio Bianchi, who is a devotee of capoeira (Brazilian wrestling.) Paulo was driving along peacefully on the deserted road when he suddenly had the presentiment that something strange was about to happen.

'On several occasions, on 15, 16, 19, 22 November, and 5 December 1971, Paulo Caetano had encountered, on this same road, the occupants of a spacecraft from another world. He had given an account of what he had seen, but he was a lone witness, and nobody had believed him. As he had no proof to support his story, the inhabitants of the region and the authorities took him to be unbalanced.

'On that evening of 19 November 1972 one may well imagine the state of nervousness that this presentiment could have aroused in him. He spoke of his misgivings to his companion, but the latter only made fun of it, saying: "Nothing can happen to you, because I'm with you!"

'A few moments later, Elvio Bianchi dropped off into a deep sleep. And again, just as on the five previous occasions, Paulo Caetano saw "the mysterious object" coming towards his car. He made desperate attempts to awaken his companion. In vain: Elvio seemed as though dead. Paulo lost control of the car. The electrical system had been neutralized, and the car left the road. Meanwhile the mysterious object had landed beside the road. Here is Paulo Caetano's account:

"The door of my car opened of its own accord, as if by magic. An intense luminous beam drew me irresistibly towards its source (the craft) and I felt myself rising all on my own without my making any sort of movement. I entered the machine quite naturally, just as if I were entering my house. At the very centre of the craft there was a table, and, without knowing why or how, I found myself stretched out on it, my legs dangling over the end. An instrument came up on my right: two things like claws came down towards me. One seized my wrist and fixed it to the table — not at all roughly — and the other claw seized me by the biceps. A sort of ashen-grey coloured tube injected a liquid into my arm, slightly above the elbow. The 'three little men' (there are always three of them) began making an incision in my arm without my feeling any pain. I did not realize what they were doing until I saw that they were taking a transfusion of my blood into a very fine tube about 20 centimetres high. Then the instrument dropped down again. I got up and the 'three little men' showed me two pictures hanging on the wall: one showed a map, and the other was a photograph of an atomic explosion. When they showed me the second picture, they made agitated movements in all directions, but without making a sound. Then they pointed to a sort of oxygen bottle, like the ones in hospitals. And once again they made lots of agitated movements. The bottle was all white, almost silvery. I didn't understand a thing. They didn't attempt to talk to me; I don't know why. I, for my part, did not manage to speak to them, or rather, I don't recall having tried to do so. Later, at the police station, I tried to pinpoint on a map the region they had shown me in the first picture: it was to the north of the State of Rio de Janeiro.

"Finally, I came down out of the machine, but I don't remember how — no doubt by the same way that I had gone up into the mysterious craft. I was completely stunned."

At that moment Elvio Bianchi woke up. He too tells his part in the adventure:

'All I saw when I woke up was that *Piston* (Paulo Caetano's nickname) was lying flopped out in the car, with a wild look in his eyes. He had a nasty cut on his arm. The car was standing askew on the lower side of the road and I thought we had been in an accident. I took Paulo by the arm and he was literally "all in". A bus came along the road, and I signalled for it to stop.

'Paulo was taken to the casualty department of the Itaperuna Hospital. There Dr Humberto C. Tinoco diagnosed him as having a third-degree burn (like those from fire or boiling water.) He was only treated for this burn. According to Dr Muniz Bussold, a burn of this type takes a week to heal, with the right treatment. But a characteristic scar remains. What, then, was the doctor's astonishment when, the next day, he examined Paulo Caetano: the burn had mysteriously disappeared. There remained only a small v-shaped scar at the spot where the incision had been made in his arm.

'The technical services of the Itaperuna Police, who had photographed Paulo's arm the day before, took a new picture, showing no burn, about ten hours after the happening had occurred. The Itaperuna doctors met together in an extraordinary session but they were unable to reach any conclusions — except that the affair involved something unknown to our Medicine and at present inexplicable.

'In addition to the doctors and the police of Itaperuna, only the driver of the bus and its passengers know about the strange encounter of Paulo Caetano with the "unknown beings". This same bus driver, on 9 October, between Italva and Itaperuna, had had his attention drawn by one of the passengers to a strange luminous object which was following them high above. All the passengers could see it; it followed them as far as the entrance to the next town through which they had to pass. The bus had to stop there, so adamant were the terrified passengers that they would not continue the journey by night.

'This supplementary account was recorded by Police Commissioner Airton Teixeira, and confirmed by Omar Salema Armond, the passenger who had been the first to see the mysterious object following the bus and who had given the alarm.'

PART THREE

*The Opinions of the
Scientists Broadcast on
France-Inter*

A MANIPULATION OF SPACE-TIME?

Interview with Jacques Vallée, consultant in Statistics at Stanford University, U.S.A., by Michel Anfrol.

With Dr Jacques Vallée, we now come to the final part of this UFO enquiry: the attempts at an explanation supplied by the international scientists who have delved into this problem. On behalf of *France-Inter*, Michel Anfrol made a tour of the American universities, meeting the leading experts on UFOs in the U.S.A. On the Stanford University's computer Dr Jacques Vallée has docketed over three thousand cases of landings observed at close quarters by witnesses. This means that he knows his subject:

●

—Jacques Vallée, what type of sighting accounts do you collect?

—I am interested in the cases which indicate that the witness has been close to one of these objects, and for a number of reasons. Firstly, because in this way you get far more information regarding the physics of the phenomenon. You can ascertain the distance, the size, the true luminosity of the craft, etc., and study the physical traces of the landing. Then, and this aspect also appeals to me very much, there are the descriptions given by the witnesses regarding the physical effects that follow upon the sightings. Here we discover a whole range of astonishing findings, which are extremely difficult to classify in the present state of our ignorance regarding psychical or mental phenomena. I am not telling you anything new when I say that a large part of human folklore has to do with legends in which there is talk of meetings with beings that have come from elsewhere in celestial objects. You come across it in statues, on rock carvings, and in religion. Unfortunately it is difficult to reconstruct, merely on the basis of a legend, what really took place.

What is striking in the cases where there has been a near approach by a flying saucer — and there are thousands of such cases — is that the eyewitnesses describe a fundamental change in their ideas on a whole host of problems.

For example — their ideas about life and death. Often the victim remains in a state of shock. The sighting makes such an impression on him that he calls into question every idea he has ever had, everything he has ever thought about existence.

This does not mean to say that the phenomenon is necessarily of an intelligent character. Many things that are natural and that are explained produce the same phenomenon: the mountains of India, Niagara Falls, make such an impression on certain people that their whole life is changed, their way of looking at existence is modified. In the case of the Saucers, the witness seems to be describing something else. It evokes not merely a new awareness of certain phenomena, but also psychic effects which are apparently verifiable. It is difficult to say more about this at present: research on these matters is in hand. However, certain witnesses seem to have developed unusual talents after contact with the phenomenon: for example — talents of an extrasensory nature. It will be interesting to follow the development of this type of research in the future.

—*Could the thoughts of people in contact with the phenomenon be linked with what is called extrasensory perception?*

—Yes, in many cases they can. The problem is to know whether the UFO problem is itself a psychic manifestation or whether it is simply a question of a physical phenomenon which makes such a deep impression that it influences or disturbs the functioning of the human brain. The fact that the witnesses describe extrasensorial phenomena does not signify that there is any intention on the part of the objects to produce these phenomena in the witness. Opinion is divided on this question. People are ready to reach conclusions because they would like to have an extraterrestrial saviour. American opinion, at this very moment, is experiencing, with the 'Watergate' affair, a vast hunger for purity. The flying saucers, as myths and not as physical phenomena, can supply this to a public opinion which is thirsting for purity, and which seems to be expecting an extraterrestrial intervention. There is thus certainly a phenomenon of a sociological order. It will be difficult for the scientists who embark on this work to sort things out and conduct valid experiments.

—*Now, you yourself, after having studied thousands of landing cases, can you reach any conclusions as to the origins of these UFOs?*

—I am a statistician, and not a physicist. What interests me, in the close range UFO sightings, is the semantic side — in

128

other words, the nature of the information which can be derived from this encounter. It is then for the physicist to decide whether the performances which seem to be in flagrant violation of physics could be explained by a change in our ideas about the structure of the Universe. It does not seem to me impossible that we might discover new theories in physics according to which the nature of time might be far more complex than what we know about it at present. Our ideas on the structure of space-time are still primitive. They are in contradiction with the experiments made daily in modern physics. I am not revealing any secret of the physicists if I remind you that there are flagrant contradictions between Quantum Mechanics and Relativity. Everywhere, in all the universities, they are looking for new theories that could reconcile the series of observations being made in their experiments. From this point of view, the UFOs are only one new phenomenon among a whole host of others which seem to contradict the present laws of Physics. The fact that the UFOs exist does not imply that we are being visited by an extraterrestrial civilization — it is simply a *possibility*. It is certain that there is a very high probability that life exists in the Universe. Consequently there are certainly beings in this Universe that are capable of travelling and possibly of visiting us. The problem remains to calculate the probability that these beings would discover us, and then what interest there would be for them in visiting an outer suburb of the Galaxy such as the area where the Earth is. It is much more interesting to find that the UFOs have apparently been seen throughout the whole history of Mankind, and that they do not seem to have evolved during the past two thousand years. This seems to indicate a manipulation of the structure of time. Regard this merely as a hypothesis. ...

From my point of view as a statistician, and to come now to the semantic side, I am interested in the fact that the dialogue (whenever there has been dialogue between the witness and the supposed occupants of the UFOs) is always absurd. It is absurd in a characteristic fashion. For example, in 1954, a witness who was passing through a wood at 4.00 o'clock in the morning, near a little town in Alsace, met a man dressed in a one-piece suit. He took him for a pilot. The dialogue between them was laboured: the witness, who was of Polish origin, knew nothing of the language of the supposed pilot. Finally they managed to understand one another when the witness spoke in Russian. The so-called pilot understood a few words of Russian. Here is the gist of their dialogue:

—The pilot asks: 'What time is it?' '4.30', says the Pole. 'That's not possible! It is 2.00 o'clock', replies the pilot, who now asks a second question: 'Am I in Germany or in Italy?' 'You are in France.' retorts the witness.

The unknown individual thereupon plunges into the forest, making signs to the witness not to follow him. Puzzled, the Pole disobeys. Coming to a clearing, he sees an oval-shaped object standing on the ground. The pilot climbs into the object, which takes off at great speed. At this moment the witness realizes that the supposed pilot is no pilot, and that he has been speaking with someone else. Later on he is told that it was probably the occupant of a UFO. ...

—*What can one deduce from this piece of testimony?*
—In the first place, that it is improbable that it was a hoax. When they occur, hoaxes are usually logical, not absurd. Furthermore, the witness knew nothing whatever about the UFO phenomenon. The descriptions and details given by him are consistent with what we know about the phenomenon. Secondly, the dialogue was confined to two absurd questions. The first question was an absurdity to do with time, and the second was an absurdity to do with space. We find these constants in all these discussions. It is therefore interesting, because when one tries to express a truth in a language that transcends our view of the world, one is obliged to do it in the form of an absurdity. All the languages of the great mystical texts are based upon absurdities of this type.

THERE ARE OTHER FORMS OF
LIFE IN THE UNIVERSE BESIDES OURS

Interview, by Jean-Claude Bourret, with Jean-Claude Ribes, radio astronomer, graduate of the Ecole Polytechnique, Doctor of Science, in charge of research at the C.N.R.S. (French National Centre for Scientific Research.)

●

Today, Friday 8 March 1974, as on every Friday since the beginning of this series of broadcasts, a scientist answers the questions which recur most frequently in the letters we have received. In these letters the question of the extraterrestrial hypothesis is often mooted. Obviously there is nothing yet that would authorize us to link the UFOs with extraterrestrials. It is another problem. Between the probabilities of life in our Galaxy, and Flying Saucers, there lies the abyss of the Infinite, bridged by a hypothesis. So it is merely a hypothesis. Is it a likely one? Jean-Claude Ribes* replies:

—*Jean-Claude Ribes, taking into account the recent explorations by unmanned space probes, have forms of life been discovered in our own solar system?*
—No. Within the solar system, the possibilities of life are not very convincing. The planets around us are either cold, or very hot. I am not talking even of the distant planets, such as Jupiter, which are freezing, and contain either methane or ammonia, and other substances that are not very favourable for life. The planets which we have in mind are Mars and Venus — the nearest planets to the Earth. Mars is a little further from the Sun than the Earth, and so a little colder. It has very little atmosphere, and virtually no oxygen, but it is not ruled out that certain forms of life may exist there. We won't know this for certain until after the landing of probes which go on working sufficiently well after they have got

---

* Co-author with François Biraud, of *Dossier des Civilisations Extraterrestres* (Pub. Fayard, Paris, 1970 and in *J'ai Lu Series* [*L'Aventure Mystérieuse*] 1972.)

there to be able to give us the information. This has not been the case so far. On Venus, conditions are the reverse of Mars: it is very hot, almost 300°. An enormous pressure (one hundred times our atmosphere) is prejudicial for any life there might be — though we cannot totally dismiss its possibility. We possess no information as to what might be found to be living on the surface of that planet. It remains certain that there is no form of evolved life there, and in particular no advanced technical civilization possessed of radio or possessing lighting. Illuminated cities — on Mars for example — would be perfectly visible to us during the Martian night. If such possible inhabitants there had radio or television we would be receiving their waves in enormous strength compared with the waves we receive in Radio-Astronomy.

—*So no intelligent life seems possible inside our Solar System? But inside our Galaxy ...?*

—The word 'galaxy' is one that requires a little explanation. It is what we see in the sky, and what we call the 'Milky Way'. It is the Universe in which we live. That is to say, a collection of about one hundred thousand million stars, of which each is a Sun greater or smaller than our Sun. ...

—*You say a hundred thousand million stars in our Galaxy: how have they been counted?*

—Obviously we haven't counted them all, one by one! The method used is to add up the stars, one by one, in a quite small square of sky. In this way we find several hundreds or several thousands of stars. Then you recommence the same operation on other small squares of sky. Then by extrapolation and by a simple rule of three we deduce from it the existing density of stars. We arrive at the total number without the risk of being very far out in our calculations.

—*So our Galaxy contains about a hundred thousand million stars? But are there other galaxies?*

—There are probably tens of thousands of millions of galaxies like ours.

—*That's fantastic. What is the diameter of our Galaxy?*

—A hundred thousand light-years. The speed of light being 300,000 kms. per second, in relative space, that represents the astronomical number of kilometres, which you can work out for yourself on the basis of 86,400 seconds in a day, thus 31,356,000 in an ordinary year, etc.

—*That's a fine piece of multiplication.*

—Certainly. But in order to give an idea of what that distance is, let us make use of a comparison. The Earth and its Sun are separated by a mean distance of 149.5 million kms. The light of the Sun takes eight minutes and eighteen seconds to reach you. The light of the nearest star to the Sun takes four years. That gives some idea of the space separating the stars.

—*Inside our own Galaxy are there other planets like the Earth, other forms of intelligent life?*

—It is virtually certain. To begin with, we have known theoretically for twenty years or so that the formation of a planetary system constitutes part of the normal evolution of a star. Probably the planetary system is formed at the same time as the star, or maybe later, but it is a natural stage of evolution. In other words, around almost all the stars of our Galaxy, there exists a planetary system similar to our own. Consequently, in very numerous cases, there is a planet roughly similar to the Earth, and offering favourable conditions for life.

—*What we don't know is whether a form of life will appear on every planet similar to the Earth? Have you tried to make contact with these other civilizations of the Cosmos?*

—Certainly. One of the best possibilities for making contact is wireless waves. Since 1960, radio-astronomers have begun setting up listening programmes. In the United States, Professor Drake set up *Project OZMA*. It consists in listening in the vicinity of the wavelength emitted by hydrogen.
. . .

—*We ought perhaps to emphasise that this hydrogen is found everywhere in the Galaxy.*

—That's right. Hydrogen is a fundamental constituent of the Universe, whence the interest in its study in astronomy, and particularly in radio-astronomy. It is characterized by the presence of a line in radio, that is to say, an emission on a narrow band, comparable to a radio emission on a precise wavelength.

—*Whence the choice of this wavelength?*

—Yes, because it is universal. YOU FIND IT IN ALL THE GALAXIES. Any radio-astronomers who might exist, around no matter what star, will know that it is one of the most important wavelengths in radio-astronomy.

—*Let us come back now to Project OZMA.*

—The idea was thus to study the area around this wavelength for hypothetical intelligent radio emissions. The stars selected were fairly similar to our own Sun. They are situated at six light-years from us. Drake had a telescope of very modest dimensions compared with our modern instruments. He listened for three months. Not continuously, but on and off, and on pretty primitive receivers.

—*What did he get?*

—He picked up nothing at all. His research was negative. But that is normal. There was virtually no hope that he would have the luck to get something at the first attempt.

—*Indeed it would have required a great number of coincidences. The stars have to possess planets; the planets have to be like ours; there has to be an intelligent form of life there; these intelligences have to be at precisely the same technological level as we are; and our brothers of the Cosmos also have to have radio.*

—That's it, precisely. You see that the probability turns out to be quite small. It can be accepted that around the majority of the stars there has been, there is, or there will be, a civilization passing through the same stage of development as we are now at. But for the two stages of development to coincide — what a poser! In other words, are these other civilizations of the Cosmos a hundred thousand years ahead of us, or are they behind us by a hundred thousand years, or by ten thousand years, or by a thousand years, or by a century? Even a century might be decisive for any possibility of contact. What would it have been like, say, a hundred years ago, when radio had not been discovered? And what will things be like here in a hundred years from now? Herein lies the difficulty for contacts between different civilizations in the galaxies.

—*Can we visualize that there might be other ways of getting in contact with these other civilizations?*

Yes, we can. But I think that wireless waves are the best means. We know a lot about wireless waves. We know that they propagate themselves right through the Universe. We are receiving natural signals emitted by the Universe and which have taken hundreds of thousands of light-years to reach us. In addition to this, we are receiving artificial signals from our own space probes which traverse millions of kilometres. Radio is still an excellent means for making contact. The essential thing is to have sufficient patience. It would be a good thing if projects like OZMA were repeated at regular intervals. This has in fact been done in the U.S.S.R. There have been two projects there. The first one was in 1972, and the other one more recently. Another listen-in took place in the U.S.A. in 1973. One of the biggest radiotelescopes was used for three weeks to study about fifty stars. So far as I know, no positive results were recorded. This was a project very similar to OZMA, but done with very much better equipment. That is to say, equipment with a thousand times greater sensitivity.

—*Jean-Claude Ribes, you are a radio-astronomer, and you*

*are a graduate of the Ecole Polytechnique. Can you accept
the hypothesis that the UFOs could be coming from another
planet?*

—Yes, certainly. That is quite conceivable. If indeed they are
objects that are intelligently controlled, which seems to be
clear from a good number of the eyewitness accounts, then I
think that the extraterrestrial explanation remains the most
rational one. But it raises problems: the distances and the
time necessary for such a journey. It is very difficult to imagine. In any case, if the UFOs exist, then it is an entirely rational explanation.

THE IDENTIKIT PORTRAIT OF THE 'HUMANOIDS'

Interview with Patrick Aimedieu, a research scientist with the C.N.R.S. (French National Council for Scientific Research.) Interviewer: Jean-Claude Bourret.

●

—*Over the past twenty-five years, more particularly during these last few years, the eyewitness accounts mentioning UFO landings with simultaneous sightings of humanoids have been increasing in every country in the world. What should be the attitude of a scientist towards these accounts?*
—To begin with, a completely natural attitude: not to reject these accounts *a priori*. Otherwise it would be proof of subjectivity. Secondly: to analyze these reports systematically. On the scientific level one must display a certain scepticism, and only consider a phenomenon if it can be reproduced in the laboratory. I will give an example: a researcher conducts a scientific experiment; he defines its conditions; he publishes a report; another researcher possessing the same means can, on the other side of the world, carry out the same experiment, and observe the same results.

When you find yourself confronted with the UFO phenomenon, you are placed in just the same conditions as when it is a question of observing and analyzing some rare atmospheric phenomena. The statistical evidence does not prove that the phenomenon exists (you would need to have the phenomenon 'in your hands'), but it opens up the mind and leads you to the conclusion: *there really is something there.* And so the phenomenon must be systematically observed and analyzed. At this stage, you see interesting things appearing. ...
—*Things that emerge from the statistical study of the eyewitness accounts?*
—Yes. For example, when you ask an eyewitness: 'What did you see? What was the general form of the personage?', he states a height. And so we can proceed to draw up statistics about heights. The personage is already beginning to be defined. He has a head, arms, legs. The investigator asks the

136

questions: the shape of the head, the eyes, the amount of hair, the colour of the skin. All these questions figure in the investigator's questionnaire. Next, this questionnaire is sent to the researcher, who sees a number of disturbing details appear. For example, the height. People often talk of 'little green men'. This is nonsense, because, so far as I know, no eyewitness has ever spoken of little green men. On the other hand, it is true that the beings observed are generally small: 1 m. 10 cms. or thereabouts. For the researcher, the question that arises is this: why does an Argentine farmer, a Frenchman, an African, a Russian, a North American, a Japanese, see the same thing! Everywhere throughout the world, and in every country, this type of small person is being seen. There are a sufficient number of eyewitness accounts — hundreds of them — for the researcher to ask himself the question: *'Is this true?'*

—Then what about the Identikit portrait of the humanoid?
—You can't make one. Because, when you study the question in depth, you realize that there are numerous *categories* of eyewitness accounts, *describing different beings*. It is true that there are lots of eyewitness accounts about the little beings. But witnesses have also seen larger entities. There are some who resemble us: same height, same colour of skin — and who speak the language of the eyewitness. Some of the big ones are two metres high. Some are cyclops (one-eyed). Others appear to be wearing a diver's suit: so you see how difficult it is to establish the Identikit portrait! All the more so, because the witness who has no knowledge of the UFO problem will describe the phenomenon in terms of his own knowledge and his own vocabulary. Despite it all however, we do end up by defining some general features.
—All this is baffling. It is already hard enough to accept that little men, coming from no one knows where, are visiting us, but that the eyewitnesses should affirm that they have seen giants and cyclops, in machines of varying shapes, this is even harder to believe. Don't you have the impression that some proportion of these extraordinary accounts have been made up?
—It doesn't seem so. It must be borne in mind that investigators (I refer to the professional investigators, such as the Gendarmes or the Police) are in any case all sceptics at the outset. They 'grill' the witness, if you will permit my use of the expression. When the witness is an adult, it is easy for professional investigators to get him to contradict himself — if he has been lying. When a witness is able to give all the same details for several hours on end and repeat them in

interrogations spaced at intervals of several weeks, doubt is scarcely possible. Or you would have to suppose that the witness is possessed of exceptional imagination and memory. That is obviously not an impossibility, but, once again, there are thousands of eyewitness accounts in the world, which come from all social levels and which confirm each other. Some people have put forward the theory that the eyewitnesses are narrating a sort of interior fantasy common to all men, which explains why the accounts tally. This problem has been studied in Psychology. The question has been asked: why do the witnesses see a being with two arms and two legs? Is this not because the witnesses have projected a sort of unconscious desire of their own to see the 'beings' who are 'visiting' us resembling our own image?

—*There is an argument that refutes this interpretation: namely the marks left on the ground, confirmed by the authorities; the UFO pilots; the physiological effects. An inner fantasy does not leave marks in fields, and cannot be photographed.*

—Precisely. And now take the Valensole case. Why should that farmer, a reliable and respectable man, tell stories that have in fact brought him nothing but trouble? On the other hand, the beings described by the eyewitnesses have curious behaviours. Some walk. This was the case at Valensole. Some fly, as at Cussac. If it is a chap who is not an addict of science fiction stories who is giving evidence, who is in close touch with Nature but never reads, his evidence carries far more weight.

—*How can you be sure that a farmer has not read any novels?*

—It is easy to find out. You ask around him, his neighbours, the village bookshop, the schoolmaster. You can get a precise psychological profile of him. There are moreover certain objective features which confirm the reality of a sighting. There are cases where eyewitnesses have fired at little beings or at UFOs. When the bullet strikes the UFO, the impact is heard. When the bullet strikes the humanoid, he retreats under the effect of the impact. So here we have fantasies that obey the law of ballistics and mechanics. In 1954, long before man went into Space, we had descriptions of humanoids dressed in a sort of supple, metallized overall, like chocolate wrapping-paper. Now we are making metallized plastics ourselves. We weren't doing so in 1954. Consequently, the witness has not been influenced by a 'reality' that he himself has projected. It is this that makes the evidence credible, especially as there are hundreds of other simi-

138

lar cases, scattered throughout the world.

—*Which, among all the accounts, is the type that recurs most frequently?*

—The little entity.

—*1 metre 10, 1 metre 20? ...*

—That's right. A humanoid presenting a certain number of characteristic features: big head, little feet, little hands, eyes which look at you, eyes of varying colours. Certain witnesses have described eyes which look at you and which therefore resemble our own organs of vision. Others have described a sort of luminous discs, red or white luminous surfaces. One can speculate that in such cases the witness is mistaking something else for eyes, and that the visitor is wearing a sort of overall with a helmet which gives a distorted image of the face. Everything is possible!

EXTRAORDINARY CREATURES?
BUT WE HAVE THEM ON EARTH!

Interview with Rémy Chauvin, Professor of Biology at the Sorbonne, by Euloge Boissonnade.

Rémy Chauvin is a particularly likeable man. His mind always wide awake, curious about the world around him. He has examined the UFO problem from the angle that interests him: have other forms of life appeared to us? Are beings different from us even imaginable? Can one, for example, imagine the existence of life-forms in a toxic environment?

●

—There is no need to go far to find beings with a biochemistry different from that of man. To start with, we know of larvae of certain insects, certain mosquitos, which live in the water of geysers at 65°C. That is a pretty high temperature. Bacteria and lower forms of vegetable take sulphuric acid into their metabolism. Some larvae of flies live in petrol. Not only do they live in petrol, but they can *only* live in petrol. In their intestines they carry bacteria which hydrolize the paraffins in the petrol in order to live on them. There is talk now of making proteins from petrol. These flies have long been doing just that. Finally, we have made an even more astonishing discovery. This is the story of the *Kakabekia*. An elementary organism has been found in the urinals of the miners in Wales. These worthy miners always emptied their bladders against the same wall. Odd growths were noticed. These were analyzed, and a microorganism was discovered, which had previously only been known in the fossil state. It dated from Silurian times; it had survived here, in an environment that was quite special, because it needs ammonia. It can only survive where there is an atmosphere with a very high ammoniac concentration; admit that this is curious! Even on Earth you find creatures whose biochemistry is special. Others, like the rotifers, live in the dessicated moss of roofs. When the moss is dessicated, they enter upon a period of diapause and shrivel to a very small curd of dry substance which you would swear is dead.

Several researchers have demonstrated that these creatures can be lyophilised. That is to say, they are dried in a carbonic vacuum at —60°. All their water is removed from them. Then they can be plunged into liquid air, that is to say, at —183°. The curd is taken out of the liquid air and put on a blotter with a drop of water. After a short time the creature reinflates itself and proceeds about its normal occupations as though nothing has happened. Here we have the typical interstellar traveller. Had it, for example, say, been stuck to a meteorite, it could go travelling around indefinitely in the cold of sidereal space. Thus, even on Earth, we see extraordinary examples of abnormal biochemistry.

—*Have you other examples, Professor?*

Yes, there is a little beetle called the bombardier beetle.

—*Why such an extraordinary name?*

—Because, when it is captured, it emits a sort of explosion, with a puff of yellowish gas. A short time ago we found out what happens. In the rectal vesicule of this insect, oxygenated water is secreted — concentrated oxygenated water. When the creature is disturbed, it injects into its oxygenated water a peroxydase — that is to say, a substance which renders the oxygenated water explosive. It is indeed a real explosion! Thus the animal has developed an elementary form of rocket propulsion. The decomposition of oxygenated water is in fact used as the propellant of some of our rockets. So we already have, here on Earth, living organisms developing systems that we would never have expected to see functioning.

—*Well, now, Professor — two hypotheses. If beings from elsewhere are visiting us, they can either resemble us like brothers, or they can be totally different beings since they would live in a different environment?*

—Yes, both cases are indeed possible: they are the two extremes. Let us remain on our good old Earth, so as to get a better grasp of the possibilities. Worthy folk imagine that intelligence has developed in one direction only — in that of Man. Naturally Man appears as the 'prince' among the animals living on the planet. But, if you look a little more closely, it all becomes a lot more complex. Firstly, you know that cerebral development is often measured by the weight of the brain relative to the weight of the body. Of course this is only a rough index, but an index all the same. Now there is already an exception: the dolphin. He has a 'brain weight-body weight relationship' which is identical with that of Man. We know relatively little about dolphins, because the Americans have assumed charge of the science of dolphin-ology — as it is called — and are keeping their work secret because of its military applications. All we know is that dolphins can detect military swimmers, and can place mines on the hulls of enemy ships. Friendly ships are protected by a special metallic plate which the dolphins have learnt to recognize. It is also known that dolphins use an extremely complicated language. They have not managed to decypher it so far. And there are other examples too. In the phyla — or if you prefer so to put it — in the families, of creatures extremely distant from ours — as in the *Mollusca*, for example. Among these there are the octopuses. Thanks to their enormous and extremely developed brains, they can use their complicated appendages, for example, to get a crab out of a bottle. As for their enormous eyes — I don't know if you have ever been looked at by an octopus — but it is anything but a comforting glance. These molluscs, therefore, on some hypothetical planet or other, could have seized the opportunity that Man has had on Earth. A planet run by octopuses? That's a nightmare: a bit of Science Fiction. But let us just imagine it! In any case, there is, once again, nothing intrinsically absurd in it — in the present state of Science. So there are the dolphins who could have developed, there are the octopuses — and then also there are the birds. The birds have no hands of course, but in their beaks they have a precision tool with which they can do a lot of things. Not long ago it was discovered that the brains of birds are capable of performances that, in certain respects, are equal to the performances of chimpanzees. The birds could have had their opportunity too. Thus there are two possibilities: either the hypothetical travellers would be similar to Man, which is not unreasonable, or they could be from other families which have not had the opportunity on Earth but have had it on other planets. I can't decide which would be the more likely of these two versions.

Are all the eyewitnesses of saucer sightings crazy? One would be tempted perhaps to say 'Yes' when listening to the explanations of the 'anti-saucerites'. During the discussion on the *Actuel 2* television programme, where Pierre Guérin faced four journalists, of whom I was one, certain of my colleagues brought up the results of a psychological study which had been made of witnesses. According to this study, the eyewitnesses who see UFOs are in general frustrated people. Either because they occupy a position which is above their intellectual possibilities. Or because, on the other hand, their position is below their capabilities. Can the whole UFO business be boiled down into a sort of complex of frustrations? Professor Rémy Chauvin gives his view:

—Those who claim that saucer eyewitness accounts come solely from people not possessed of a satisfactory mental equilibrium have not examined the UFO dossier, and don't know what they are talking about. In particular, they are unaware of the existence of numerous photographs and marks left on the ground. In fact, over the past five years a large number of UFO landings have been reported by a whole lot of witnesses. These landings have sometimes given rise to panic situations — notably in the United States. Naturally these witnesses have hastened to give the alert at the nearest police station. Generally they display a state of considerable fear, and policemen are despatched to see what it is all about. Well now, a large proportion of the marks prove the recent presence there of something material: the soil is as though scorched, and the marks of supports are found, as if some more or less heavy object has landed there. I will not give any examples. They are innumerable, and you have already given quite a lot yourselves in the course of your broadcasts. Your listeners are thus extremely well informed.

—*Do these marks permit us to draw conclusions?*

—We can scarcely draw any conclusions from these marks — except that they are of large diameter, sometimes twenty or thirty metres, and that they do not correspond to any identified terrestrial machine. These precise facts, plus the existence of photos that have been judged authentic after investigation and scrutiny — including some photos, incidentally, in the Condon Report itself — plus the marks on the ground and the statements made by eyewitnesses of good faith (some of them themselves astronomers) cannot be denied. It would consequently be preposterous to say that there is nothing to the UFO phenomenon. To do so would be to display an un-scientific sectarianism.

—*It is not very likely that life — at any rate intelligent life — exists within our Solar System. Must we therefore conclude that these UFOs come from elsewhere?*

—Yes. Obviously. I don't see where evolved and intelligent life could develop within our Solar System. There is nothing on the Moon. On Mars there are still some unknowns: let us say there is a faint chance of life; if there is life there, it would probably be a primitive life. My own personal opinion is that, if there are machines visiting us, it is doubtful that they

143

could come from our Solar System. But are they machines? Telepathic projection has been mentioned. All sorts of things could be suggested. I myself however am inclined towards the explanation that they are machines from elsewhere. As a matter of fact it would be a difficult problem if they were coming from elsewhere than in our Solar System — that is to say from the Galaxy — or from even further. Indeed it is difficult to accept this — in the present state of course of our own Science. However, we must never tire of reminding ourselves of one true fact — and that is that our Science, such as we know it today, is an altogether recent creation of the human mind. At what stage was Physics a hundred years ago? It wasn't very advanced, you have got to admit that. I think Galileo would be pretty astonished if he were taken now and put in front of a nuclear reactor, don't you?

So, Science is recent. It is evolving rapidly, which nobody can deny. The science of 1974 will provoke a few smiles among the scientists of the year 2000. Everyone is in agreement about this, in theory. In practice however nobody agrees with it. We musn't say: it is impossible for interstellar craft, if there be such craft, to be visiting us, because of Einstein's equations! In the present state of affairs, and given what we know at present, it is indeed quite impossible! I repeat: in the present state of affairs. Let us therefore leave the decision as to whether such a thing is possible or impossible to a Physics that will be more evolved than our own is at present.

— *You are a biologist, and consequently you are particularly well qualified to reply to one question which everybody asks: could these beings who have come from elsewhere resemble us?*

—There is an enormously high number of chances that planets of the same type as the Earth have been created, by stellar evolution, in large numbers. I do not understand how anyone could support any other theory. Or, if of course you do, we are back with the old geocentrism: 'the Earth was the home of intelligent men, the place where the Redemption took place. Consequently the Earth was distinguished among all the planets, and there couldn't be another planet like it in the Universe.' Well, for some time past we have ceased to follow that sort of thinking. It seems however that a certain number of scientists, possibly out of fear of the consequences that might result from an infinity of planets throughout Space, are now reverting to the old geocentrism. So I think that if craft were arriving here from worlds biochemically similar to ours it would seem probable that their passengers would be roughly similar to us. It does not seem an impossibility.

—*Could they have come from the same 'original soup'?*

—In some sense, yes. You talk of 'original soup'. Do you know that for some time already we have no longer been limited to mere hypotheses? We can do experiments. If I remember rightly, we must go back to the 1950s: a young student, whose name was Arthur Miller, and who was a pupil of Urey (Nobel Prize for Chemistry, 1934), had asked Urey for permission to carry out an experiment. He said: 'I am constantly hearing people talking about "original soup", about the primitive ocean in which life must have proliferated. Why not try an experiment on it?' 'An experiment?' asked Urey, 'How would you want the experiment to be?' 'Well', said Miller, 'What if I put into a flask what we believe was in the original soup, namely water of course, some gases like methane, some ammoniacal salts — in short, purely mineral substances, with nothing living? Then I would set off a number of sparks in the flask, since it is claimed that a certain number of the reactions presiding at the birth of life came from the influence of the electricity produced by the frequent thunderstorms over the primitive ocean. What do you think of the idea?' Urey said: 'I think you are crazy.' 'Then', said Miller, 'Are you forbidding me to perform the experiment?' 'Oh', replied Urey, 'If I were to forbid you, you would do it all the same; but I'll bet you $2,000 it will fail'. 'It's a deal', replied Miller. The sequel is well known. Miller did the experiment. After eight hours, he notices that in the bottom of the flask, where he has set off the sparks, a reddish substance has appeared. He analyzes it. He finds, among other substances, peptoids, that is to say, the first bricks that go to building proteins. What are proteins but the very fabric of our bodies! Since then, the experiment has been repeated many times. Whole congresses have been devoted to biogenesis, that is to say, to the improvement of Miller's apparatus. It has become so technical and so complicated that it is difficult to explain. The essential thing to know however is that at the present time, and in a quite commonplace fashion, work is being done on the original soup, on biochemical evolution. Hope has not been abandoned of manufacturing — I say *manufacturing* — elementary organisms. Oh, admittedly they haven't succeeded yet ... What they have observed are all sorts of vesicles which contract and which divide, but which merely remain caricatures of cells. Starting from there, two hypotheses present themselves. Firstly, the hypothesis that we shan't succeed, which, personally, I would hardly find surprising. And then the conclusion will be that it can only have happened in altogether special circumstances.

Or, alternatively, that we shall succeed one day in synthesizing it. This is not entirely impossible, because progress towards biogenesis is going forward very fast at present. It would be an extremely exciting result. It would show, as Teilhard de Chardin had already hoped to show, that matter is a sort of immense machine, blind and deaf, you understand, *but which is only there in order to create life.* If we could show that life must necessarily arise when matter is in a particular state, it would indeed be quite astonishing. This would enable us to say with absolute certainty that this life is very widespread throughout all the galaxies. For this reason the experiments which we are conducting at present could perhaps yield us some probabilities or, on the contrary, some improbabilities, regarding the possibilities of life developing outside the Earth.

ARE THEY ROBOTS, OR LIVING BEINGS?

Are we sure that the humanoids seen by numerous eyewitnesses are, if one may so put it, creatures of flesh and blood like ourselves? Or, alternatively, could they be highly perfected robots? This latter hypothesis cannot be ruled out. There are many surprises in the realm of Ufology. Patrick Aimedieu, a research scientist with the French National Council for Scientific Research (C.N.R.S.) is once again our guest to discuss these hypotheses.

●

—*The humanoids are fairly well known, thanks to over a thousand sightings of them throughout the world. But all we know about them is more or less their outer envelope. Can one attempt to say whether they are living or mechanical?*
—We are unable to give an answer. But we can exercise our imagination. Robots? Let us take a precise case. An eyewitness sees a flying saucer appear one day over a pond. It takes up a stationary position near the pond. Then little beings appear. They go around the saucer. The witness says: 'they walked with a jerky gait'. Well — were they robots? We can't tell. One can only speculate, on the basis of our own technology, our own culture. Some specialists have thought that these might be modified human beings, on to whom certain special organs have been grafted. In this sort of thing one rapidly falls into Science Fiction, and that is not a scientific attitude. To exercise one's imagination is natural. At times it is necessary, but it is very important to remain cautious and to *base one's reasoning only on what is certain.* Now, in the subject of UFOs, there are no certainties. Obviously some folk would like the humanoids to be truly visitors from other worlds. Or maybe visitors from the future who have invented a machine for time-travel into the past. Such a thing is for us, in 1974, a technical impossibility. But it would be rash to say that men will never succeed in time-travel.
—*What other hypotheses are there to explain, or attempt to explain, these UFOs?*

—One can imagine that they might be beings coming from another Galaxy and who have taken several hundreds of years to get here. They might have founded a civilization which could have spread throughout the Universe, a civilization that is not associated with any one planet in particular, and that dwells in Space. ...

—*How could we make contact with 'Them'?*

—The problem is to know if it is we who ought to contact them or they who ought to contact us. That is, if 'They' exist, and if UFOs are not the fruits of I don't know what sort of imaginings.

—*We don't,* a priori, *have the impression that they are all that keen on getting in touch with us, since they run away every time they come face to face with eyewitnesses.*

—Not necessarily. There have been certain cases in which the humanoids ran away. In other cases, there have been contacts. Witnesses have said that they have been addressed in a language that they could not understand. Was the speech borne through the air from a vocal organ, or were the humanoids projecting a thought into the mind of the witness. We simply do not know.

—*Are you thinking of telepathy?*

—Yes. Telepathy has been envisaged by specialists in the UFO question. We are in a domain here where we have to exercise our imaginations. But — I must repeat this — that is no longer Science.

—*Is contact possible between totally different psychisms?*

—Let us take an example in order to understand the problem better. Between the mind of a child and the mind of an adult it is clear that there is an insuperable gulf. There are lots of problems that a child cannot comprehend. And yet the child and the adult both speak the same language. Maybe we are in a similar situation, with this difference, that the gulf is no doubt even greater between us and the humanoids, and that we do not speak the same language. In that case it is necessary to imagine the gulf which, say, separates the ant from Man. ...

—*Have these sort of relationships been studied?*

—Yes, researchers have studied animal psychophysiology and animal sociology. It seems that Man can communicate with a living being, but a living being of a lower mentality. Man can speak to his cat or his dog and be understood by them. Man, in the same way, can understand his dog if he puts himself on a lower mental level. But can we generalize from this reasoning and from this fact, and make it applicable to beings possibly coming from another planet? Especially if they are very different in structure and nature from us.

—*We have already discussed this problem of other 'humans' in the Cosmos. But what do you think about it, Patrick Aime-dieu?*

—One would like to say that life follows the same laws, or almost the same laws, everywhere. There are the same chemical elements throughout the Universe. Of that we can be sure. The laws of nuclear physics necessitate it. But how can one cause life to be born from those chemical elements? One would like to say that it starts from carbon, and that then you go on to make aminoacids and so forth right up to living organisms. And that these will have the same form, along with a certain symmetry. But obviously all this is only a hypothesis. Given the particular conditions prevailing on that other planet, will the minds of the living beings that are going to inhabit it develop in the same fashion as we ourselves? Maybe they will. But maybe not.

—*Are Mathematics, our Mathematics, a result at which an evolved society is inevitably bound to arrive?*

—One may well start by wondering whether or not an advanced civilization will even use Mathematics. Would 'They' have a decimal system of numbers? Would 'They' have Euclidean — or non-Euclidean — Geometry? Would they have followed the same line of intellectual progress in the sphere of Mathematics? Would they see the Universe in the same way as we do?

—*And what about Physics?*

—On the basis of our own astronomical observations, it seems absolutely clear that the laws of Physics are valid everywhere. If not, then we would have to call in question all our models of the Universe. In conditions of pressure and temperature identical to those on Earth, you will have water boil at 100°C at the other end of the Universe. The light emitted by hydrogen atoms on Earth is the same as the light emitted by those same atoms at the other end of the Galaxy. Thus there are laws that are identical. So, if a psychism sets itself to the task of trying to comprehend the Universe around it, that psychism will have to go about it in the same way as we do. That is, of course, insofar as the entity has the same sense organs as ourselves. . . .

—*This brings me to my next question: would an evolved being, but a being living on another planet than ours, necessarily possess the same sense-organs as we do?*

—When you analyze Man, you realize that, living in a gaseous environment which is transparent to light, he has ears,

149

that is to say, organs sensitive to the vibrations of the air, eyes sensitive to certain wave-lengths of light, a skin sensitive to shocks and heat, and a nose and tongue sensitive respectively to smells and to taste. In other words, organs designed to enable him to survive in his environment by giving him a maximum amount of information about that environment and by enabling him also to comprehend his own position in the Universe, when he has reached an advanced stage. So one can imagine that it is the same everywhere in the Universe, and that there will always be beings possessing sense-organs for surviving and moving about in their environment. Perhaps they will have more sensitive organs that ours, with a wider field of perception. They might perhaps be able to see in the ultra-violet or the infra-red, for example. They will have a different corpus of knowledge about the Universe right from the start. Perhaps they will have progressed more rapidly than we have done? But that is not certain. Would a psychism that is different from us have developed in the same way as we have done? We have to ask ourselves the question, without being able to give the slightest answer for it.

—*If there are beings travelling around in machines, then one feels tempted to say; yes.*

—Obviously, but we are obliged to ask ourselves the question. Look at our own little humanity. It has already got to the Moon. Soon it will be Mars and Venus. In 200 years, if there is no cataclysm, we shall be much further. Perhaps we shall then confront other psychisms, discovered by *us*. And we must ask ourselves the question: *What are we going to say to them?* If indeed any dialogue with them is possible. Why not start preparing ourselves now to get used to the idea of other types of faces? In the United States, Frankenstein masks represent horrible and terrifying forms. Certain folk have thought that, unconsciously, mankind is in this way getting itself ready to meet faces which to us would not be all that agreeable. Extraterrestrials who maybe really would have weird heads. . . .

IS THE ROLE OF THE UNIVERSE TO CREATE LIFE?

Interview with Jean-Michel Dutuit, a palaeontologist in charge of research at the C.R.N.S.

Obviously one cannot reject the hypothesis of extra-terrestrial visitors as an explanation for the origin of the UFOs. It would mean that intelligent life exists in our Galaxy or elsewhere. And here is the great question — *is life itself the purpose of matter?* In other words, is life a part of the normal processus of evolution in the Universe?

Jean-Michel Dutuit replies to the questions:

●

—*Does your training as a palaeontologist enable you to contribute any concrete data to the search for the truth about the UFOs?*
—No, I don't think so. I think that at present no scientist can make any direct link between his own researches and the UFO phenomenon. On the other hand, a scientist, whoever he may be, can contribute a method of study to help in tackling the problem that we have to solve. An astronaut or an astrophysicist will be well equipped to answer the question: was it a meteorite? A meteorologist will contribute other details about lenticular clouds shaped like saucers. But the connections are minimal. The UFO phenomenon has so many forms, and one is obliged to contemplate such a range of material phenomena, that it is impossible for one single man to find his bearings in this imbroglio.
—*All the same, Jean-Michel Dutuit, let us try to benefit from your scientific talents. A certain proportion of international scientific opinion is beginning to accept the idea that the final aim of matter is life. Do you agree with this view?*
—I don't think the whole scientific community accepts it entirely. There is just a tendency developing that way. Twenty years ago it wasn't possible to see how the transition from inert matter to living matter could take place. There had, it is true, been laboratory experiments. The experiments proved that it is possible to accept the 'construction' of certain ele-

mentary organic bodies. But, as regards the later sequence of events in the process, it was thought that an enormous amount of chance was involved in the phenomenon. Even to-day, I don't say the majority, but at any rate a large number of scientists, still think that life is a very exceptional phenomenon which occurs only on Earth.

—*How do things stand now?*

Over the course of the past twenty years the tendency has been to reduce this part represented by chance in biogenesis. In particular, since we have been employing frequency spectometry, we have been able to detect the presence of numerous organic molecules in the Universe. These are as it were the basic building bricks which enable us to envisage the possibility of constructing life. There is more or less general agreement now in saying that, on Earth, the first elementary bacterium made its appearance about 4,000,000,000 years ago, the Earth itself having been formed 5,000,000,000 years ago. It will be observed that the birth of life was thus already almost immediate, viewed of course on the geological scale. Thus, going back through all the stages, you find that bacteria already existed 1,500,000,000 years ago. After that, things go much faster. 800,000,000 years ago there were already all kinds of multi-cellular organisms inhabiting the seas and even the shores or the land. Then, after that, 600,000,000 years ago, at the beginning of the Cambrian, we find a fauna and a flora that are extremely complex. ...

—*And what about Man?*

—As far as Man is concerned, the latest scientific theories lead us to think that we might perhaps be able to include him among the primates of ten or twenty million years ago. It has thus taken 4,000,000,000 years to produce Man. Or even 4,500,000,000 years. ...

—*Is it possible to visualize that, on another planet like our own, there might be such a span of time as these 4,000,000,000 years available for producing a form of intelligent life?*

—It is difficult to give a reply to that. You fully grasp of course the complexity of a question that involves too many unknowns. But, so as to remain very cautious, we can speak of *tendencies*. One may say that, for about ten years past, the *tendency* — in these days when we are still in the early, faltering stages of Biology — is to say that life is not an accidental phenomenon. It is highly possible that life appears from the very moment when the right conditions come together on a planet. As to the problem of knowing whether

152

GROUPE DE SCIENTIFIQUES DE L'OKLAHOMA (U.S.A.)
ÉTABLI LE PORTRAIT TYPE D'OCCUPANT DES M. O. C.,
RES LES DÉTAILS DE QUELQUES 300 CAS D'ATTERRISSAGES
(Interprétation de M. TALLÉ)

supplied by French UFO investigation group *Lumieres Dans La Nuit* of
nbon-sur-Lignon. Caption reads: 'A group of scientists in Oklahoma, USA,
wn up the typical portrait of a UFO occupant, based on the details in some
300 landing cases.'
(Interpretation by M. Tallé)

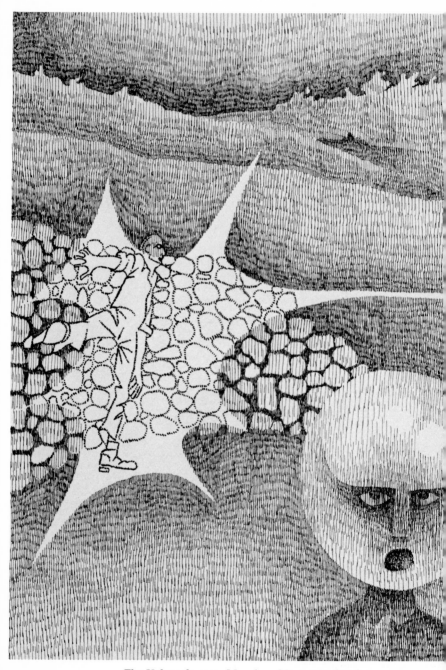

The Valensole case. Monsieur Masse paralyzed.
(Sketch by Pierre Giroud)

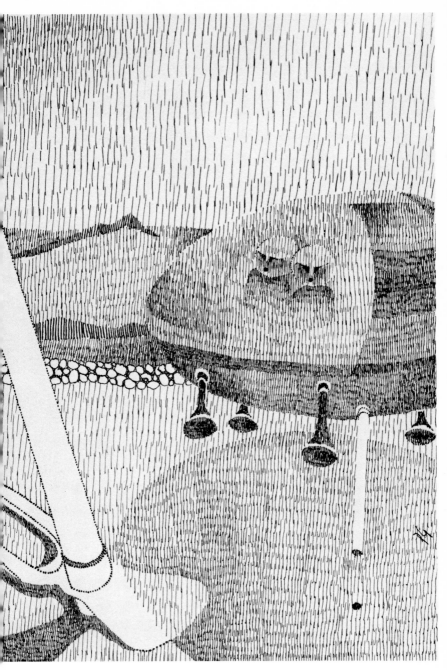

The Valensole case. Departure of the UFO.
(Sketch by Pierre Giroud)

The Black Robot: 'I saw something that was eyeing me . . .'
(Sketch by Pierre Giroud)

such life will evolve as far as Man — that of course is another question. . . .

—*Have you grounds for thinking that the development of life on another planet would end in a symmetrical system, with two eyes, two arms, two legs, etc.?*

—We do indeed have grounds for thinking so, insofar as Nature always ends up with the simplest solution. As regards the arms and legs, the historical record is quite simple — our limbs have developed from the folding back of a sort of longitudinal fins underneath the body of a species of fish. This lateral swimming fold concentrated itself into two groups of fins on each side, one fin in front and one behind. With the help of millions of years we have ended up with articulated limbs that permit the animal to move around on land.

—*And in the case of Man?*

—The matter is complex not only for Man but for all the mammals and all the insects. There has been a parallel process going on, which concentrated the nervous system in the skull. The scientists say there has been *cephalisation*. One can thus imagine, or admit, that the same phenomenon may have taken place elsewhere, because on Earth Nature has always preferred the simplest solutions. But always provided that the conditions on that other hypothetical planet are the same as here, and provided that the process started out at the beginning from the same elements as here. Yes — it is possible, if these similarities in conditions continue to hold good.

We were unable to broadcast on *France-Inter* all the
interviews which Michel Anfrol secured in the
United States. However we give them further on in
the book. By a happy coincidence Claude Poher,
Head of the Rocket Probe Division of the French
Space Research Agency, has been over to the U.S.A.,
and met all the American scientists who are interested in the UFO problem. I think I am giving away
no secrets if I reveal that in March 1974 a meeting
was held in the U.S.A., at the highest scientific level,
of all those university scientists who are investigating the UFO problem. It is not for me to say
whether or not Claude Poher took part in that meeting, but he was in the United States at the time when
the meeting took place. That is why it will be very interesting for us to hear now what Claude Poher has
to say after making that trip:

●

—*Whom did you meet in the United States?*
—I met about thirty scientists. The best-known of them are
Dr Hynek, Dr Jacques Vallée, and Dr Saunders. They are all
engaged in normal academic work, but all of them also devote a proportion of their spare time to studying the UFO
problem. I also met representatives of the American Institute for Aeronautics and Astronautics. This body has set up
a UFO sub-committee, which publishes articles in the AIAA
journal — so that the scientific community may become familiar with the problem. These people of the UFO sub-committee are not actually doing any research themselves on
the subject. Nevertheless, they have published some very
interesting cases, and will continue to do so.
—*How does the UFO question now stand in the U.S.A. Is
there a better approach to the problem there than in France?*
—No. It seems that in France the UFOs are more readily accepted by the scientific community than in the United
States. This is the result of the work of the Condon Committee, which was negative, and which is still producing sterile

effects in the U.S.A. In France we have not had these negative setbacks: the majority of our scientists are unfamiliar
with the Condon Report.
—*The Condon Report is not negative for anyone who is pre-*
pared to read it right through — a thousand pages. It con-
tains cases of UFO sightings, and also photographs, that
were judged to be authentic by the Committee — which
nevertheless was not favourably disposed towards UFOs,
since it had been given, as its mission, the job of whittling
down the whole UFO phenomenon to bad interpretations of
known phenomena. . . .
—Yes, that is the very least that one can say about it. I met
Dr David Saunders, who was a member of the Condon Committee, and who resigned from it. He is the man who has the
largest computer catalogue of UFO sightings in the world.
The last I heard was that he has 85,000 sighting cases in his
computer.
—*Can you recall for us why it was that Dr David Saunders re-*
signed from the Committee?
—Quite simply it was because he did not agree with the working methods of the Committee and the conclusions they produced.
—*You say he has 85,000 cases, Claude Poher. Are those all*
landing cases, or are they sightings plus landings?
—No. It is a mixture of all types of sightings. Ten per cent of
the cases involve landings. Among the scientists in the
U.S.A. who are interested in UFOs, there is a certain degree
of specialization. Dr Saunders collects together all the reports and, on the basis of that, he then compiles statistics at
the request of the other scientists. For example, I asked him
to do a certain number of jobs for me, and he was kind
enough to do them.
—*What sort of jobs would those be?*
—Well, for example, it is easy for us to obtain all the French
cases. But certain foreign eyewitnesses have also seen
UFOs in France and have reported their observations after
returning to their own countries. This type of sighting is
interesting; you can compare them with the descriptions
given by French witnesses. Such comparisons furnish us
with proof that the description of the UFO phenomenon is
identical — whatever the nationality of the eyewitness.
—*What about the landings?*
—There are at present 546 cases of landings with marks,
which have been thoroughly investigated by the American
scientists. Comparing the marks left in these landings and
the marks that have been investigated and analyzed in

France, we find precisely the same features.

—*What kinds of features?*

—Well, for example, the time-distribution of the landings follows precisely the same laws in America as in France. This is disturbing. For, if it is a question of a sociological or psychological phenomenon, then there is no reason whatever why Frenchmen and Americans should be induced to make reports that coincide precisely on all points, when the way of life in the two countries differs considerably.

—*All through this whole series of broadcasts I have met many scientists. Some were 'against' the UFOs, and some were 'for' them. I purposely use this simplistic vocabulary: it has the merit that it defines their attitudes. Well now — I have not met a single scientist who, having made a serious study of the UFO question and, in particular, having himself conducted investigations on the spot, is to be found in the 'against' category after a thoroughgoing study of the subject. How is it in the U.S.A. in this respect?*

—An important study has been carried out in the U.S.A. on this very question. Its findings are quite recent. Out of 195 scientists who were involved, be it closely or be it distantly, in the study of UFOs in the U.S.A., forty per cent were 'for' at the start and sixty per cent 'against'. But after a more or less prolonged study of the subject (ranging from a few days to several years) we find that ninety-five per cent of them were 'for'. And the residual five per cent contained more 'reserved judgements' than 'againsts'. And of course these were in any case the ones who had given the least time to studying the problem: a mere few days or a few weeks. This is the upshot of an analysis covering a span of fifteen years. These figures are consequently highly interesting. It was the scientists themselves who furnished the answers to a questionnaire that had been sent out to them. Consequently it is clear that this is their answer, and this is their position on the UFO question.

—*Claude Poher, we have now reached the point where we shall have to draw up our balance sheet. We are now turning the final pages of this UFO dossier. Can you please tell us, then, what theories do the American scientists have for trying to explain the UFO phenomenon?*

—More or less the same as those put forward in the course of this programme of yours. The extraterrestrial theory is far from being the only one capable of explaining the phenomenon. There are others, difficult ones to verify. Hypotheses concerning the manipulation of Space-Time. At the present moment, we are still at the stage of trying to grasp the characteristic features of the phenomenon. These features are being gauged solely through the intermediary agency of human testimony, with all the inexactitudes that this entails. The approach made in the United States, as here in Europe, is many-sided. We are trying to improve our knowledge by making our investigations more and more thorough and more reliable, by using more appropriate skills and methods, particularly in the interrogation of eyewitnesses. Better use is being made of the investigations of landings. Another approach which we are also making to the problem is via the methods of statistical analysis. It is being realized that when you have got thousands of eyewitness accounts at your disposal, certain characteristic features appear. When reliable investigations are available to us in very great quantity, we shall be able, merely by statistical studies, to secure a far more precise knowledge of the whole UFO phenomenon.

—*Is this where the future of UFO studies lies?*

—It isn't only that. We can hope that, in the fairly near future, we shall be able to set up a certain number of automatic recording stations, which will be capable of giving more objective data on the phenomenon. At the present time we do not know whether the emissions of light that the witnesses declare they have seen are or are not confined to the *visible* spectrum. These emissions of light may very well extend into the infra-red, and into the ultraviolet too.

—*Talk of 'automatic scientific stations' means 'funds', doesn't it?*

—Yes, and that is the nub of the whole problem. But the outlay would not actually be very great. With about 10,000 Francs or so we would be able to further our objective knowledge of the phenomenon quite considerably. For more elaborate stations bigger sums would obviously be needed — which our Scientific Research people won't release to us — at least not at present!

PIERRE GUERIN: MY PHILOSOPHY IN THE MATTER OF UFOs

At his observatory on the Pic du Midi, where he was working, Pierre Guérin was good enough to take time off to reply to my questions. And here is the first question:

•

—What conclusions may we now add to the UFO Dossier?
—Well, Jean-Claude Bourret, now that we have reached this stage in this long series of broadcasts on the UFO Dossier, I think we must try to draw some conclusions. The listeners must indeed be asking themselves many questions. First of all, some of the points already raised have not yet been answered. Perhaps the most important of them is this one: several people who have been questioned have agreed in saying that we do not know what UFOs are, that we do not know their origin, and that the theory that they are extraterrestrial spacecraft is not the only possible one. On the other hand, all these same individuals have agreed in saying that the UFOs seem to behave like intelligently controlled machines that cannot have been constructed by Man owing to their observed performances — which defy anything that we are capable of achieving. I imagine that quite a lot of listeners must be racking their brains over this apparent contradiction between the non-human origin of the UFOs and the doubt as to their extraterrestrial origin. And indeed it is easy to get out of one's depth in all this business. and many other points too deserve an answer. And, right at the very outset, this question of the proofs for the existence of the UFOs: do we have, or do we not have, *proofs* that we are dealing with physical objects or physical phenomena, and not with psychological phantasmagoria? If the answer is *yes*, then why hasn't the existence of UFOs ever been recognized *officially*? How does it come about that Ufology, the importance and seriousness of which are defended by genuine professional scientists, is at the same time stigmatized and ridiculed by a great number of other scientists? How does it come about that the big Parisian daily newspapers virtually never mention the UFOs on their general news pages, as

though the problem were non-existent, while, at the same time, the provincial dailies report such and such a landing or such and such a low-altitude flyover in their regional pages, as furnished by civilian eyewitnesses and, in some cases, even by the gendarmes called to the spot to investigate? And, finally, how does it come about that, the minute it is merely announced that research on UFOs in an important French research laboratory may possibly receive official recognition, pressures seem at once to be brought to bear by university people for the rejection of such a project? Why this 'religious war' between supporters and opponents of Ufology? Well, I will try to reply to these various questions.

I will start with the proofs: as regards the proofs, you know as well as I do that the diehards in the opposition always say: 'You are merely quoting reports — not scientific proofs'. Now, does such an argument make any sense? My answer is: no, it does not. Let us suppose in fact that we did secure 'scientific proofs'. In reality you don't prove the existence of an object or of a phenomenon scientifically. By 'scientific proof' most folk understand — wrongly — recordings, measurements, made in an impersonal fashion. LET US SUPPOSE THAT WE DID SECURE SUCH RECORDINGS, SUCH MEASUREMENTS. These documents could never be known except via the testimony of those who had secured them, and who would display them and publish them. And the retort could always be hurled back: 'We have no confidence in you. We do not know whether these documents have not been faked.' And so we go round and round in a circle. When people don't want to accept the reality of something, there is nothing, absolutely nothing, that will convince them: every time you produce a proof, they ask for ten more. For us, who have been studying the UFOs for twenty years past the proofs of their reality are as follows:

Right at the outset, certain extremely precise and detailed accounts have come from people who are of sound mind and of high moral and intellectual calibre. They relate unquestionably to things *having the appearance of machines, with performances that are beyond terrestrial capabilities, and which move and behave as though intelligently controlled.* Furthermore, we have this enormous number of reports, of varying value, which have been collected throughout the entire world over the last twenty-five years, and the global statistical analysis of these reports brings out the fact that there are common features which the individual analysis of each case on its own could not have revealed. In other words, the personal equation of the eyewitness is becoming

159

less important, and is yielding place to an 'invariant' — which is the UFO itself. And this UFO is not behaving as a hallucination would behave. For example: the law of the frequency of the appearances of the UFOs, in relation to local time, is the same in Spain, in France, and in the U.S.A. — in other words, in every latitude. And here is another example:the different shapes the UFOs are alleged to have are also found, with precisely the same frequency, in every country. Yet another example: the descriptions given of distant UFOs never occur in misty or foggy weather, but only when the sky is clear. All this, and a whole lot of other things too, not to mention authenticated radar echoes and rare authentic photos (there are even some of these in the famous Condon Report) shows very clearly that the phenomenon exists physically, and right outside of the imaginations of the eyewitnesses.

—*If the proofs are so well founded — and, like you, I think that they are — then what is the reason for all this contempt and this cantankerous peevishness, on the part of an entire intelligentsia, against the idea of the reality of the UFOs?*

—I think this is due to the extreme caginess with which the phenomenon itself operates — even at peak periods, as at the present moment for example. It is all the result of this caginess. Let me return now to the question of the apparent contradiction between the non-human origin of the UFOs and the doubt as to their being extraterrestrial spacecraft.

Our Physics isn't 'completed'. Many modern theoretical physicists, some of them among our greatest, are becoming more and more convinced that our ideas of Space, of Time, and of energy are inadequate. We are aware of a Space with three dimensions — width, length, and height — in which we move and have our being, and we are aware of a uniform Time which unfolds in one direction only, from the past towards the future. All our classical Physics has been constructed by us within the entirely intuitive framework of such a scheme, which corresponds to what we see and what we experience. Our Physics describes very conveniently our astronomical Universe, within which the speed of light cannot be passed or even attained by an 'object' in the classic sense. Now, one can begin to ask oneself, more and more, whether this astronomical Universe in which we feel we are living, is not just one particular aspect of something that is far more complex and that is quite inconceivable for our senses. A sort of Super-Universe, if I may so call it, not necessarily more extensive, but in which there exist other dimensions of Time and Space such as would permit — not the violation of the laws of our Physics, which are, and will remain, valid in three-dimensional space — but such as would permit of their being circumvented, transcended. We would then be running up against certain other phenomena that are just as difficult to accept as the UFOs are, and regarding which I do not propose to speak today, except to say that they are dubbed — quite wrongly — with the epithet of 'supernatural'. This word 'supernatural' is a nonsense; everything that exists in Nature, is, by definition, natural. The phenomena in question, impugned because they apparently violate the laws of Nature, only contradict the latter if you hold that the whole of Nature is reducible to the three-dimensional Universe and the astronomical Universe that are accessible to our senses. But from the moment that a more complex Universe exists, of which our three-dimensional Universe would be only one particular aspect, then many phenomena might well exist that would transcend the laws of our Physics without ceasing to be entirely rational at their own level. You see no doubt what I am getting at. If the UFOs are extraterrestrial spacecraft, what we know about them shows that they transcend the known laws of Nature — the law of inertia in particular — and they consequently testify to a mastery of a more extensive Physics than our Physics, utilizing the properties of an enlarged 'Space-Time'. But then, in that case, one may equally well imagine that the UFOs are something other than spacecraft that have come from the stars by physical routes unknown to us. We don't know what this enlarged Universe is, of which I have just been speaking, nor do we know whether, *inter alia*, it harbours within it the possibility of directly engendering the intrusion of the UFOs into our world.

In either of these two cases, we would find that the UFOs defy our Physics, and we would have no criteria for deciding between the two possible hypotheses. Naturally all this isn't yet Science, but, if we accept the existence of the UFOs, then we are logically led to the consideration that our own present-day Physics is fantastically limited.

So I return to the question that was asked: why this scorn, this opposition, to the idea of the reality of the UFOs?

If the UFO phenomenon were an everyday one; if we 'lived with it'; if every one of us were used to encountering it several times in his life, perhaps we would not comprehend it any better than we do now but at least we would no doubt accept it. Such, however, is not the case, and everything stems from that. Our Science has been built up gradually, bit by bit, neglecting the phenomena wrongly called 'supernatural', because they are rare, and, while doing this, our Science has constructed a blueprint of the Universe which is pretty coherent but which only describes the properties of our three-dimensional world. It is obvious that the phenomena which transcend this blueprint have ended up by being rejected, on account of their rarity. At the same time, due to a lack of frequent contact with a phenomenon like the UFOs, man himself has ended up by feeling himself to be alone in the Universe and at the summit of the Creation.

My conclusion is that, in these circumstances, it is not in the least bit surprising that the UFOs should trigger off such impassioned reactions of negation — and it isn't all over yet, not by a long shot. Believe me, Jean-Claude Bourret, when I say it won't be even tomorrow that — except in rare places here and there — there will be any consent to their being made a subject for official research.

MICHEL MONNERIE:
THE BIG NIGHT OF THE UFOs

Here is the last broadcast dedicated to the UFOs in this series, and sent out on *France-Inter* on Friday, 22 March, 1974. Claude Villiers, my companion in all these evening sessions, asks me to draw up the balance-sheet for these two months of broadcasts — a balance which, when all is said and done, has been on the positive side.

What struck me first of all, during these eight weeks of broadcasts, was the quantity — and the quality — of the letters received. University professors, schoolmasters, lawyers, mayors, investigators, students, and schoolboys, have written to us. Now I can admit that, when I began this series of broadcasts on the UFOs, I was particularly afraid that we would get a mass of letters from the mentally unbalanced. Out of the thousands of letters received, in fact only two or three gave rise to any doubts as to the cerebral health of those who had written them.

●

—*Claude Villiers, I think we can also talk about the unfavourable reactions; a certain number of criticisms were levelled at us.* ...
—Oh, yes — the attempts to make the UFOs a political matter — that amused us enormously. ...
—*It was quite good too, because we were criticized from both sides.*
—Yes, once by the Left and once by the Right. Let us be honest — what pleased us greatly was that there was one weekly journal — a bit to the Right. ...
—*To the extreme Right.*
—Yes, to the extreme Right — don't let us be scared of labels. That particular paper dragged us through the mud, just as the other paper on the Left did. It proves anyway that this programme has many listeners, both on the Left and on the Right. That is very gratifying.
—*There were also the criticisms, weren't there, from certain scientists who don't like to contemplate the existence of*

something that isn't being taught in the universities?

—Yes, indeed. But why isn't there, in the programme, a single scientist 'against'? Quite simply, it is because one meets lots of scientists who are against the UFOs, but one doesn't find a single scientist WHO HAS STUDIED THE UFO PROBLEM AND IS STILL 'AGAINST' IT. What these scientists of the opposition are offering is consequently purely a human opinion on the problem — and not the result of a serious study.

—*In any case, these broadcasts have had quite an impact on public opinion. And even in the scientific world too, haven't they?*

—Yes, this series of broadcasts has loosened up a situation that has been jamlocked for twenty years. Don't forget that we got the first official statement ever made on the UFO question by the French Minister for the Armed Forces. It created quite a stir. It got top front-page treatment not only in many French newspapers, but also abroad. Many scientists who at first did not want to give an opinion on the subject (even though they are quietly studying it on the side) have now dared to speak about it.

—*But you yourself, Jean-Claude Bourret, what are your own thoughts now on the UFO problem, if indeed it be a problem?*

—The thing that struck me when I started these broadcasts, and when I had the good fortune to meet eminent scientists like Claude Poher, Jacques Vallée, Pierre Guérin and Aimé Michel, was my privileged position as a journalist. I thought that in two minutes, to me alone, they were going to give the completely clear results of twenty years of research. But not a bit of it. *We don't know what the UFOs are.* The more you study them, the more complex the phenomenon becomes, and the more bewildering. We don't know if they are extra-terrestrials who are appearing here. We don't know if it is a manipulation of Space-Time. We don't know whether it is an intelligent phenomenon, so impossible for our minds to grasp that, and precisely for that reason, it will always remain a mystery for us. All that we can say is that they are material machines, because they leave marks behind on the ground, and are probably occupied by humanoid beings. Where do they come from? Who are they? It is impossible to answer these questions. What is certain however is that there is a real phenomenon and that it is high time the scientific intelligensia paid a bit of attention to this problem. I personally think that it is one of the biggest scientific problems of all time. To contribute today to this study of the UFO problem, we have with us in the studio Monsieur Michel Monnerie of the French UFO Investigation Group, *Lumières Dans La Nuit.*

—Michel Monnerie, you are organizing for tomorrow, Saturday 23 March, 1974, a national sky-watch. So can we please have your explanations and your instructions for all the France-Inter *listeners who want to participate in it?*

—Yes. Tomorrow evening, Saturday, we are organizing a *sky-watch.* This type of evening is organized two or three times yearly by *Lumières Dans La Nuit,* whose address is: Les Pins, 43400 Le Chambon-sur-Lignon. Thanks to you, Claude Villiers, and to you, Jean-Claude Bourret, we are going to be able to try a big experiment. This will be the first time in the history of Ufology. We shall be able to measure the impact of an intense psychological preparation on the possible eyewitnesses. Will there be a considerable increase in the number of sightings, and what will be the value of the sighting-reports we receive? All this is only possible with a great number of observers. So, thank you once again, *France-Inter.*

—What do we have to do?

—We are requesting all those who want to try the experiment of carrying out a watch over the whole sky of France to listen in tomorrow evening between 9.00 p.m. and midnight, or longer if possible. The ideal thing would be for everyone to have a camera.

—What photographic advice have you to give?

—You must have a camera loaded with sensitive film, that is to say at least 125 ASA and up to 400 ASA. Black and white is preferable to colour. Preferably use your camera on a stand. If you have a telephoto lens, use it. If you have the luck to see a UFO, take as many photos as you can, using different speeds.

—So, tomorrow evening, you get your camera, you keep a look-out between 9.00 p.m. and midnight, you photograph any UFOs you see, and you send the photos to Pas de Panique* programme, Maison de la Radio, 75016 Paris.

—And, anyway . . . don't panic!

Results of the National Skywatch

Organized by *Lumières Dans La Nuit* and *France-Inter* Radio, this national skywatch received maximum publicity. We had talked about it for several days over the air, and our colleagues of the Press also alerted their readers. It was diffi-

---

* English translation: 'No Panic', or 'Don't Panic'. G.C.

cult not to know about the scheme. Millions of Frenchmen 'knew' and tens of thousands of them kept watch here and there all over the country, cameras at the ready. And what was the result. *Nil. We received not one single photo, not one single sighting report of any value whatsoever from that famous night.* This is a very signficant result indeed. It is still a little early for drawing conclusions from it, but the first conclusion that forces itself upon us is obvious: *the sensitization of public opinion to the UFO problem via the audio-visual channels produces no increase in the number of sighting reports.* In other words, talk of 'saucer hysteria' or of 'the saucer bush-telegraph' smacks of the most pitifully stupid of attitudes — the attitude of folk who are totally ignorant of the UFO problem. We had not of course mentioned it over the air, for obvious reasons, but in fact that was precisely the aim of our experiment: *to test the consequences of a psychological preparation of public opinion.*

The results are there, obvious to all: not one single photo, not one single sighting report of any significance. Now it is up to Aimé Michel, Pierre Guérin, Claude Poher, or Jacques Vallée to extract still further lessons from the experiment.

AN EXCLUSIVE INTERVIEW:
THE VOICE OF THE CHURCH

Father Russo belongs to the Jesuit Order. And he is a scientist. He is a graduate of the Ecole Polytechnique, a historian, a scientific philosopher, and a counsellor to the Catholic Centre for UNESCO.

●

—*Père Russo: Have you looked into the UFO problem, and have you an opinion on it?*
—Yes. I have looked into the problem, but I confess that for a long time I was very reticent about it. I thought that it was not a very important problem. But I must admit that for several years now, and above all during these last few months, seeing how the number of UFO sighting reports has increased, and seeing conscientious astronomers taking an interest in the subject, I have thought it difficult to say that the problem is not one worthy of attention. In my view you can't say that everything in this business is illusion or hoax. We must remain openminded, and ready to accept the existence of certain objects which so far we have been unable to recognize and identify. But all the same I am somewhat uneasy about it in one sense — namely that the subject nourishes a somewhat unhealthy curiosity among the general public. The scientists would like to work on the problem free of emotional considerations. But, anyway, I don't deny that the problem exists: I think it ought to be examined.
—*What is interesting about your attitude, Father Russo, is that in the beginning you thought that it was all a hoax, just like the majority of the scientists who have not studied the problem. Then you looked into the question, and now you have arrived at the opposite conclusion. . . .*
—I don't think in days to come we shall be able to prove that this business is all pure illusion. It might of course turn out that way, but I think it would be very difficult to prove. But it is one thing to say: we must study the problem. And it's another thing to hypothesize regarding the nature of these objects. On this precise point, the opinions vary.
—*Many listeners have written in to ask: 'what if God were an extraterrestrial?'*

—Well then, I regret to have to say that my answer to that theory is that I reject it totally. There are indeed allusions in the Old Testament to activities of extraterrestrial origin, but the advances made in Biblical exegesis lead us to think that those stories relate to a fanciful imagery which has no relation to reality. Please permit me to emphasise this very firmly.

—*Scientists are accepting more and more that in the Universe there are thousands of worlds inhabited by intelligences superior to our intelligence. Does this present a problem for the Catholic Church?*

—I don't think it presents any real theological problem. The Revelation which we have received through the message of Jesus Christ, at the beginning of the Christian Era, did not envisage that there might be other living beings outside of the Earth, then considered to be the centre of the Universe. But the Revelation gives us a perspective which lies outside of the concrete conditions in which it is expressed. The Christian Revelation in now way excludes the possibility of other forms of life far from the Earth, and even of other forms of intelligent life. Personally I would be more inclined to the view that in the whole Universe only the Earth contains thinking beings. But this is just a personal view — I don't want to impose it on others. I remain open to the hypothesis of the existence of other intelligent living beings on other planets.

—*You say, Father Russo, that you are an open-minded man. I would like to be able to say as much about all those who know nothing whatsoever about the UFO evidence but who attack it violently just the same.*

—I would like to make a point here, in parentheses: I am as prepared to accept the existence of unidentified flying objects as I am to refute the so-called predictions of Astrology. Whereas the UFO business contains positive data, Astrology is based on incoherent and unacceptable data: in short, on nothing.

—*Some people have reproached us for having concocted this UFO programme 'out of nothing' in order to avoid discussing what they hold to be the real problems: the high cost of living and the inflation. . . .*

—Well, I must say that, like your listeners, I too am interested in the high cost of living, and in the environment. In short, I am interested in all sorts of practical questions! But I am struck when I see that such a large number of young people are so completely obsessed with the immediate questions of the moment; no speculative problems seem serious to

them. I think this is a deplorable intellectual regression. . . .
—*Let us return to the UFOs, Father Russo. Do you accept the extraterrestrial theory as the most likely explanation for the phenomenon?*
—As a hypothesis, I see no *a priori* reason for being against it. But there immediately arises a problem which is at once both theological and scientific: the problem of communication with these beings. We cannot take these extraterrestrials into consideration unless we can communicate with them. Now, there are immense factors here that are unknown to us: in particular, there is the problem of the synchronisation of civilizations in Time, if those other civilizations exist. . . .
—*If those extraterrestrial civilizations exist, do you think that Jesus Christ has taken upon himself the task of bringing salvation to them?*
—One may think so. One may also think that there have been others who have been sent by God, although that raises some very serious difficulties.

PART FOUR

*Opinions of Scientists that were not
Broadcast on France-Inter*

THE PHYSICAL MANIFESTATION OF THE
UFOs:
A TENTATIVE EXPLANATION

Jean Goupil is a friendly, bearded type. He has smiling eyes, an intelligent look, and makes friends easily. Jean Goupil was born in 1933. In 1955 he got his engineer's Diploma from the E.N.R.E.A. (The French National School of Applied Radio-Electricity). He was top of his graduation class. He took an engineering post with the French Centre for Nuclear Studies at Saclay where, until 1963, he was engaged in research on detection systems in reactors, and after that he took part in Space experiments in Gamma-ray Astronomy. In 1963 he became the technical director of a firm which studies and assembles electronic aggregates for computers. Jean Goupil has been a member of G.E.P.A. (French Group for the Study of Aerial Phenomena) since 1962.

I interviewed Jean Goupil in studio 141 in the Maison de la Radio in Paris. And I was scheduled to broadcast this interview in the Second Part of our UFO Dossier — the part which we had reserved for the suggested explanations by the scientists.

But an incredible thing happened: the tape-recordings were stolen! The tapes had been stacked, in a metal press in the Editorial Offices of *France-Inter*. All the tapes vanished, except for those already broadcast. Who would have had an interest in causing those tapes to disappear? I don't know the answer. But this gesture is the finest compliment that could possibly have been paid to our broadcasts. When folk are reduced to gangsterism in order to prevent the dissemination of the truth about UFOs, that's a very good sign. It proves that not a single 'contra' argument against the UFOs exists. Jean Goupil was not the only victim of this theft, which I decided, at the time, to pass over in silence, without mentioning it in our radio programmes. Pierre Kohler (astronomer), Cardinal Daniélou (who, alas, died on 20 May 1974), Dr J. Allen Hynek, Dr David Saunders, Gordon Creighton, and several Swiss witnesses and Swiss scientists, as well as several Belgian scientists, all were unable to express their views on *France-Inter*, because the tapes of their interviews had been stolen. Unfortunately I was unable to make fresh recordings of all of them. Jean Goupil, although a very busy man, has since agreed to write down for me what he had said for the *France-Inter* microphone, and you will read his exciting theories below in a moment. In the United States Michel Anfrol, who had kept the original tapes of his interviews, was able to make good the losses. Gordon Creighton's taped statement had already been transcribed by me, curiously enough, almost as though by premonition, and so his text was available for this book, although not for the broadcast programme. Unfortunately, Cardinal Daniélou, Dr Pierre Kohler, and several Swiss and Belgian scientists and several Swiss witnesses, could not be contacted again in time for fresh tapes to be secured. Their statements had consequently to be left out of the broadcasts. In the meantime we hope that they will excuse us, and, above all, we hope that they will perhaps forgive the mysterious thief. . . .

●

Here now are the reflections of Jean Goupil on the UFO problem:

The unbelievable and the impossible.

Through the agency of the UFOs, and for the first time in the history of Mankind, our Science finds itself in confrontation with the products of a civilization that is more advanced that we are in the technological field. Nothing has prepared our Science for it, and no methodology exists for this situation. The scientists who approach this problem are generally baffled, indeed definitely repelled, by the inverisimilitude of the events related by the eyewitnesses. In fact the physical manifestations of these strange objects are particularly unbelievable: they fly without making any sound, even at speeds that are largely supersonic, they accelerate like lightning, do right-angle turns, at times become invisible, emit truncated beams of light that go through people and through walls. As for the occupants so frequently described, they can fly, are insensitive to bullets, they paralyze the wit-

174

nesses, and at times are themselves luminous or trans-
lucent. . . .

It is possible that our own intellect may be for ever incap-
able of grasping how these machines (?) work, and what are
the intentions of those who have conceived them, but we do
not have the right to adopt the pessimistic answer without
having first attempted to define the limits of our own understanding — if indeed those limits exist.

Technician of the Future.

In order to advance in the field of UFO study, we propose
that we set about it in the following way:

1. Assume that a new property of matter has just been revealed (for example, a force field, a particle, etc.) Define the limits of this working hypothesis while avoid-
   ing, to the extent that is possible, going against the
   fundamental principles, such as the conservation of
   energy, the equality of action and reaction, etc.
2. Then put ourselves in the position of a 'Technician of
   the Future', and attempt to list the practical applications of this hypothetical discovery.
3. Compare the consequences envisaged with the effects
   alleged in the eyewitness reports. It will be advisable
   at this stage to pay great attention to the secondary effects, which could constitute valuable indications
   that would either support or invalidate a working
   hypothesis.
4. With a view to deciding as between the various theories which we can, and must propound, we will draw
   up a comparative table that will select the most probable theory, on the basis of the undermentioned criteria:

   — simplicity of the hypothesis.
   — minimal contradiction with principles already ac-
     cepted.
   — technological probability.
   — scope of the explanations, i.e., the number and vo-
     lume of the normally inexplicable facts that might
     be comprised wthin the framework of the hypo-
     thesis formulated.

In the UFOs, we find ourselves confronted with phenomena that are not reproducible in the laboratory — that is to

say, we shall not be permitted true certainty about them, but at any rate we shall be able to extract from it a whole range of presumptions, just as in a police investigation. The aim of these speculations will be twofold: firstly, to know more about the UFOs (for there is nothing which authorizes us to assert that they are inoffensive) and then, secondly, to suggest to the physicists ways of possible research.

Such an enterprise cannot be the task of one isolated scientist, but must be done by a group of specialists resolved to play the game with all the open-mindedness required. Let us, meanwhile, pay homage to one pioneer, Captain Plantier, who was the first to attempt to explain the propulsion of UFOs by anti-gravity.

The repulsion field.

We will illustrate our remarks with an example: the hypothesis of the repulsion field.

Let us accept that it may be possible to create a repulsion field with the aid of a hypothetical generator. This field, of limited range, is supposed to be such that any mass, M, is repelled, in the direction away from the generator, with a force, F, equal to the product of M multiplied by the strength of the field at the given point. In order not to go against fundamental principles, we will accept that the energy hypothetically communicated to the repelled masses will have to be supplied to the field generator, and that the latter will be subject to a strength of reaction equal to, and opposed to, that resulting from the actions on the surrounding medium.

What might the practical applications for this generator be? The first concerns propulsion: in the vicinity of large masses considerable forces are produced by a very weak field. For example, in a cube of soil measuring ten metres to the side, the creation of a field equal to a hundredth of the weight of the Earth would produce a reactive force of 20 tons. If this is so, the UFOs are capable of accelerating more strongly upwards (repulsion against the Earth) than downwards (repulsion against the atmosphere.) Here we have a possible explanation of the 'lightning-fast' departures vertically, and of the 'dead leaf' descents that are so characteristic of the phenomenon.

The second application concerns aerodynamism.

We can, in fact, imagine the use of our hypothetical 'repulsor' to thrust aside the air molecules lying in the trajectory of the UFO. In these conditions, the machine is moving in a bubble of partial vacuum, which it carries along with it. This has two very important consequences: firstly there is neither sound nor shock wave, as the successive layers of air would slip, one over the other, without abrupt discontinuity. And secondly: there is no impact on the wall of the machine, as a result of which there is no heating up, and this permits speeds higher than the technological limit known as the 'thermic wall'.

But we can go still further in this investigation. We can show by calculations that the most rational shape for a machine using an atmospheric repulsor would be precisely the shape that is most frequently described (the frustrum of a cone, like a reversed saucer, surmounted by a dome or mast), whereas this shape would be of no interest to anyone examining it from the standpoint of standard aerodynamism. (See the G.E.P.A. journal, *Phénomènes Spatiaux,* No. 14, December 1967.) We also find another very curious thing: you can demonstrate that there is a two-to-one relationship between the maximum speed permitted by a given repulsion field, and the degree of the partial vacuum obtained at the wall of the craft if we suppose that the same field is applied when the machine is stationary. This relationship is completely independent of the law of the diminution of the field with the distance. The calculations give us the following values: for a maximum speed of 3,600 km.p.h., the vacuum is of 1.9 mm of mercury; for 4,200 km.p.h. it falls to about 0.2 mm of mercury. Furthermore, it has been discovered that the UFOs emit quite powerful electro-magnetic radiation. Now, it turns out that such radiations are capable of producing red light in a vacuum of the order of 2 mm of mercury, and bluish-white light in a vacuum of 0.2 mm. This corresponds precisely with a large number of eyewitness accounts, which indicate that the UFOs are surrounded by a red light which changes to blue when the speed increases. (See *Phénomènes Spatiaux* No. 11, March 1967.)

The Invisibility of the UFOs.

Let us mention one final consequence of the use of the 'atmospheric repulsor', which is not the least strange of its features. . . .

We have seen that the device would give rise to the appearance of a vacuum bubble with the machine at its centre.

There is thus a difference in refractive index between the atmosphere and the partial vacuum prevailing near the machine. This condition suffices to produce the phenomenon of the mirages which we have all seen in summer on roads heated by the Sun: the pools of water which we imagine we can see in the distance represent, in fact, a fragment of the sky, the light beams of which have been bent by the difference in refractive index between the overheated air at road-surface level and the denser surrounding air.

In the case of the UFOs, the difference in the density being much greater, this effect is consequently all the more perceptible. You can say that, depending upon the shape of the vacuum bubble, and upon the position of the eyewitness, it can occur that the machine becomes invisible at the moment when its atmospheric repulsors are brought into operation.

Conversely, if one tries to illuminate (for example — with a car headlight) a UFO when its repulsor is in action, it can happen that a curvature of the beam occurs, and it fails to light up the object. This is in fact precisely what is reported in a certain number of eyewitness accounts.

'Lightning-like' Accelerations.

So we have a machine endowed with most interesting performances, but which can only utilize them fully if its passengers are capable of enduring the great accelerations. We measure this acceleration in terms of 'g', this letter representing the acceleration due to the weight at the surface of the Earth (9.81 m/s^2). A trained man can only stand 10 g, and even then only for a brief time. Why this limit? Quite simply because, from the ox-drawn waggon to the cabin of *Apollo*, we have made no progress whatsoever as regards the method of accelerating the passengers: it is still through the intermediary of the seat that the acceleration is communicated to the whole body, which becomes painful, and then dangerous, when the acceleration is stepped up.

It is entirely different, if, here again, we employ our repulsion field: let us suppose that, behind the passenger, a cluster of small generators is placed with the purpose of creating, in the volume of space occupied by the passenger, a field that is uniform in direction and in intensity, this intensity being adjustable at will. This field will have to be *nil* so long as the speed of the machine does not vary, particularly when it is stationary. It will only come into operation in the acceleration phase. It will then be necessary to reduce its intensity, so that the passenger is kept at a constant distance from the cluster of small generators. The position of a small indicator mass, detected by standard methods, will serve to assure this reduction.

In these conditions, what happens? During the accelerations, the passenger literally 'falls' into a constant field, which acts upon every point on his body, and consequently there is no painful restraint. The only limit relating to the maximum intensity of the field is of a technological order: this concerns the absence of uniformity. If the field is uniform to better than 1% in the cabin, then accelerations of 1,000 g can be contemplated.

A simple calculation shows that a stationary UFO, on undergoing this acceleration, is 5 kilometres distant after one second. In 0.5 second, the time it takes to blink, the distance travelled is already 1,250 metres, so that the visual effect is in fact tantamount to a veritable sudden 'disappearance' of the machine.

If we now suppose that the internal repulsors are employed to compensate for the centrifugal forces (the cluster of repulsors being set towards the centre of the turn which is to be made) we can likewise calculate the time needed for making a right-angle turn. If the UFO has a speed of 1 km. per second (3,600 km.p.h.) this time is 0.16 of a second for a centrifugal acceleration of 1,000 g, the radius of the turn being only 100 metres.

How to build a UFO . . .

The structure of a UFO utilizing repulsor fields would thus be as follows:

At the top, that is to say on the dome, is the atmospheric repulsor. It will be noted that, at high speeds, the saucer tilts so that it points the dome in the direction in which it is moving. (This fact is frequently mentioned by eyewitnesses.)

On the lower part, that is to say beneath the disc, are installed a minimum of three repulsors which, in stationary flight, balance out the force produced by the upper repulsor. To secure an acceleration of the machine, it suffices to increase the fields of the three repulsors. All the repulsors which we have just mentioned must be directed towards the exterior, so as to produce no field inside the machine itself.

Finally, in the cockpit, is the cluster of generators of the uniform field; it only comes into play when the speed is altered. Braking is effected by reversal of the machine, or, better still, by means of a second cluster opposed to the first.

Invulnerability as a bonus.

Let us visualise the machine stationary, with its repulsors working. The field generated by the repulsors permits a certain maximum speed V (for example, 1 km./s.) This means that any projectile fired towards the machine at a speed lower than, or equal to, V, will be repelled and will be unable to strike it.

Thus, if you decide to fire your gun at a UFO, understand that it has every likelihood of being useless and ... watch our for the ricochets.

If portable repulsors are conceivable, everything inclines us to the belief that the UFO occupants themselves are equipped with them, which would, in particular, explain the very curious landing case at Kelly (Kentucky, U.S.A.) on 21 August 1955. Little humanoids appeared to float in the air, and the shots fired by the eyewitnesses had no other effect than to knock the entities down.

Luminous Phenomena.

If it is well founded, our first hypothesis would explain the 'incredible' manoeuvres of the UFOs — so incredible, indeed, that some folk saw in them conclusive proof that UFOs either do not exist or are non-material, while other people went so far as to envisage journeys in Hyper-Space, and even in Time ... But there is another class of unwonted phenomena which our hypothesis does not help us to comprehend: namely the luminous phenomena.

Some of these light phenomena are particularly baffling: stationary UFOs have frequently been seen to emit one or more truncated beams — that is to say, beams of light that terminate abruptly. These 'tubes' have a diameter varying from a few centimetres up to several metres, and a length varying from a few metres to several kilometres. They seem to make a careful exploration of the surroundings, all the while changing in length. Their brightness is uniform, quite similar to that of a neon tube. But — and this is the strange fact — they pass through obstacles (partitions, walls — and the eyewitnesses), so that they cast no shadows.

One eyewitness, who had one of these beams shine on him, felt a general sensation of heat. (See the case at Trancas, Arg-

entina,* in *Phénomènes Spatiaux*, No. 33, September 1972).
Sometimes the light beam is fragmented or is even curved.

Finally, to lend body to the problem, let us quote the following case: a car, caught in a luminous beam emitted by a UFO, became transparent; the eyewitness could see the engine through the dashboard. Then, having fled, he had, so he said, a perfect view of the inside of the vehicle, through its walls. After the beam of light was turned off everything returned to normal. (See the case at Catanduva,** Brazil, in *Phénomènes Spatiaux*, No. 37, September 1973.)

Maybe we can classify in this same category the 'foo-fighters', a species of luminous globes, apparently tele-guided, which accompanied aircraft during the Second World War (this relates to those cases that are not explicable as ball-lightning.)

Particles with modular interaction.

Using the same intellectual process as before, in order to attempt to make progress on this new series of enigmas, we have been induced to define a second hypothetical entity: particles with modulable interaction.

We know that contemporary Physics has revealed evidence for the existence of about 200 fundamental particles, at the rate of ten per year. ...

As a general rule, these particles interact with matter, their probability of interaction being in terms of the particle, of its energy, of the nature of the target, and of its specific mass. One particle, the neutrino, is distinguished by its very weak probability of interaction, to such a degree that stars and planets seem far more transparent to it than a pane of glass is for a beam of light. It is consequently not at all unthinkable to say: 'Let us suppose that a particle (or group of particles) is capable of penetrating several metres of water or of material of a density akin to water'.

And this is our hypothesis: under the effect of a specific agent, the probability of interaction of this particle in a given material can be greatly increased (which would correspond, for example, to an average distance of several centimetres in the atmosphere).

* This very well known case was reported at length in *Flying Saucer Review*, Vol. XI, No. 1 (1966) and Vol. XVII, No. 3 (1971). (Both now out of print. G.C.)

** This case has been reported in *The car that turned transparent*, in *Flying Saucer Review*, Vol. XXI, Double Number 3 and 4, 1975. G.C.

What would this mysterious 'specific agent' be? It is too soon for us to be able to define it precisely, but, for the purpose of demonstration, let us accept that it is a wave, possibly electromagnetic. In that case there would doubtless be a minimum threshold of radiated power, to produce the supposed 'modulation of interaction'.

Let us turn now to the practical applications of this.

What happens if we emit brief bursts of these particles, accelerated beforehand, so that they all have the same speed (monoenergetic particles)?

Each burst of short distance (less than 30 cms. for an impulse of one nanosecond) will move at a speed necessarily less than that of light. Let us take, as an example, a speed of 150,000 kms. per second. A microsecond after the emission of a burst, the latter is consequently at a distance of 150 metres from the emitting source. At this precise instant we will emit the modulation wave. A microsecond later, this wave, moving at 300,000 kms. per second, will catch up with the particles at a distance of 300 metres from the starting point.

The particles interact then with the matter, through which they are passing. This interaction is revealed by a transfer of energy which generates heat, radiations, and secondary particles.

If the bursts are repeated in a sufficiently rapid rhythm, we will get the local appearance of a stable luminous ball. Any variation in the phase between the burst and the wave will bring about an instantaneous longitudinal displacement. As a result of our hypothesis, this luminous phenomenon can be produced through a wall, so long as the modulation wave has not been completely absorbed by the latter. What could there be of interest about such a contrivance?

Its interest is considerable: in fact it permits the in-depth exploration of any object, for analysis of the radiations and particles emitted at the point of interaction enables us to know the internal constitution of that object; what is more, there is nothing to prevent our proceeding in the same way with a living being, the doses of irradiation received being reduced but very localized.

The same device can serve two purposes: firstly, to ascertain precisely the position of an eyewitness, and then, secondly, to paralyze him by acting selectively on certain of his motor-centres.

The idea of therapeutic applications is not ruled out, and in fact we find that there are two eyewitness accounts relating to healings directly linked with the UFOs.

Should we explain in the same fashion certain 'accursed

facts' involving the spontaneous and violent combustion of men and women when they have been alone in a closed room?

To return to the analysis of the radiations emitted at the point of interaction, it is clear that this analysis calls for a prior knowledge of the materials interposed between the point being analyzed and the emitting source, for they determine the amount of the absorption of the radiations under analysis. It is necessary therefore to keep exploring the whole of the space between the examiner and the material being examined. This is done by a repetitive variation, at constant speed, of the phase between the bursts and the trains of modulating waves.

The appearance is now no longer that of a luminous ball, but of a tube irradiating a diffuse light, passing through walls, making no shadow, and discharging a certain energy in the medium traversed.

One can easily visualize the processes of scrutinizing the surrounding space which would be obtained with a tube of light that is fragmented or curved (in combining the variations of phase with horizontal and vertical angling of the direction of emission of particles).

There still remains the problem of the transparency of the objects irradiated.

It is possible that, at the moment of interaction, a certain proportion of the particles are retrodiffused, that is to say, sent back after having lost a fraction of their energy. If the modulation wave is of brief duration, these retrodiffused particles are capable of emerging again from the medium where they have interacted, without interacting again. The following modulating wave will traverse them when they are outside the object which is undergoing examination. The light emitted will consequently be perceived by the eyewitness as if it came directly from the point of first interaction, that is to say, as if the object examined were transparent, or at least translucid.

Extraterrestrial phantoms.

But here is a second practical application for our hypothetical particles, and this one risks putting in question once more a certain number of ideas that we have acquired. ...

If our emitting device is capable of generating points of light at a distance, and through walls, there is no difficulty in associating these points together to produce an image of some kind, this image being scanned and modulated point by point, like a television image. What will the eyewitness see? A 'being of light', immaterial, seeming to levitate above the ground, capable of disappearing instantly, manifesting itself usually in darkness, and having the power to pass through walls ... It is not our intention to fit all paranormal phenomena willynilly into the framework of a hypothesis designed to explain the UFOs, but we must note, all the same, the relative frequence of this type of sighting. The reader should consult Jacques Vallée's book *Chronique Des Apparitions Extraterrestres*,** which gives summaries of 923 landing cases spread over the century 1868-1968. We have extracted the following examples from the book:

No. 44　'A luminous transparent object in the form of a pyramid'.

No. 486　'The object was luminous, and seemed as though made of glass'.

No. 716　'By what appeared to them to be an optical illusion, a third personage was near them. The machine and the creatures were very bright'.

No. 719　'A luminous man'.

No. 767　'They seemed two metres high, had voluminous heads, seemed brilliant and transparent... They returned aboard their craft "as though transported by the light".'

No. 848　'A brilliant object, transparent, and shaped like a mushroom'.

No. 857　'A silhouette wearing luminous clothes. It changed into a formless light and vanished'.

No. 862　'... a little man in shining, silvery clothes, his head surrounded by vapour'.

No. 870　'... It made jerky movements, raised a tube with its arms, and its image seemed to flicker'.

No. 915　'... a strange being, 2 m 10 cms high, was gliding through the air, its body emitting a curious light, near a brilliant unknown object'.

And, finally, a sighting account which fits particularly well with our last hypothesis: it occurred at Verona, in Italy, on 26 June 1962:

** The original English-language version of this list of landings formed part of the American edition of Dr Vallée's *Passport To Magonia* (George Regnery Co, Chicago, 1969). The British edition of *Passport To Magonia*, issued in 1970 by Neville Spearman, does not contain the list of landings. G.C.

The UFO as big as a house. 'I felt a slight tingling in my hand.'
(*Sketch by Pierre Giroud*)

The UFO that liked tractors.
(*Sketch by Pierre Giroud*)

PAUL FAIVELEY
'. . . In July 1934, in England, in the
New Forest.'

Monsieur VILLENEUVE DE JANTI
(The car under surveillance from the
sky.)

Commandant PISTRE of the Gend-
arerie, who directed the investigation
o the mystery lights at Montréal
ide) in February 1974.

Jean-Claude Bourret with Monsieur Robert Galley, Minister of Defence, during their 'historic' interview about the UFOs.

(Photo: Jacques Vainst

No. 537 'At the window a human form was seen, which was well outlined, and showed a semi-transparent body. The apparition had an enormous bald head. The witness let out a yell, woke up the two others, and they saw the apparition shrink and disappear like TV image when the television set is switched off'.

In the same book by Vallée we find the very strange account of an apparition which lasted for several hours at Knock, in the West of Ireland, on 21 August 1879. Numerous witnesses were able to observe three luminous, motionless beings at very close quarters. One of the witnesses tried to touch one of the apparitions, 'but his arms closed on empty air'.

That Day ...

That day, a UFO situated at 10,000 kms. from the surface of the Earth unfurled a blue screen one kilometre in diameter and then, slowly, approached the ground in such a fashion that the screen remained aligned with the Sun and with a well defined spot: a small valley where 50,000 people, packed closely together, awaited an exceptional event.

Simultaneously, a second UFO, 50 metres in diameter, was following a similar trajectory to that of the first. It was as bright as the Sun, and, for that reason, passed entirely unnoticed by the crowd, whose attention was concentrated on a tree, in the centre of the valley. This tree had been the scene of curious phenomena during the preceding months: the apparition of a luminous being, shock waves, a ball of light, flashes, clouds, hummings, falls of floccules, etc.

The first UFO took up position at an altitude of 50 kms., and the second at 5 kms. Thus placed, they totally blotted out sight of the Sun over an area of twenty hectares, an area greater than that of the valley itself.

At that moment a rumour began to circulate through the crowd, who gradually began to turn round and look at the Daystar.

And the expected miracle began: the nearer UFO, which all the eyewitnesses took for the Sun, modified its brightness and its colour, and approached the ground, which terrified the crowd, and then started to 'dance', whirling around on its own axis while dropping down towards the horizon, while in the meantime the first UFO was masking the real Sun, which was thus replaced by a translucid blue screen, invisible against the azure of the sky.

Finally the smaller UFO returned to its first position, and both UFOs then retraced their course, returning whence they had come. The Sun began to shine again, dazzling the astonished crowd.

All this happened on 13 October 1917 in a little village in Portugal.

The name of the village was Fátima.

What are they trying to make us believe?

Here is the big question that has been put, for if the hypotheses proposed are correct in their main lines, we are in the presence of a civilization which has all the necessary means for deceiving our senses and our understanding.

Is it really an extraterrestrial civilization that is involved?

To this question, there is no certain, scientific answer, but we will give you a few thoughts on this subject, debatable though they all may be.

Can we visualize what a very advanced civilization would be capable of achieving?

One may imagine that the problem of immortality (or at least, of quasi-immortality) having been solved, the biggest danger would be of perishing accidentally. How would other Worlds be explored in such conditions? By sending out intelligent probes capable of bringing back a vast harvest of information, and by reconstructing this information, after the return of the probes, and by recreating *in toto*, but in complete security, the scenes recorded on the particular planet explored. Would it be necessary for those robots to be humanoids?

The answer is not obvious. When we shall be capable of memorizing a mass of information in a large organic molecule, all the images that our eyes will have seen in the course of our own whole lifetime will be contained in a volume of the size of a pea. ...

It is therefore probable that these probes, if they exist, pass totally unperceived by us — which is not the case with the UFOs. Thus these UFO apparitions would appear to be intentional, and we would appear to be confronting a vast psychological action extending over several centuries. Or, on the other hand, the technological superiority over us of those who construct the UFOs may not be so great as we imagine. In this latter case it is not certain that we are dealing with extraterrestrials, but rather with 'supra-terrestrials' —

that is to say, with Humans who have acquired a high level of knowledge via paths other than those that we are exploring.

If such be the case, what are they trying to make us believe with this fantastic and marvellous masquerade?

A family man with five children, Professor J. Allen Hynek lives in a small house in the suburbs of Chicago, where he is head of the Department of Astronomy and Astrophysics at Northwestern University, one of the best known universities in the United States, notably in the realm of the sciences.

For a number of years Professor Hynek was the Technical Adviser to the American Air Force during the period when the Air Force began its researches into unidentified flying objects. This was the famous 'Project Blue Book', now abandoned. Over a period of ten years Professor Hynek was able to have access to all the official American documents and to know secret facts not yet known to anyone. To begin with, Professor Hynek had no preconceived ideas. The ideas which he expresses today are the result of fifteen years of research. The interviewer is Michel Anfrol.

●

—*Then why, Dr Hynek, if you, the No. 1 investigator, the Special Adviser to the U.S. Air Force, have been able to reach certain conclusions favourable to the continuation of the work of research, has 'Project Blue Book' been abandoned?*

—The Secretary of State for Air set a term to the project baptised with the name of 'Blue Book', primarily because of the advice given to him by the Condon Committee, a group which was supported by the Air Force and which was, in theory, to make an independent study of the UFOs.

You have referred to the research which the Air Force was to have undertaken. I find it difficult to call that *research*, since, for example, there was not the slightest attempt made to put the data into a computer, or even to double-check the statements or even to sort out the references. Everything was simply filed in chronological order. In other words, there was no attempt at all to make a scientific study of the problem.

Then you might say: 'but weren't you the Scientific Adviser? Why didn't you do anything about it?' Yes indeed, I was the Adviser, but very frequently my advice was disregarded. Several times I suggested that the material received should be taped and computerized, and I recommended that statistical studies be undertaken.

The project baptized with the name *Blue Book* was pigeonholed at the end of 1969, and after the publication of the Condon Report early in 1970, the newspapers and the radio and TV commentators all said that, as the Air Force had halted its investigations and as the Condon Report had been published, that had to be the end of the affair. We ought to have heard no more, after that, about this subject of UFOs. Everything should have been finished. One thing you can be quite sure of — that isn't what happened, and we are in fact still continuing to hear a great deal of discussion on the subject. In 1971 a few reports began to reach us, in 1972 there were more, and in 1973, particularly at the end of 1973, a wave of reports of all kinds occurred, and by 'all kinds' I mean the most diverse sorts, such as I have described in my book, *The UFO experience.** Especially the close encounter sightings, where there is no question of a far-off light in the sky or a strange object at a distance, but things very near, things that really are very close.

Thus we have had many more sightings in 1973 than in any previous year, which clearly is in contradiction with what most folk had expected.

That is why I decided, at the end of last year, that things had gone too far. We had had twenty-five years of what I will term Government buffoonery or nonsense, and it was time for us scientists to do something about it.

So I appealed to first-class scientists in different parts of the United States, from the universities, such as U.C.L.A., Stanford, Chicago, etc.

There are three reasons which induced us to set up what is officially called the Centre for UFO Studies: the first reason was that there is no place where you can learn about the UFOs, even with the help of newspapers or magazines, and even less in serious scientific reviews, which refuse to touch this material. This is why we thought that something ought to be done.

Furthermore, there is no scientific organization to which sightings and reports can be sent without fear of ridicule,

* *The UFO Experience*, by Dr J. Allen Hynek, U.S. Edition by Henry Regnery Co., Chicago, 1972. British edition by Abelard-Schuman Ltd., London, 1972. (Published in French edition as *Les OVNI: Mythe ou Réalité?*, Ed. Belfond, Paris, 1974.) G.C.

and, finally, and most important of all, there is no place anywhere where this subject is studied in a scientific fashion.

So we have set up the Centre for UFO Studies as a non-profit-making corporation, which of course enables us to receive contributions that are tax-exempt. Indeed, not long ago I received $100 from a lady in Paris who had heard about the Centre and wished to contribute to it financially. Well, this Centre is itself more a meeting-place for people and for ideas than a geographical centre, as it is situated in several different universities.**

I think this will interest your listeners very much — at least I hope so. The Centre has four principal functions: the first and the most frequent consists in the gathering of material. Luckily we have a special telephone line which enables anyone to ring us up free of charge, from wherever he may be. We have given our number to thousands of policemen, sheriffs, civil defence organs, the F.A.A. (Federal Aviation Agency), Defence bodies, etc. So, if somebody thinks he has seen a UFO, he can at once tell a police officer, sheriff, or an F.A.A. official, who will take his statement. In this fashion, just before your arrival here this evening, I received a call from an air base in Florida. Someone that had had a sighting, though I think that in this particular case there is a good explanation — as it must have been a very bright meteor. But, as you see, the facts are there: people phone us, and it is rare for a night to go by without our receiving reports from some part of the country.

Then what do we do when this happens? Let us say, for example, that something happens in Kansas, and we have a man in that region. We ring him, and ask him to go and take a closer look. We have a sort of network in which various organizations cooperate, and also several others who by their cooperation enable us to be sure that these reports do reach the Centre.

The other aspect of our activity is of course the cataloguing and analysis of the data. This is where we have access to computers. For example, Dr David Saunders, a member of our Centre, has computerized some 60,000 cases. And then of course there is the analysis laboratory, and here too we have access to the instruments of a laboratory of national importance. Thus, when we got a report of a landing in Kansas in which a bright ring of unknown material was left on the ground, we were able to have a chemical analysis done of it,

** It now has a new centralized address, at 924 Chicago Avenue, Evanston, Illinois 60202, U.S.A. G.C.

190

and we found significant changes in the soil. Clearly these three activities serve no purpose however if the data and the results of our work are not made public. This is why education plays a part in all this. We hope to be able to establish a quarterly review, not merely for the use of the public, but in the same spirit as a medical journal, in which illnesses are described.... Thus, we would like to publish serious, scientifically authentic investigations, not for their sensational aspect or for mere entertainment, but for their scientific value.

If all this succeeds — and I will say that it is under way — even though we are only operating at a limited level, more people will be informed about it. I hope, for example, that some big foundations will give us the donations for research which we need if we are really to do our job as it should be done.

— *What are the most interesting sightings that you have collected recently, and what are the most disquieting facts that have been brought to your knowledge?*

—I have a letter from a Frenchman, a Monsieur Courette, who is the Controller of the North Canadian Energy Commission, in the extreme north of Hudson's Bay, at a place called Chesterfield Inlet. It is about 2° south of the Arctic Circle, and he wrote to tell me about the experience he and three other people had had while they were out hunting caribou. They were aboard snowmobiles when they suddenly saw, coming straight towards them, a machine which was travelling at only a few feet above the ground. His account tallies with many of those I have already received. In essence, it involved the customary dome-shaped saucer and blinking lights. He told me that one of the strangest things was that the three engines of their snowmobiles all cut out suddenly, just like that, after which all they could hear was a faint hum, but which in fact was not like a true hum.

I think this is a very interesting case, because it comes from such a remote part of the world, where it would be difficult to imagine that anyone had heard talk of UFOs.

We also have another very interesting case in Missouri, and I must emphasise that I have myself confirmed all that I am now telling you about these cases. I am not content simply to quote something mentioned in the newspapers.

Before I tell you this story from Missouri, let me give you some idea of what is happening in general rather than in particular cases. The witnesses are becoming more and more respectable — and notably so on the scientific side. Thus, I recently took part in a meeting of astronomers in Arizona, and several of them came up to me to talk about the UFOs.

—*There was a time when99.9% of the astronomers were utterly hostile to all ideas about UFOs. They regarded them as tales that they would never believe at any price.*

—Absolutely, and they would have laughed at them. Today it is they who come up and talk about them without laughing or fidgeting about. In the wider public too an interesting change is taking place. In fact a recent Gallup Poll showed that 15,000,000 Americans had seen a UFO, and 51% of Americans believed that UFOs were real, and if you compare this poll with another recent poll devoted to politics, you get this rather amusing and perhaps disturbing result that it seems there are more people in the U.S.A. today who believe in UFOs than there are who believe in the President!

The people who send in these sighting reports to us are folk of a certain mental calibre, people whose evidence would be accepted by a court in no matter what other circumstances: airline pilots, air traffic controllers, radar engineers, policemen, and school-masters. It is getting harder and harder to treat all these people as liars or madmen. So there is a growth in the general interest in this field.

—*Reverting now to the most interesting sightings, which are the most disturbing cases that you have had to study?*

—Two come to mind at once. Both fit very well with the definition of a UFO report as 'an incredible story told by a credible person.' Aimé Michel has spoken of UFO phenomena as 'festivals of absurdity', and I think this is a very good description. The sightings are incredible if compared with the norms of our ordinary life. Just as incredible as television would have been a few hundred years ago.

One of these cases which I have in mind, and in which I was involved personally and on which I went to the spot to investigate, occurred in Missouri. It concerned a man who looked after the animals for the biology department of the University. He lived in a caravan outside the town, with his wife, his daughter of sixteen, and his son aged three. The wife is a nurse, who often works nights at the hospital. Often during the night, when the wife is absent, the sixteen-year-old daughter goes to get some milk from the refrigerator for the baby's feeding bottle. That night, as usual, she went to the refrigerator, and, looking out of the caravan window, she saw a light which was coming towards her. I have been there myself and have seen the surroundings and the terrain: a few trees, fields, long grass, no road — nothing could come from that side. The light was extremely bright and very big.

She got frightened, and awakened her father. He came, glanced out of the window, shut the door, and loaded two guns. He had two hunting dogs with quite aggressive natures. These dogs were beneath the caravan, and remained there. When the light had come even closer, the telephone ceased to work, just at the moment when the father tried to call the Police. Then the strangest things began to happen. The light was so bright that he could no longer make out any details outside. The trees that were nearest to the object began to sway violently, as though they were at the centre of a hurricane. The other trees around about were completely still, as the wind that night was blowing at no more than 5 m.p.h. It was a clear night, and while these trees were writhing about violently, there was a loud crack, like a clap of thunder, and when the Police arrived there some time later and inspected the area, they reported that large branches about 7 centimetres in diameter and situated some 5 metres or so from the ground had been torn off. I went to the spot a few days later and I can testify that the breaks on the branches were fresh and were definitely not something that had happened long before. Another interesting thing was that the leaves from these branches and from the neighbouring branches were all heaped together in a strange fashion and with no apparent explanation.

Now that man had no reason for inventing this story. He is a respectable individual, who works at the University, and who had nothing to gain from this affair. ...

He seemed very embarrassed by all this, and there is one additional detail that I should mention — his little boy had woken up while the phenomenon were going on and had seen the trees shaking violently. So, when one of my colleagues arrived there a few days later and was walking over the fields and chatting with the father about entirely different matters, the little boy came up and said: 'Daddy, the trees aren't moving about today as they did the other night!' That remark was a piece of quite unsolicited testimony!

Another case which I was given to study recently is the case of Captain Coyne's helicopter. He was the captain of an Army rescue team. They are used for rescuing people in accidents and for other activities of that kind. They were returning from Columbus, Ohio, where they had just passed their annual physical-fitness test, and so they were in top form. Half-way between Columbus and Cleveland, near a small village called Mansfield, one of the crew saw a red light approaching them very, very fast, a really vivid red light. I went myself to Cleveland and interviewed the crew, and I

193

sat in all the seats in the helicopter. The captain re-enacted for me his movements of that day. It was a completely unbelievable story. This intense red light they saw was as powerful as the landing light of a *Boeing 727* aircraft, only it was red instead of being white. The light was attached to a cylindrically shaped object, and when this object was right above their helicopter it slowed down to their speed, which was around 160 km.p.h. Then an intense green beam of light came down into the cabin. Captain Coyne showed me exactly what happened. He tried to call the radio station at Mansfield. He got contact with them briefly, and then suddenly his radio stopped working. He tried again several times to contact the Mansfield radio station, but then the strangest thing happened. He showed me how he had tried to take the helicopter down quickly. He did this hoping to avoid the impact which he feared, for he thought a collision was going to occur. Instead of losing altitude however, the helicopter began to rise, and he saw on his altimeter that he had gone from 700 ft. to 3,800 ft. This sort of thing has been reported several time before. A violation, as it were, of the laws of physics. He was still trying to take the helicopter down but it was still continuing to rise when the object, the UFO, suddenly made off and disappeared towards the west. It had a white light at its rear, and it made a 45° turn.

Thus we have four very experienced men telling us a completely unbelievable story. Nobody can explain how a helicopter can rise instead of descending.

I think you must have heard too of the case of the two Mississippi fishermen: it's in the book by Ralph Blum, *Beyond Earth*.* I went down there with Dr Harder of the University of California. The two men, one aged forty-five and the other about nineteen, both work in the naval shipyards. They like fishing, and were just about to start fishing from the end of the jetty when they saw a brilliant blue light which was approaching and which they quickly decided was a typical UFO. The UFO did not actually land. Two creatures came out of it, they seemed pretty grotesque, and resembled robots: two legs, two arms like pincers, and hands like pincers. So they came out and they seized the two men by the arms. They did not lift them, one of the men told us, but somehow or other they simply caused them to float aboard the craft. There was no table there; they were simply lying on their sides inside the machine, without any sort of support.

* Bantam paperback, 1974 (original American edition). British paperback edition by Corgi, 1974. G.C.

The two men were in a condition of weightlessness, just like astronauts, and then a sort of bizarre instrument, which they describe to the best of their ability as like a great eye, passed to and fro over them several times and then they were released. The younger man was so frightened that he had fainted and remained unconscious throughout.

Dr Harder, who is a good hypnotist, and I worked together on this case for about four hours. We thought that the conscious minds of the two men had been put under a block, so that they could not remember the details. With them under hypnosis Dr Harder tried to oblige their subconscious minds to reveal what they knew, but it didn't work. It was simply like this: when he put Charlie and his companion into the hypnotic state, so long as he tried to take them back to real events, such as for example what presents they had both received on their tenth birthdays, etc., all went well, but when he tried to allude to their recent UFO experience, a heavy sweat broke out on Charlie's forehead and he at once became very tense. Dr Harder had to bring him out of the hypnosis at once, for fear of possible serious consequences. Then the sheriff too played a sort of 'Watergate' style trick on Charlie. He left a hidden tape-recorder, running, in the room where the two men were put on their own. I listened to this tape, and there was no evidence on it of cheating. The two men were genuinely in a state of shock.

I went down there forty-eight hours after it had happened, and then I was asked to take part in the Dick Cavett Show with Charlie. I insisted that he be given a lie-detector test. Meanwhile, the other man had fallen into a nervous depression, and so that's why he wasn't there. But Charlie passed the lie-detector test successfully. In my press-conference I said that these two men had undergone a very real and very frightening experience. I was not able to say that they had actually seen a machine, but that something must indeed have happened, because these fine people from the South of the United States were normally calm, living at a slow pace, fond of fishing, simple, honest, intelligent folk, but not educated — and then suddenly something like this happened to them. What do you do in a case like that?

So there you have a few of the most extraordinary cases. I would also like to emphasise that I am a member of a five-man jury, five professors from different parts of the United States. I expect you know the paper, the *National Enquirer* — it is doing what I would call a reportage on this subject. They have offered a reward of $50,000 to anyone who can prove that the UFOs come from distant Space. But of course the proof in this case is difficult to establish, and what is more, it is just as difficult to get five professors to agree on anything. So, just imagine for a moment how hard it would be to prove the existence of the UFOs!

To everyone, and to all our listeners, while we await such proof, we are offering a prize of $5,000 annually for the best eyewitness report of a scientific nature, and for the most interesting case, always from the scientific point of view. Incidentally, we are going to have to decide in the next few days on the prizewinner for 1973, and I think we shall have a hard job, for it has been a good year for sightings.

After everybody had thought that this subject was finished, and that there would be no more talk about it, it turns out that the UFOs haven't deigned to read the Condon Report, and are carrying on just as they like, not only in the United States. Incidentally, people are surprised when I tell them that UFOs are also seen in France, in Spain, in Latin America. They imagine that it is only here in the U.S.A. that this sort of thing happens, and now they are discovering that it is not so. It seems that the most interesting cases occur in very isolated areas, and this agrees with the findings of Dr Claude Poher in France. For landings and encounters they seem to avoid urban areas, and so these tend to take place in isolated regions.

It was a case of this type that took place in a little town in the middle of Kansas, in an agricultural community where nothing ever happens. An eighteen-year-old boy was tending his sheep when he suddenly saw a brilliantly illuminated machine coming down from the sky. It did not land, but remained there at about 2 ft. above the ground. Then, after several minutes, it flew off. The terrified boy called to his parents, who arrived in time to see the craft disappearing in the distance. The boy's mother is a nurse. As it went, the UFO left a glowing ring about 3 metres wide, resembling a fritter in shape. The sheriff told us that the bark at the foot of the trees was glowing just as brightly, and he took a photo showing it. The mother has a *Polaroid* camera, and although it was loaded with colour film for day photography, the brightness of the glow was so intense that, when she photographed it, it affected the film. This is one of the most interesting photos that we possess. We have taken bits of the bark of the trees for analysis. The most interesting thing about the soil where this brilliant ring was left is that, up to the present, it has remained totally impervious to water. You can pour as much water on it as you like, but the water just lies there, and doesn't penetrate the soil, whereas, a few centimetres from there, outside the ring, the water penetrates into the ground as though into a sponge. On the other hand, as you might expect, we have tried to get things to grow on that ring, but without any success. It genuinely is a very interesting case, and it is this case that won the $5,000 prize. I repeat that these people are simple farmers, and I do not think them capable of making up a bogus story of such dimensions. This case is a very good example of physical traces left by a UFO, and it is this sort of thing that interests us at the UFO Study Centre quite particularly. We are trying to concentrate on these cases where something is left behind that can be studied: photographs; damaged cars; broken branches of trees; or indeed anything that can be examined in a laboratory.

—As a scientist yourself, Dr Hynek, what explanations can you offer, and what conclusions can you draw from all these eyewitness accounts?

—The most likely explanation is that we are being visited by extraterrestrial intelligences, and there is no doubt that this phenomenon presents signs of what we might call intelligence.

As an astronomer, it is very difficult for me to deduce that this is the proof that we are being visited by extraterrestrials. It is as though we were to have dozens of *Apollo* launchings daily! When you realize that the nearest star to us, apart from the Sun, is a hundred million times as far from us as the Moon, you will realize that getting here would represent a tremendous undertaking. It is something that our technology could not do. So we can discuss it on this basis. And, on the other hand, you can also say that we have progressed from the Wright Brothers' aeroplane to the landings on the Moon in less than seventy years, and that we have gone from the horse-drawn carriage to the *Boeing 747* in scarcely more than a hundred years. There are stars that are millions of years older than the Sun. It is very probable that there are civilizations which are older than us, not by a hundred years, but by millions of years, and they will certainly know things that we don't know. I do not deny the idea of visitors from Space, but I do think we ought to look in another direction as well. What other direction? Well, we are in a situation where we don't know what to investigate. An example: Everyone knows who Benjamin Franklin was. Suppose now that someone had asked Benjamin Franklin, who was a very good scientist in his own line: 'Ben, what makes the Sun shine?' There was nothing whatsoever in his knowledge of Physics and of Science which could have sug-

197

gested to him the idea that the Sun is a type of nuclear reactor. How could Benjamin Franklin have been able to guess what makes the Sun shine? Well, now, we may be in exactly the same situation as regards the UFOs. If they are not extraterrestrial, well then, we are touching here on a domain which is just as alien and as unknown for us as nuclear energy was for Benjamin Franklin.

We have, too, an interesting paradox. At times I like to think that if I were no longer a scientist I would be a science fiction writer. Suppose that one day we discovered that there is something like the domination of spirit over matter, as some parapsychological investigations today seem to indicate. Suppose that in a million years from now we were to learn (perhaps a civilization somewhere in Space has already learnt it) how to project a thought-form from here to Mars instead of sending a physical machine there. Suppose that we sent a type of thought, and that we could materialize it there in a fashion that is still completely unknown to us today. I have not the slightest idea as to what might be done. Just as I have not the slightest idea what the state of Science will be in a million years from now. Certainly anyone transported suddenly forward to millions of years from now and seeing what might be taking place at that future time would be puzzled and unable to understand anything, just as an African pygmy suddenly brought here now would be dumbfounded by television. For example, how would you prove to anyone that at this present moment, while we are talking, there are television images passing through this room? Try to explain that to an aborigine, and he will simply tell you that you are crazy, that you are talking nonsense. But it isn't nonsense. The UFOs are something like that. I sometimes think that reality is perhaps a multidimensional continuum, and that the physical world which we see around us merely represents a momentary sample of that global reality, and that another momentary slice of that global reality would be in another sort of world. Perhaps there are inter-laced universes? Perhaps the UFOs are manifestations, glimpses, of another world? This business of time-travel has often been mentioned. Thus, we are now in the present, but suppose that there is another world ten minutes behind us, or another one a million years ahead of us? We cannot cross that distance, any more than we can transfer ourselves instantaneously from this room to another room of the same kind at the same moment in San Francisco, even if we know that it exists. Evanston-Chicago is separated from San Francisco by space, but suppose that two places situated in the

198

same location are separated not by space, but by time, like a train running ten minutes behind another train and passing through the same place. .... Perhaps from time to time there might be a way in which we could cross this gap and have a glimpse of that other world.

Please remember that at this present moment I am no longer speaking as an astronomer or as a scientist, but as a simple human being using his imagination.

—*Dr Hynek, all the eyewitness accounts speak of phenomena which occur right on the ground or at a very low altitude. But have astronomers ever said that they have seen flying objects during their observations of the night sky?*

—Yes. The answer is yes, but none of them have allowed their names to be mentioned.* I have received excellent eyewitness accounts from astronomers, but always under the seal of secrecy and anonymity. As you can well realize, it is one of the most disturbing, most complex of problems. We will perhaps have to revise our way of looking at certain things. When the classical laws of Physics were not capable of explaining atomic spectra, we had to turn to Quantum Mechanics, and when the classical laws of Physics could no longer explain certain things, we had to take an extraordinary leap in the direction of Relativity. Bernard Shaw said: '*Every great idea begins as a heresy*'. We are still trying to explain things by the natural approach. One of the most famous examples happened in France, when the French Academy of Sciences tried to deny the existence of meteorites, seeing them merely as stones that had been struck by lightning, because it seemed to them preposterous that stones could fall from the sky. And yet stones do fall from the sky. If you were a doctor, ten or twenty years ago, and had talked about Acupuncture, you would have been rejected by all the medical associations of the entire world. Today, people are beginning to accept that science of Acupuncture. Nobody knows how it works, but it is recognized. It is the same with hypnotism, which started as a sort of carnival spectacle, branded as ridiculous, absurd, unbelievable, by the most sober scientists, and yet today hypnotism is used in Medicine and is recognized as being a medical technique. I am always impressed by what I call our 'temporal provincialism'. When we look at the ancient civilizations, such as the Egyptians and the Babylonians, we think that they were nice folk but awfully stupid, and we think how many things we know

* See the anonymous testimony of the French astronomer given in Chapter 1 of this book.

that they did not. But what we tend to forget is that in 5,000 years from now our Science will have evolved greatly, and that when people then will speak condescendingly of us, they will be thinking of us just as we now think about the Egyptians. Maybe they will say of us: 'They were splendid people, but a bit limited; they didn't even know what the UFOs were.'

—*The NASA astronauts had some astonishing sightings at the times of the first Mercury and Gemini flights, but for several years past it seems as though NASA no longer allows them to tell the truth about what they have seen. Have you had anything from the astronauts?*

—Yes. I can even prove that the astronauts have been forbidden to speak. I have talked to some of the astronauts, to McDivitt, for example, and it is now certain that Collins and Aldrin (in *Apollo XI*), while on their way to the Moon, saw a strange object, not in orbit around the Moon but in flight, in front of them. Other astronauts have also said they have seen strange things. The whole UFO question has been controversial — we call it 'a hot potato' — so you can see why NASA don't want to be mixed up in it. NASA have to ask Congress for their budget funds, and if it was said that NASA were not getting on with their own business, but were interested in Flying Saucers, that could endanger their budget. So I think if I had been the Director of NASA, I would have acted in the same way.

—*Dr Hynek, you went round the world last year, collecting information and eyewitness accounts. Are there any differences between what you have gathered in the U.S.A. and what you have heard and collected in the most outlying areas of the world, such as, for example, the Pacific Islands?*

—That is precisely the reason why I made that trip. I wanted to find out whether the things seen in Australia were different from those that occur here in the U.S.A. I found that there is no difference. The same things are reported here as they are over there, and one of the principal reasons for my journey was to go to the old Anglican Mission at Boianai in New Guinea. It was there that, in 1959, Father William Gill, along with thirty other witnesses, had the remarkable sighting of a machine descending towards the Earth, with some sort of creatures standing on the deck as it were. The priest waved to them, and they waved back. Then he waved again twice, and again they answered him twice. They did not land, but rose up into the sky and plunged into the clouds and disappeared. I went to Boianai to see for myself the place where this had happened. I took some photographs, I drew some maps, and I found six eyewitnesses, natives who still remembered the event. The priest himself is no longer there, but lives in Melbourne. So then I went to Melbourne, and had a very long chat with him. He is a highly educated man, certainly not the kind of man who would stoop to the least sort of hoax, and this case, like those at Socorro in New Mexico and Valensole in France, remains profoundly mysterious.

—*And now, finally, I think all those who have just heard you would like to know, Dr Hynek, where to write to you if anyone wants information or especially if anyone wants to send you information and to collaborate with your Centre for UFO Studies.*

—Contact me directly at the Department of Astronomy, Northwestern University, Evanston, Illinois, or at the Centre for UFO studies, 924 Chicago Avenue, Evanston, Illinois 60202, U.S.A.*

* Amended address. G.C.

Dr David Saunders is Professor of Psychology in the University of Colorado at Boulder, near Denver. It was precisely to this university that the American Government had entrusted the task of preparing an enquiry and an exhaustive and definitive report on the phenomenon of the unidentified flying objects. And Dr Condon, who was in charge of the general synthesis of the work, concluded finally that the UFOs did not exist. But David Saunders protested vigorously, and his protests received at least as much airing as did the conclusions reached by the Condon Committee.

Michel Anfrol accordingly arranged to interview Dr Saunders on behalf of *France-Inter*:

●

—*Dr Saunders, what was it that induced you to take the opposite view to the theories put forward by your colleague, Condon?*
—I think there were many things that happened. After a certain length of time it had already become apparent that the 'Condon Project' was not going in the direction which it should have been following on the basis of the documentation gathered and the evidence which was accumulating. There were several of us who had the feeling that what was considered important was not what was happening inside the framework of the Condon enquiry, but that, right from the outset, it had already been decided that the Report was to be formulated along the lines which it did eventually have.
—*How do you explain the conclusions reached in the Report written by Dr Condon when the documentation built up by most of the scientists and the investigators had arrived at totally different explanations?*
—The simplest way to explain this is to recognize that, at the psychological level, Dr Condon was essentially a *political individual.* He was a scientific politician, if you like to employ such a term, because he certainly had some very impressive scientific qualifications. But his role within this UFO study was in my opinion, the role of a politician carrying out a polit-

ical mission, and his reactions to everything that happened, as our work proceeded, can be grasped very easily indeed from that aspect.

—*What has been your attitude since?*

—When working on the Condon Project, I began collecting together all the statistical data, with the aim of doing an analysis of it on the computer, and I have continued to add to these statistics, to such a point that they now represent a total of 60,000 UFO reports of all kinds. And I have now begun — just recently — to draw a number of conclusions from these basic statistics.

—*Do you classify it all under different categories of sightings and eyewitness accounts?*

—Yes, there are those reports which, unfortunately, shall we say, are very easy to explain, and then it ranges right across from the simplest categories to the sightings that are extremely difficult to evaluate and to classify. The particular system of classification which I use comprises nine categories, which run from what I call Type 1, that is to say, the report of something which has never been seen moving, up to Type 9, which is a report in which the witness declares that something happened, a physical wound, say, or again something else which does not disappear when the UFO departs. Perhaps 80%-90% of the cases in this documentation are relatively routine affairs, if indeed one can talk of routine in the matter of UFO sightings. The really interesting cases represent maybe 10% of the documentation. But even so, that amounts to several thousand cases. Anything that *Project Blue Book*, for example, would have declared inexplicable is certainly a good case, a case for which, it seems, ridiculous explanations have been given, these explanations serving simply to throw a smoke screen across the trail. A case that is reported by highly qualified and credible witnesses, and which contains elements that are difficult to explain, must certainly be a good case. And especially so is a case in which a witness declares that the UFO came right close to him, and he begins to think that he may have been able to communicate individually with the UFO or exchange something with it.

—*What did the other members of the Condon Committee do? Did they just remain neutral, or did they decide in favour of Condon or of you?*

—We were a gathering of individuals on the Condon Committee, and if you present a complete sampling of questions, I am sure that you will find that there were points of disagreement among all of us on at least one count. There were no two persons among us who saw everything in exactly the same way. As for myself, personally, I think that, at the moment when the Condon Project was reaching its conclusion, had they chosen to put it to a sort of majority vote, the majority would have said that there really was something in the UFO problem, that it was an area that deserved a more intensive, more thorough, and more complete enquiry. I would have liked to have seen at least some sort of summary which would have said precisely that.

—*Your domain here at the University is psychology. Well, now, how can you use psychology in research on unidentified flying objects?*

—Well, of course, psychology can play a part in numerous ways. Some of these ways relate for example to the psychology of perception, to which there will be frequent recourse. Thus, we have to know what it is possible for a human being to see or hear in the memories that he may bring back. There can be several psychological aspects to hypnosis, which aspects can furnish very fruitful techniques of enquiry. Psychology also means the possibility to spot those individuals who are seeking publicity through UFO reports, and to distinguish them from those who really are telling the truth because they feel the need to make something known. There are certainly mentally unbalanced individuals among all those who have contributed to my studies, but I do not think that they represent the majority in my files, and I think I am in a position to spot them — thanks precisely to psychology.

—*Have your researches led you to formulate any conclusions as to the origin of the UFOs?*

—I have not come to anything that you could call a conclusion on the subject. There seem to be several possibilities. The most common view is what is known as the extraterrestrial hypothesis, that is to say, the idea of creatures that have succeeded in getting here from out there while acting within what we consider to be the laws of Physics. We cannot eliminate this hypothesis — I don't think we can. Another equally attractive theory suggests that there are people who have come among us, having travelled a very short distance, and moving through a dimension which is unknown to us. I don't know how to term it, because we don't know what it could be, but let us say that the notion of a parallel universe or the notion of a psychic dimension would correspond to this possibility.

—*Incidentally, this idea seems to be more and more widespread.*

—Yes, this hypothesis is being examined with relatively more attention in the publications of the various UFO study groups. *Flying Saucer Review*, which I consider to be the best of its kind in the world, certainly puts forward this idea. Certainly a number of investigators approach the whole subject with this idea as their first hypothesis, and it is not one that I wish to reject.

—*Have you talked to many people who have witnessed the appearances of UFOs?*

—I have not talked personally with many of these people. I have found it better if I maintain a certain distance between myself and the witnesses. This gives me a greater feeling of perspective about the whole subject. I have been invited several times to take part in an investigation, and I have always been inclined to refuse. Obviously if I were to see a UFO myself it would certainly cause me to be a different person.

—*And, incidentally, most of the scientists who are interested in UFOs have never seen one themselves. But in the cases of those individuals who in fact have seen a flying saucer, can a change of behaviour be detected in them?*

—Yes, there are indeed many reports which indicate changes of behaviour, changes in appearance, changes in philosophical attitude, and changes in the mere ability to perform elementary chores. There are dozens of reports like that. I find it very difficult to evaluate the least report, and to say: That's how it happened. This is the reason why I prefer to maintain a certain attitude which will allow me to see a much wider picture, rather than to be confined in a situation where I would have to pronounce judgement on a particular event.

—*How many sightings have you in your computer?*

—I now have 60,000 eyewitness reports in my files, and more than 40,000 of them relate to separate events, and 4,000 of them refer to very interesting cases that happened on the ground or very close to the ground. This figure of 4,000 is a good number for statistical work, but if you start going into the details and start classifying these 4,000 reports, saying that some individuals suffered electromagnetic effects, some suffered psychological effects, and others loss of memory, etc., you will see that in the end you have only a few cases that you could use in each category, and that puts the statisticians in a difficult position, as in the end they have to make do with only a small sample of the material. One of the first things that I did was to classify the sighting reports according to the day of the week. I did this for my own amusement, and did not expect anything special from it. So I was indeed astonished when I discovered that every day of the week did not produce the same number of sightings, and perhaps even more astonished when I found that it was not the weekends that produced the most reports, but quite the opposite. In other words, it was something very different from the idea that one might have of the people who provide the reports — that is to say, of folk who are drunkards, or who are having a game, or who are seeking publicity.

I have also classified the reports by counties, with the object of seeing which regions were most closely connected with the bulk of the sightings. The population obviously plays a great role in this, for obviously you have got to have witnesses before you can have sighting reports. And then it turns out that, in a most surprising fashion, it is the people with the best education in each county who furnish most of the reports. This is understandable if you reflect that a person already has to have a certain amount of knowledge in order to perceive that the thing moving about in the sky over there is maybe neither an aeroplane nor a helicopter. It turns out, too, that the sighting conditions are particularly important, and that the existence of a place where one can make a statement, a report, is likewise very important.

All these things are very important facts which have to be sifted and classified among the mass of data, because there will be, on the whole, numerous influences that come into play, and it will be necessary to differentiate between them all and to recognize the part that each of them plays. This should enable us to extract from it a line of enquiry which will perhaps be more important than the phenomenon itself.

—*How is it that far more eyewitness reports are received from rural or backward regions than from great cities like New York or Chicago where it must be said that sighting reports are indeed pretty rare?*

—Yes, certainly the population is a factor that is closely linked to the number of sightings, and you would be justified in expecting more sightings from a city like New York than from a village in Mississippi. But that is not the only factor which influences the number of reports that are published. The essential factor so far as New York is concerned will certainly be the number of newspapers that are published and that are likely to mention these things. Thus, New York has excellent papers, like the *New York Times*, but which won't print things of this sort, while maybe newspapers in the suburbs might be likely to print such things, but the chances for eyewitness accounts are less. If you go to Pascagoula, in Mississippi, you will find as many papers there as in New York, with far fewer people, and we see at least as many sightings in them, limited perhaps on the score of the need for a place where they can be recorded. One of the biggest difficulties in knowing about this subject arises from the fact that we are almost entirely limited to reports and stories published in the papers at this or that period.

—*Do you receive any reports directly, which have not first been published by the newspapers?*

—Very, very few. I have not put myself in such a position where I would have to encourage that sort of thing, and in any case Dr Hynek is taking the lead with his Centre for UFO Studies, and he is well placed for making it as widely known as possible.

—*When you receive a report, are you quickly able to check its accuracy and its degree of truthfulness thanks to the guidelines which have emerged from all the cards already in your possession?*

—I cannot check them as regards truthfulness. But I can check them against what I know already, that is to say, what is happening in the same period of time or in the same geographical area, or indeed whether the same witnesses have already produced other reports, or, again, whether the contents of this new report present similarities with earlier sightings. But I don't think that, at the stage where we are today, we know enough about the subject yet for us to be capable of saying that a report that speaks of such and such a thing is true and that a report which says something else cannot be considered.

—*Do certain regions furnish interesting sightings several times, or does the phenomenon appear in different regions each time?*

—I think there are a number of places, or rather I should say several geographically definable regions. I am thinking in fact of certain lines which produce more than one simple sheriff's report during a given period. One of the things that I am trying to investigate is this matter of the places which produce more than just a simple sheriff's report, and, looking at it from the opposite angle, I am trying to seek, in these particular counties that stand out, the particular reasons which could explain why so many sightings come from those areas. It is getting interesting to work on finding a corollary to our basic hypotheses. Thus, for example, the possibility that sightings are more numerous in the vicinity of atomic installations would be an interesting hypothesis if it could be verified. But there are too many places of that type to enable me to get such a precise definition in my researches. I would like to arrive at some conclusions by approaching the subject from various different directions, and to be able to say, for example, which are the most interesting places, and the most unexpected places, or the most extraordinary places. Do they in fact correspond in some way or another with the places which we find already in the history of the UFO phenomenon?

—*What, then, can you conclude from it all?*

—I draw no conclusions, but I must say that, even after having spent a certain time studying all this, the only thing I can say is that I still need to study it for a while yet.

—*Dr Saunders, how do you now plan to obtain the information that you still need?*

—The principal thing that would contribute to the studies I am making would be the creation of an important new source of data. Maybe Dr Hynek and his new Centre for UFO Studies will start sending us something along those lines. I would like to develop a method that would enable me to hear and learn more about these UFO occurrences, and most especially about those that are not mentioned in the newspapers. I would like to find a means, perhaps via an approach to public opinion similar to what is done with the opinion polls, to discover witnesses who have never made their UFO sightings public. And then do a study of samples of this material, using a different method from the one that we are dependent on at present. I don't know whether or not this would lead us to fresh material, but it would be very important to see whether it could be done.

BELGIAN RESEARCHERS AND THE UFO PROBLEM

The Belgian Society for the Study of Space Phenomena (S.O.B.E.P.S.)* defines its position as follows:

The activities of S.O.B.E.P.S. had their genesis in the fact that, as we had discovered, the problem of the UFOs is still not solved.

Article 3 of the Rules of the Society, published in its official journal, states: 'The Association has as its aims the observation and the rational and objective study of Space phenomena and related problems, as well as the diffusion of the reports received via a bi-monthly Journal called INFORESPACE.'

What is S.O.B.E.P.S.' position as regards the UFO problem? S.O.B.E.P.S. declares that there is a problem worthy of scientific study. This affirmation does not rest solely on the human testimony, with all its possible errors and exaggerations, but principally on what one may term the 'physical evidence', such as:
—marks on the ground.
—detection by radar.
—deviation of magnetic compasses aboard aircraft.
—electromagnetic effects on cars and on circuit-breakers in power plants.
—physiological effects on the witnesses.
—effects on animals, etc.

All this constitutes a pattern of elements which are frequently verifiable scientifically. Photographs and films do not constitute proof in the opinion of S.O.B.E.P.S., given all the possibilities of forgery and fraud by means of present-day photographic techniques.

Such documentation as films and photos can only give an idea of how the UFO problem is seen by investigators.

As to the nature and origin of the phenomenon, we have to say that we know neither what it is, nor whence it comes. We are here to study the phenomenon.

* *Société Belge d'Etudes des Phénomènes Spatiaux*, (S.O.B.E.P.S.), 26 Boulevard Aristide-Briand, 1070 Bruxelles.

Euloge Boissonnade of *France-Inter* went to Brussels to interview the S.O.B.E.P.S. scientists. But, as you know, the tapes were stolen. However, Lucien Clerebaut, General Secretary of S.O.B.E.P.S., has authorized the O.R.T.F. (French Radio and Television) to reproduce here the article which appeared in Issue No. 7 of their excelllent magazine INFORE-SPACE. This article sets out the guidelines for the UFO research undertaken by S.O.B.E.P.S. It is signed by Lucien Clerebaut and André Boudin. The former is a professor at the Nuclear Institute and is on the staff of Lovanium University, Kinshasa. André Boudin is a specialist in Nuclear Geology.

●

I. *A Problem Exists.*

Few people nowadays have never heard the expression 'flying saucer'. However, those who have gone into the problem are few. In every human group three attitudes can be discerned, three fundamental attitudes in the face of this thorny problem:

1. Firstly, there are those who admit to the reality of the problem. But capital distinctions must be made among them, for there are many different ways of accepting this reality:

   (a) There are those, trustworthy witnesses, and honest investigators, isolated or grouped in associations like S.O.B.E.P.S. or numerous sister societies abroad, who, after examination of the facts, *recognize the existence of an original phenomenon,* worthy of being studied in depth, without pronouncing themselves yet as to its exact nature, which is not at all the same thing as 'believing in flying saucers'. This group does not desire to pit itself in sterile opposition to orthodox science, but rather to try to interest orthodox science in the UFO problem.

   (b) There are also those who, with the greatest sincerity, 'believe' in flying saucers, in the religious sense of the term 'to believe', and who feel no need for any scientific proof to support their conviction. Their clubs, of very variable quality and displaying a more or less excessive mysticism and taste for the occult and the fantastic, are usually more interested in philosophical or moral studies than in a real study of the UFO phenomenon. It can at times go so far as the cult of the 'Cosmic Brethren', whence the label of 'cultists' given to some of these groups.

(c) There are, finally, alas, those who must be called the hoaxers and the crooks, when they are not actually mentally sick, who furnish the public with ready-fabricated eyewitness accounts and claim to have actually experienced their splendid science-fiction stories, which would have been huge hits had they been advertised as such, with their romantic trips to Venus and their handshakes with the Jupiterians. ...

2. In the class opposed to this first category, there are many scientists, and not of the least eminent, who condemn the subject and think that even to take it into consideration is anti-scientific behaviour. It is clear however that no problem is, *a priori*, anti-scientific in itself: it is merely the method of studying it that is good or bad, and to study it seriously is not to fail to be serious, as was pointed out very opportunely by the editors of *Sciences et Avenir* (No. 307, September 1972, p. 696) in their editorial heading the remarkable article by Pierre Guérin.

3. Finally, between these two positions, there are many scientists and investigators whose interest in this particular problem is no greater than in any other problem lying outside the field of their own work, and who simply rely on the official studies published on the subject. Now these official studies, or at any rate those that have been made public, are, so far as we know, without exception all negative. A large proportion of scientists have been induced to adopt this

official position more as a reaction against the excesses of folk in groups 1(b) and 1(c) than as a result of any critical work done by themselves personally. This is a great pity, for nothing short of the impartial examination of the record authorizes one to form an opinion — not psychological reactions or preconceived opinions.

So far, there has been too much desire to make the data serve some official truth selected in advance. What is required now is a reversal of this process and the realization that the 'flying saucer phenomenon' is a permanent one, even though the leading newspapers only mention it occasionally, and that it involves every part of the world without exception, including the socialist countries, whence we receive reports from time to time.

Unfortunately, while the fundamental problem is the problem of knowing what UFOs are, the real difficulty is to find the material for a proper scientific study. The scientific community, alas, lacks experimental data, because it does not take the problem seriously, and it does not take the problem seriously because it lacks experimental data, as was very justly pointed out by Dr James D. McDonald.* The result of this vicious circle is that *bona fide* UFO sighters who could furnish this data do not do so for fear of ridicule. The only way out of the situation is for a few scientists to accept openly to devote themselves to the subject, in many cases of course at the price of drawing down upon themselves the suspicion of their colleagues.

II. *The Facts*

The data available to us are the reports compiled by eyewitnesses and obtained via the press or through official channels, as well as the reports of investigations con-

* *Symposium on Unidentified Flying Objects: Hearings before the Committee on Science and Astronautics, U.S. House of Representatives, July 29, 1968.* Oral communication from Dr James D. McDonald. See resume in INFORESPACE No. 2, pp. 34-37.

ducted by specialized private organizations, sister societies to S.O.B.E.P.S., such as L.D.L.N. or G.E.P.A. in France, N.I.C.A.P. and A.P.R.O. in the U.S.A., etc. Each of these reports furnishes three categories of information:

a. The place.
b. The time.
c. The description of the phenomena.

The *Type 1 Report* consists of three elements:

Longitude.
Latitude.
Precise Details.

It is objective: whatever the number of witnesses, their ages, their characters, their degree of education, we can always give witnesses these three coordinates. Likewise, on the basis of this *Type 1*, we can investigate whether the topographical distribution of the UFO sightings obeys an exact law, and what methods can be employed for checking this. The theory of Orthoteny for example.

The *Type 2* sighting is more complex; it is only possible to treat cases in which it occurs by more precise analytic and descriptive methods. An example is the study of the phenomenon of the 'UFO wave'.

The *Type 3* sighting is extremely complex, for it is the result of an intimate interpenetration between the physical sciences and the behavioural sciences. Which makes the pure scientist very ill at ease. The category can be divided into two elements:
—the first describes the *conditions* of the sighting (number of witnesses, meteorological conditions, cameras at their disposal. ...)
—the second describes the *features* of the sighting, i.e., all the remarks relating to physical conditions contained in the description given by the witness, or the marks which were left behind by the UFO (speed, shape, colour, size, marks on the ground. ...)

In any case, it is urgently necessary to contradict once and for all time certain statements made concerning UFOs:
It is in effect claimed that:
—Only those who have an *a priori* belief in the UFOs and who have already read a great deal about the sub-

213

ject submit reports of sightings. *Nothing is more false.* Most of the time the witnesses are total novices in the subject and have no preconceived ideas.

—that the bulk of sighting reports come from mentally unstable individuals or folk who find their lives humdrum: this can indeed happen and does happen, but the great majority of the eyewitness accounts come, on the contrary, from socially stable and trustworthy people. These are the observers who make the best reports and consequently it is they who carry the most weight in the analysis that we are able to make of the phenomenon.

—that sighting reports never come from scientists. *This is also false*, unequivocally so. Some of the very best reports come from scientists. It is true that, in general they jib at writing a report for publication, and that they prefer to remain anonymous. Whence this allegation that no reports have ever emanated from them. A Gallup Poll taken in the U.S.A. among astronomers showed that 12% of them had seen a UFO at least once. The best known case is that of Clyde Tombaugh, who discovered Pluto. One cannot believe that all these people would mistake bladders for lanterns and sonde-balloons and helicopters for UFOs.

—that sightings are always vague, and give very few practical and precise details. *This is false.* There are several thousands of extremely detailed cases.

—that the U.S. Air Force has no proof that the UFOs are extraterrestrial or represent an advanced technique: *This is true*, but neither does the Air Force have any proof that these two hypotheses are not true. So long as these flying objects remain unidentified, the debate will remain open.

—that publicity generates sightings: *this is true*. The great number of cases published encourages amateurs and hoaxers to see UFOs where there are none; but this is very far from being the only cause of reports.

—that UFOs have never been photographed with the special cameras which are used to follow meteors and satellites: this is possibly true, but, on the other hand, these cameras did not yet exist when the great UFO waves of 1947 and 1952 took place, and, on the other hand, these instruments do often register unexplained trails and objects. Furthermore, N.I.C.A.P. received in 1963 several photographs taken by the Smithsonian Astrophysical Observatory and showing trails, made by objects, which did not correspond to the trails of known satellites.

Once all these truths have been established, we believe it is best to adopt the system of sighting classification made by Dr J. Allen Hynek, who was for 18 years the scientific consultant to *Project Blue Book* and who consequently had access to all the secret files. We strongly recommend his recent book, *The UFO Experience*, published by Henry Regnery Co., Chicago, 1972.

Dr Hynek's Classification System

Category 1 : Observations at a distance.
    1.1: Nocturnal lights.
    1.2: Daylight discs.
    1.3: Radar-Visual sightings.
Category 2 : Close Encounter Sightings (at less than 150 m.)
    2.1: Without interaction with environment (witness and surroundings.)
    2.2: With interaction with the environment.
    2.3: With description of occupants (Ufonauts.)

In addition to these, Hynek proposes the use of two yardsticks:

1. *The Strangeness Rating* (S), which is a measure of the number of 'information bits' contained in the sighting (1 to 10).
2. *The Probability Rating* (P): the assessment of the credibility of the witness himself. It is very hard to evaluate; Hynek tackled it by taking into account the number of the eyewitnesses and their respective qualifications. Examples: 1 witness, P = 3; several witnesses, P = 3.5; 1 witness with scientific or technical knowledge, P = 5, and so on.

III *Examination of the Different Categories*

  1.1: *Nocturnal Lights.*
    We omit from this category everything in the sky which an uninformed public could call abnormal but which has in fact an ordinary explanation (whereas the Condon Committee accepted *a priori* 'every sighting which is unusual for the observer').

Prototype: The typical nocturnal light is a bright light, generally not a point source, of indeterminate linear size, of variable colour but most often yellowish-orange, although no colour of the spectrum is absent from the descriptions: it follows a path different from the path of a balloon, an aircraft, or any other natural object, and often gives the appearance of intelligent action. The light gives no direct evidence of being attached to a solid body, but presumably may be.

The risks of error and confusion are greatest in this category, especially when the observers are inexperienced, and so we shall not dwell at length on it.

1.2: *UFOs observed during the day: daylight discs*
Hynek uses this appellation, for the majority of the objects seen in daytime appear in the shape of discs; these reports are less numerous than those for the nocturnal lights. The daylight disc seems to follow the contours of the terrain over which it is flying (undulatory movement) and often stops over stretches of water. Most of the cases in this category examined by *Blue Book* end without any conclusion being reached or with the notation 'unidentified'.

Prototype: The object is of metallic aspect, circular or oval form, usually luminous or shining; it performs manoeuvres which could be termed 'deliberate', accelerating or slowing down at will. No sound is associated with the majority of these cases. One can only be amazed at the methods of *Blue Book*, which never took the trouble to translate the subjective reports given by witnesses into objective data (example: 'very bright': translate as *'lumen'*; 'the object was displaying an undulatory movement': translate as *'frequency'*, etc.)

1.3: *Radar and Visual Sightings*
According to Hynek, the radar stations of the NORAD network do actually capture indeterminate echoes from time to time, but as these echoes do not correspond to the ballistic trajectories under surveillance, they are discarded

216

without examination. And yet it would be easy to introduce into the programming of the computers controlling the radars a sub-routine charged with the task of isolating these indeterminate echoes. Hynek made a suggestion along these lines, but *Blue Book* categorically turned it down. Consequently it is impossible at present to say how frequent radar observations of this type are.

In any case, it is clear that we are losing here an extremely valuable source of information, for it could yield very rapidly, and in advance, data as to speeds, directions of flight, UFO waves, any groupings that occur, etc., etc. Figure 1 compares the speeds of UFOs detected on radar with the speeds of aircraft and rockets.

2.1: *Close Encounters of the First Kind:* Reports of sightings of very bright lights at a distance of less than 150 metres from the observer, but without tangible physical effects.

Explanation as 'misinterpretation' becomes virtually impossible here, given the close proximity, the coherence of the reports, the number of the eyewitnesses, and their 'credibility rating'. The occupations, education, and mental make-up of the eyewitnesses are very varied. The reports in this categoy present the following feature: it is difficult to separate the reactions of the witnesses from their description of the event; the two things go together.

Prototype: Brilliant luminosity, size relatively small (of the order of tens of metres rather than hundreds of metres), generally oval form, sometimes surmounted by a dome, absence of conventional wings or wheels or other protuberances, ability to hover and to accelerate very rapidly to high speeds.

Let us note here that all the objects in this category are silent, which is the case for only 60%-75% of UFOs, as some 10%-15% emit humming noises, 10%-15% emit whistling noises, and the remainder make varied noises. (Study extracted from *Sciences Et Avenir*, No. 307, see Fig. 2.)

Figure 1: Comparison between speeds of UFOs and aircraft and rockets, expressed in m.p.h.
1 = record speed for aircraft
2 = record speed for rockets
3 = speed of UFOs captured on radar.
(From NICAP's *The UFO Evidence*, p.81)

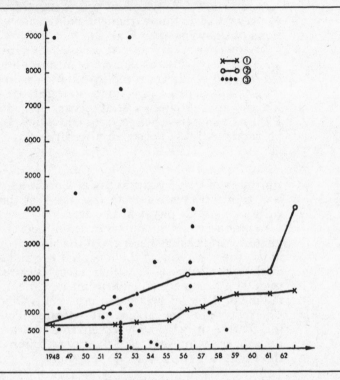

Hundreds if not thousands of cases of this category are known, as also of the others. Note that the amount of information is generally greater (Hynek's *Strangeness Rating*) than for the Category 1 sightings, and this is normal, since the witnesses are closer.

Although there are no visible marks, disturbance of the surroundings is sometimes noticed. Electrical perturbations are an example. It often happens in fact that during sightings car drivers find their engines stopping and their lights going out. It can also happen

Figure 2. Of a total of 273 cases, worldwide:
1. Silent object
2. Various sounds
3. Whistling
4. Hum.
(Document supplied by Claude Poher)

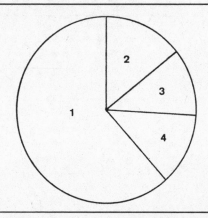

that UFOs cause breakdowns in the general electricity distribution networks. Figure 3 illustrates this supposition. Examination of the correlations between these two curves provides food for thought. ...

2.2: *Close Encounters of the Second Kind:* This category differs from the preceding one only by the fact that the sighting leaves visible and detectable traces. The question of why some close encounters leave traces and others do not is a mystery.

Here is a list, which is not exhaustive, of recorded traces and effects: marks on the ground; burnt vegetation; disturbed animals; psychological effects on man; temporary paralysis, sensation of suffocation, heat, weakness, or burns; interference with the local magnetic field (deviation of compasses); rupture of electric current. Here we have solid data on which we can employ the arsenal of scientific methods. The actual question is however still not: '*how* could this have happened?' , but rather:

Figure 3. Comparison between the number of UFOs recorded by the US Air Force and the number of power failures (electricity) between 1954 and 1966, on basis of data supplied by the Federal Power Commission.
1 = Number of electricity failures
2 = Number of UFOs observed (according to US Air Force.)
(From APRO BULLETIN, March-April 1970, p. 5)

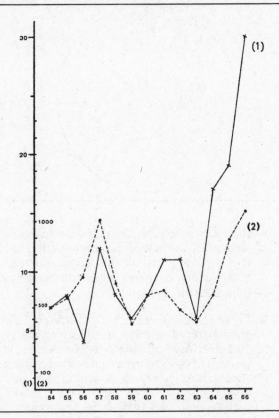

'did this happen more or less as it has been reported?'

Prototype: Hynek here illustrates rather than defines the prototype, noting as a habitual feature the presence of circular marks (burned vegetation), about 10-15 m. in diameter, on the ground.

In our view this category is one of the most important, for we are dealing here not only with the witnesses, whose stories it is always possible — *a priori* — to doubt, but we have, if we may so put it, proofs in our hand. For we have in fact marks on the ground, samples, and suchlike, the examination of which can often enable us to say whether or not something abnormal has ever happened there, even though nothing was ever found there that definitely clarified the question.

2.3: *Close Encounters of the Third Kind:* Sightings with occupants (Ufonauts) and frequently with visible or detectable traces.

This is the trickiest of all the categories. Psychologically, Man is in fact ill-prepared to accept the presence of 'Ufonauts', even if the possibility of unknown craft is accepted. This reticence when faced with the possibility that strangers might come here to us is linked with the struggle for life in which we are still engaged, and we are afraid lest we may not be the winners. Moreover, Science nowadays estimates that, in certain conditions which are very prevalent in our Galaxy, life is bound to appear, and thus is itself probably also widespread.

In this category, we often find ourselves without solid scientific data and we are obliged to centre everything upon the reporter, and this poses for us the terrible problem of the interaction of the exact sciences and the behavioural sciences, particularly so inasmuch as the investigators, who are ordinary folk like you and me, have not received the training of an examining magistrate. At times however it is people whose profession it is to discover hidden truths, such as psychologists and psychiatrists, who conduct the investigations. A typical case of this kind is the story of *Betty and Barney Hill** in the U.S.A., which was the subject of an article in our Journal *INFORE-SPACE* No. 4, pp. 22-31.

* *The Interrupted Journey*, by John G. Fuller (Dial Press, New York, 1966).

Is that story true? Is it false? You can reach no conclusion, for it must not be forgotten that statements made under hypnosis conform to the subject's own concept of truth. In many cases it is indeed also the actual truth, pure and simple, but not always. In fact it seems that it is easy to concoct a story which will later be repeated under hypnosis. To do this, you hypnotize the person and tell him the story. Subsequently, he will only repeat it when under hypnosis again. As you see, in cases of this category, when they are not just simple sightings, there are often two possible explanations.

Obviously the reasoning can be quite different from this if, in addition to the statement by the witness, who seems well balanced, and who has never 'been in trouble', who has an excellent reputation or who is under oath, there are also material traces to confirm the veracity of his statements. We know of such cases as Valensole, Socorro, Quarouble, etc., and these are just a few examples selected from hundreds of others. In his *Catalogue* Jacques Vallée reports more than one thousand close encounter cases, of which 750 are landings, 300 of them with 'Ufonauts'.*

It has been possible to compile an 'Identikit portrait' of the latter: the size is generally small (about one metre), large head, often bald, wide shoulders, and arms long in relation to the body. The eyes are often round or of the slit type, the lips thin, and the nose absent, replaced merely by two nostrils. He is often wearing a one-piece overall or a 'diver's suit'.

IV. *Two Aspects of the Work Done on the Basis of Categories 1 and 2*

We think we can at least be sure of the following points:

* Dr Jacques Vallée: *A Century of Landings*. Published as an appendix to the American edition of *Passport to Magonia* (Henry Regnery Co., Chicago, 1969). The English edition of *Passport to Magonia*, issued by Neville Spearman Ltd., does not contain the appendix. The title of the French edition is *Chronique des Apparitions Extra-Terrestres: (2e. Partie). Un Siècle d'Atterrissages* (Editions Denoël, Paris, 1972.)

(a) A phenomenon exists, as described in the UFO reports, which merits systematic and thorough study. The number of eyewitness accounts is so enormous, and certain of the effects so unexpected, that it is impossible for it to be simply a huge collective joke.

(b) If we consider point (a) as established, then it seems that this phenomenon is connected with an unexplored domain of technology, if not of science.

(c) Consequently it is not frivolous to occupy oneself seriously with this problem.

But if there is certainly no lack of sightings, it seems on the other hand extremely difficult to extract anything positive from them. Few studies have so far succeeded in isolating invariants in the problem.

The first study that appeared to yield some results was that of Aimé Michel, a celebrated investigator in the UFO field and author of several books on the subject. It was in 1958 that he published his theory of Orthoteny,** based on the French UFO wave of October 1954. Taking the sighting accounts one by one, he discovered in fact that UFOs seemed to be employing preferential flight corridors.

Aimé Michel's approach can be summed up in a few words: the probability that a psychological phenomenon would occur along a random alignment is zero. The existence of witnesses and the order of their succession in time and their geographical distribution in space are irrefutable objective facts. If the places where sightings have occurred are entered on a map and we find straight lines, there is no subjective stage in the reasoning and hence the process is unassailable. Moreover it seems that 'cigars' are often seen at the points where the orthotenic lines intersect, as if these 'cigars' are collecting the 'flying saucers' that have gone off along the straight lines to explore the territory.

However, there are areas in this theory which are a matter for debate. Jacques Vallée* produced a system

** Aimé Michel: *Mystérieux Objets Célestes* (Ed. Arthaud, Paris, 1968.) An expanded version was brought out by Editions Planète under the title of *A Propos des Soucoupes Volantes*. (No English language version of either of these two works has appeared.) G.C.

* Jacques and Janine Vallée: *Les Phénomènes Insolites de l'Espace*: Editions La Table Ronde, Paris, 1966.

for giving UFO sighting places at random, based on a classic programme for the production of random numbers on a computer. He showed, for example, that after 25 sighting points the probability that any isolated points remain becomes practically nil, and that the number of four-point alignments, to within 2½ kilometres, on a map of France is already five for thirty sightings.

The number of alignments created by chance is consequently far from negligible, and it seems that the alignments of three or four points could all be explained in this way, if the number of sightings is big enough. Vallée emphasises moreover the effect that accuracy of coordinates can have on the number of alignments that can be determined. But straight lines with five or six points or more have a chance probability that is virtually zero. Even the famous *Bayonne-Vichy Line*, or BAVIC, which has six of the fourteen French sightings for 24 September 1954, seems to be particularly resistant to all attempts at analysis.

The discussion has now moved towards becoming a problem for the statisticians, partisans or opponents of Orthoteny as the case may be, politely refuting one another in the columns of *Phénomènes Spatiaux*, the three-monthly journal issued by the G.E.P.A. investigation Group.* The debate is thus far from being over, but it seems that the supporters of Orthoteny are getting fewer and fewer.

Establishment of another type of phenomenon is also reported — not at the spots where sightings have taken place, but as regards the time of their occurrence. We call this 'the wave phenomenon', that is to say, the periodicity in the appearances of the UFO phenomenon. These reports based on the time factor are very interesting, for it might perhaps be possible to correlate their periodicity with such or such a type of physical interpretation that shows a similar periodicity.

This distribution in the frequency of UFO appearances can be divided into four headings:

1. Long-term movement or tendency.
2. Cyclic variations.
3. Seasonal variations.
4. Irregular variations (rumour).

In the work done by Jacques Vallée it was found, after

* G.E.P.A., 69 Rue de la Tombe-Issoire, 75014 Paris.

elimination of a general tendency to long-period variation — possibly attributable to the generation of false sightings by the public — that there remains a distribution of sightings which in essence pertains to the cyclic component, which is the principal unknown factor. Vallée found, after calculation and rechecking to eliminate errors, that there were two cycles, of fifteen months and twenty-six months respectively. This second figure is precisely the same as the cycle of the close approach of Mars to the Earth.

Obviously we must not 'go overboard' about this and believe the problem to be solved; to attribute the UFOs purely and simply to some hypothetical 'Martians' would be just as absurd as to explain them away by sonde balloons, helicopters, or mirages, for the data at our disposal are very inadequate still, and the concordance in the 26-month periods could be a mere coincidence: in fact it would be practically always possible to find some astronomical phenomenon whose frequency corresponds approximately with the UFO periodicity. The question could only be resolved definitely by the establishment of a centralised, codified world-wide register and by the furnishing of extensive funds for the treatment of the sighting waves as well as of Orthoteny by means of computers.

The results could give cause for reflection. For if several hundreds of Hindus and several hundreds of Brazilians, for example, describe the same phenomenon, in roughly the same fashion, then it is hardly rational to talk about hallucinations, collective psychosis, or 'press rumours'.

In conclusion, one can simply say that if there is no doubt of the fact that the UFO phenomenon makes its appearance in waves, it is certain that it also exists outside of the waves; and, on the other hand, even if the correlation with Mars still seemed to be a fact after thorough study, that still would not in any way prove that intelligent life exists on Mars: that planet might well be serving as a relay-station, or base, for travellers who have come from somewhere far more distant. . . .

But, all the same, this shows the sort of studies that can be made, and the type of precautions that *ought* to be taken.

V. *A Discussion of Possible Interpretations*

Here we certainly come to the nub of the question. Let us say straight away that the possible hypotheses are many, but they fall into two large groups-

—Hypotheses based on reality.
—Hypotheses based on imagination. (See Figure 4: *Diagram of Hypotheses.*)

Let us see first of all what is meant by so-called 'imaginary hypotheses'. Among them, those of a physical nature can be distinguished from those of a purely mental nature.

Hypothesis 1 comprises all the *imaginary hypotheses of a physical nature.* By this apparent contradiction in terms we mean the sightings which derive from a physical cause but which the eyewitness, in all good faith, transforms in exaggerated fashion until he ends up by seeing something that does not exist.

As examples, we can quote mirages, optical illusions caused by some pathological condition of the eye; the pressure of wind on the eyeballs, which causes light to be experienced in the eye; or again the reflections of car headlights on high tension power lines covered with hoar frost; on sheets of water, etc., etc.

Needless to say this hypothesis, which is valid in certain cases, is far from explaining the sightings by seasoned pilots and astronomers or the marks left on the ground.

Hypothesis 2 is of *an exclusively mental nature*, and comprises all the cultists, the announcers of salvation or of occult truth, and the mounters of hoaxes, who construct novels based on bogus contacts with extraterrestrials. This group of people, who are all too evident, are frequently believed by the scientists to represent the totality of those who take the UFO problem seriously. To confound folk who are attempting to study the subject seriously with these groups of eccentrics is a grave mistake, the effect of which is to discredit the UFO problem as a whole in the eyes of officialdom.

This category also includes the phenomenon of *rumour*, this sort of autocatalysis, as the chemists would say, or this sort of positive retro-action as the electronicists would say, as the result of which, when the press makes but one single solitary reference to UFOs, the following evening several hundred amateur

226

observers scan the skies and see, or think they see, yet more UFOs, which in turn brings about more articles in the press and so extends the rumours by degrees until a peak is reached when the journalists have had enough of reproducing the same eyewitness accounts and the same denials, and abandon the game because it is no longer journalistically interesting.* And so the phenomenon dies away of its own accord. This hypothesis does not take into account the fact that the sightings are neither more nor less numerous in terms of illiteracy percentage.

Hypothesis 3 is also *of a purely mental nature.*

This concerns individual or collective hallucinations among people who are predisposed to these troubles. This hypothesis can certainly explain some cases, but fails as soon as groups having no contact with each other see the same phenomenon, as soon as marks are found on the ground, or as soon as there is a confirmation by radar. Furthermore, the professions and the psychological characters of the eyewitnesses are as varied as it is possible for them to be, whereas the tendency to mystification and hallucination is often associated with precise psychological groups.

Let us turn now to the Hypotheses which we have defined as based on reality.

Hypothesis 4 is the hypothesis of *erroneous explanation,* by the uninitiated, of well-known natural phenomena, such as ball-lightning, Venus, Mars, will-o'-the-wisps, corona effects, etc. Its principal advocate was Dr Donald H. Menzel,** astrophysicist and ex-director of the Harvard Observatory, who claimed to explain all phenomena in terms of atmospheric physics, including, for example, the sighting by Clyde Tombaugh, the well-known astronomer who discovered Pluto. Menzel has been attacked in the U.S.A. by a specialist in atmospheric physics, Dr James McDonald,*** who claimed that Menzel's arguments were perhaps qualitatively reasonable but never quantitatively so. In other cases,

---

* Chapter 38 of this book shows that our Belgian friends may be wide of the mark! G.C.
** Donald H. Menzel: *Flying Saucers,* Harvard University Press, 1963, and D. H. Menzel and L. G. Boyd: *The World of Flying Saucers,* Doubleday, New York, 1963. (Dr Menzel died some years ago. G.C.)
*** James D. McDonald: *Unidentified Flying Objects: The Greatest Scientific Problem of our Time?* Paper circulated privately. A French version of it appeared as a special number of the G.E.P.A. *Phénomènes Spatiaux.*

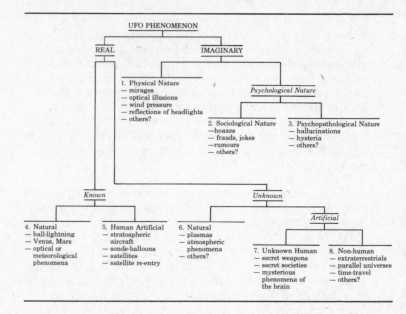

UFO PHENOMENON

REAL — IMAGINARY

1. Physical Nature
   — mirages
   — optical illusions
   — wind pressure
   — reflections of headlights
   — others?

Psychological Nature

2. Sociological Nature
   —hoaxes
   — frauds, jokes
   —rumours
   — others?

3. Psychopathological Nature
   — hallucinations
   — hysteria
   — others?

Known — Unknown

Artificial

4. Natural
   — ball-lightning
   — Venus, Mars
   — optical or
     meteorological
     phenomena

5. Human Artificial
   — stratospheric
     aircraft
   — sonde-balloons
   — satellites
   — satellite re-entry

6. Natural
   — plasmas
   — atmospheric
     phenomena
   — others?

7. Unknown Human
   — secret weapons
   — secret societies
   — mysterious
     phenomena of
     the brain

8. Non-human
   — extraterrestrials
   — parallel universes
   — time-travel
   — others?

again according to McDonald, Menzel simply ignored all arguments that ran counter to his own theory. We are not going to quote or discuss here the interpretations given by Menzel for a number of sightings, and will simply say that his favourite explanations are the planets Mars or Venus, even in cases where an echo was captured on the radar or there were marks left on the ground. ...

Another supporter of this hypothesis is Philip J. Klass, one of the editors of *Aviation Week*, who tries to explain the entire phenomenon in terms of plasmoids or corona effects, those luminous effluxes which appear around high tension power lines when they are dirty or are loaded with ice crystals. Here too, some proportion of the phenomena might certainly be explained in this fashion, but reports of the many sightings relating to discs flying high in fine weather or following aircraft cannot possibly be classified either among Menzel's planets or Klass's plasmoids.

Hypothesis 5 also relates to the *misinterpretation of a well-known phenomenon*, but this time artificial, such as a stratospheric aircraft, a sonde-balloon, a satellite, or a satellite re-entering the atmosphere ... It calls for no particular comment. It is obvious that this sort of error does occur frequently, but nevertheless it does not explain everything.

Hypothesis 6 brings us to the category of the most probable of the hypotheses. In this group we have assembled *all those natural phenomena that we do not yet understand and which might explain the UFO sightings.* It suffices to see the exponential growth of discoveries to realize how obvious it is that in atmospheric physics, just as in the field of any other science, we could still have much to learn.

Most of the sceptical scientists, who only have a limited knowledge of the UFO subject, generally think of some combination of Hypotheses 2, 3, 4, and 5, and if they have given rather more than a rapid glance at the subject they will add that maybe Hypothesis 6 merits further examination, inasmuch as something offering real scientific interest — let us say in atmospheric physics or in plasma physics — might well be finally discovered through a careful study of the UFO reports. Consider on the one hand the almost certain existence of ball-lightning and, on the other hand, the efforts made by whole teams of scientists to confine plasmas for a few milliseconds.

Certainly, numerous lights resembling plasmas are mentioned in many high-probability-rating reports of night sightings. But once again it is difficult to classify in this category daytime reports of disc-shaped objects of metallic appearance flying in formation high in the sky or following aircraft in fine weather. Consequently this Hypothesis 6 may perhaps contain some portion of the truth, but it too does not explain everything.

Hypothesis 7 comprises — admittedly a bit of a rag-bag collection — *everything that could be of human origin but that is unknown.* We refer for example to secret experimental craft of one or other of the Great Powers, although the simple fact that these craft should have been in existence for more than twenty-five years now, and that they have been tried out all over the entire world, surely suffices to show that this hypothesis is absurd.

The category also contains all the hypotheses concerning paranormal phenomena due to the human brain, such as, for example, the projection of images at a distance which can vanish just as UFOs sometimes do. According to this theory, the UFOs would only differ from phenomena of the poltergeist type or ectoplasm materialisation type by virtue of an immensely greater intensity. This is certainly the most tricky of the categories of hypotheses, for we are here stepping into a domain where the scientific data are most lacking and where the facts, if they exist, pertain only to privileged categories of individuals. While we are unable to reject them totally, it nevertheless remains difficult to believe that these unknown powers of the brain could shoot down a military aircraft in the air or make marks on the ground suggesting pressures of several tons.

Finally, there is *Hypothesis 8*, which implies the intervention of *non-human intelligences*, be they extraterrestrials, or from parallel universes, or be they time-travellers.... Our heart — not our head — tends to reject it for the purely animal reasons of the struggle for life to which we have already referred above.

However, this hypothesis presents one objection. If its defenders can certainly account for everything (and not prove scientifically): the metallic appearance of the discs, the marks left on the ground, the presence of humanoids, the radar sightings, the high speeds, nevertheless it is at first sight absurd because, technologically speaking, we are totally unable to conceive of what source of energy would enable them to cross the enormous interstellar distances in a lapse of time comparable with *our* ideas concerning life, and taking into account the limits of speed imposed by relativity.

However, let us be mindful of the great astronomer Simon Newcomb, who demonstrated, in 1903, that the piloted flight of a machine heavier than air was out of the question; his calculations were indeed perfectly correct, but he had based himself upon the weight/power ratio of the steam-engine. ...

Consequently the extraterrestrial hypothesis, or the theory of universes of other dimensions, is maybe in the end the most likely of all, for who can say how far our own technology will have got in several centuries — or even in only several decades — from now?

On the other hand, if we recall the frequent presence of humanoids in the reports, and the relatively consistent descriptions which have been given of them, we are bound to ask ourselves whether it is possible that these hundreds of sightings can all be absurd. It would suffice if one single sighting were true for the problem to acquire immediately a fantastic importance and become, as Dr James McDonald in the United States has long maintained, the most important problem of all times, and one which involves the question of our very existence.

Other investigators, like Jacques Vallée* and John Keel** have directed their thinking along a somewhat different line, further away from orthodox science, and bordering upon Hypotheses 7 and 8. According to both these writers, there is a large parapsychological element in the UFO phenomenon, but they suggest that possibly a source exterior to Mankind induces these manifestations to some extent. One is bound to state that the importance of the UFO phenomenon would be no less great were the truth to be found to lie in that direction.

One of the arguments frequently put forward against *Hypothesis 8* is that, if 'They' were here, 'They' would have contacted us long ago. The argument is invalid for at least two reasons:

Firstly, we cannot study interstellar psychology before that science is born. Very often, already, we do not understand the motives of our fellowmen. How then could we understand those of living species which maybe have no biological links with us?

Secondly, our human psychology can already explain this abstention by 'Them' from contact: for example, the successive phases of approach as described by Frank Edwards*** do not yet seem to have reached their final point; for example, too, let us put ourselves in the position of scientists, biologists, or others, who have had the chance to study, from Space, an intelligent, living species in an exponential stage of development within the closed system of its own planet. Isn't that a fantastically interesting subject of study? Our own ethnologists and explorers have done precisely the same thing when encountering unknown peoples.

Two of the great study techniques of science are:

---

* Jacques Vallée: *Passport to Magonia*, published by Henry Regnery Co., Chicago, 1969, British edition by Neville Spearman Ltd., London, 1970. French translation: *Chronique des Apparitions Extraterrestres*, Editions Denoël, Paris, 1972.
** John A. Keel: *Operation Trojan Horse*. Putnam, New York, 1970. British edition by Souvenir Press, London, 1971.
*** Frank Edwards: *Flying Saucers — Here And Now!* U.S. edition, Bantam paperback, 1967, Chapter 5. French translation: *Du Nouveau sur Les Soucoupes Volantes*.

(a) to examine a system in all its aspects, while endeavouring to disturb it as little as possible, so that it can remain in its original state (i.e. the use of 'foo fighters', close approaches to aircraft, the taking of samples. . . .)

(b) to provoke small localized disturbances, and then examine their effects (i.e., landings, electricity failures, chance contacts with a few humans. . . .)

Within the framework of *Hypothesis 8* these considerations offer a perfect explanation for the absence of contact.

VI. *What Should We Do?*

The most important step towards the solution of any problem is, above all, to recognize that the problem exists. The human community as a whole will only take this step after a considerable number of qualified people have made a sufficiently thorough study of the UFO evidence to realize that:

1. An astonishingly vast body of sightings made by trustworthy witnesses, and sometimes confirmed by radar, indicates the persistent presence of objects that are completely unknown, having the appearance of machines, and performing manoeuvres in the air-space around our planet and frequently leaving material traces behind them;

2. The frequency of the phenomenon, which has in fact been present during all the epochs of our history, has increased in a fantastic manner since the end of World War II;

3. There has never been any serious scientific and public study of this aggregate of sightings.

Once this basic step has been taken, a number of working parties should be set up to make a study in depth of certain questions:

1. There must be a programme for educating the public, with the help of the principal newspapers, and involving the issue of summarized reports on the state of the problem and also giving outlines of Astronomy, Meteorology, and

Atmospheric Physics. The objective of such a programme would be to dissipate the aura of ridicule which at present permanently envelops the UFO problem. People will thereafter be better informed and more free to express themselves, and one may expect that the number of serious reports received will augment accordingly by five- or ten-fold. The UFO study groups and the scientists would have to cope with the task of gathering in this sudden increase in the volume of sighting reports.

2. At least one team of researchers should set themselves to the task of studying the problem of the electromagnetic effects ('EM effects') of the UFOs, engine stoppages, radio disturbance, electrical failures, and so forth.

3. Historical studies should be made into the numerous sightings prior to our century, which present fascinating similarities with today's sightings, and at the same time also show certain differences.

4. Psychologists and psychiatrists should make a particularly thorough study of the many reports in which paranormal phenomena seem to be associated with the presence of UFOs.

5. The problem of the 'occupants' should be minutely studied by psychologists and biologists, and these psychologists and biologists should be furnished with the most complete collections of reports from all parts of the world.

6. In order to determine the invariants of the phenomenon, as also to assist the research of the various aforesaid groups, it ought to be possible to put the hundreds of thousands of 'bits' of data which will by then be available into a computer with a wide band of programmings, so as to extract all the potential information contained in them.

7. Military radar installations throughout the whole world should be programmed to register UFO flight paths. (This is rather a lot to hope for, but one can always dream. ....)*

Once all these various programmes have been put in hand, new research projects would automatically appear after a few years, and in this way a serious and sustained study would no doubt lead, in less than five years, to a clarification of the main lines of the phenomenon and to the determination of at least some of its invariants. For all this to come about, official funds would of course be necessary, since the resources of the private groups everywhere are very limited, and the regular use of a computer is alone enough to involve high outlay. But what Ufology needs, even more than subsidies, is cooperation, both between the societies like S.O.B.E.P.S and official scientific circles, and between the various investigative societies themselves, which, alas, is far from being the general case at present. We would recall that S.O.B.E.P.S. has never ceased to favour closer collaboration at all levels. But the question may be asked: would the existence of private research groups still be justified if the scientists were to establish a truly objective study of the phenomenon at the official level? We think that the answer is: *yes*, for, thanks to their experience and their networks of investigators already in the field, and thanks also to their more direct contacts with the public, they can gather many reports very rapidly for delivery to the scientists for study.

Such, in our view, is the present situation of Ufology. We have been obliged to omit mention of certain aspects of the problem — for example the possible connections between UFOs and geological fault lines, as suggested by the French investigator Fernard Lagarde, as well as the work of many lone invesigators, and it is possible that we may have dwelt too lengthily on certain other aspects which did not deserve it such as the UFO waves, or Orthoteny. Inevitably we have only been able, within the limits of this study, to show a few of the problems with which the UFOs challenge our intelligence. In any case, reflections such as this paper, which enable us to take stock, show that the whole UFO problem still remains unsolved, in every one of its aspects, and that the work of the investigative groups such as S.O.B.E.P.S is far from being finished. Maybe indeed it is only just beginning.

André Boudin,
Lucien Clerebaut.

*As our Belgian friends say, 'one can always dream. . . .' To imagine however that, particularly as the overall crisis of our species rapidly deepens, there could be the slightest expectation that any of their suggestions would ever be carried out by any government or any country would indeed be the wildest form of dreaming. *And, incidentally, why should it always be assumed that governments do not know what UFOs are? Is it not rapidly becoming obvious that governments DO know what UFOs are, and what their occupants are, and that governments probably know by now that overmuch probing and prying into matters that are not Earthman's concern is likely to bring a speedy rap over the knuckles from his Masters and Owners?*

G.C.

Britain's *Flying Saucer Review* is one of the best UFO journals in the world. Everyone is in agreement in recognizing this. Mr Gordon Creighton, a former British diplomat, is one of the Directors of this Review. He speaks French admirably. Mr Creighton is not a scientist. Nevertheless the point of view which he expressed to Henri Di Donna is interesting, even if the philosophical side of it takes precedence over the scientific side.

●

—*What is the present situation in Great Britain in the field of UFO studies?*
—Here, in England, we have a very small nucleus of people who are interested in the subject. We have a *Review* however which has a world-wide readership. But the proportion of British people who take an interest in UFOs is minimal. The majority of our fellow-citizens are in fact convinced that 'Flying Saucers' don't exist.
—*In your opinion, are the UFOs just a joke, or are they a scientific phenomenon?*
—They aren't a joke. A 'scientific phenomenon' do you say? But that depends on what you call a 'scientific phenomenon'. I think, in fact, that we are witnessing the manifestation of the science of other beings far more advanced that we are. Believe me, however — there are plenty of governments or official scientific bodies who would like to persuade you that it is all a joke. And they have been working to make you think so for a long time. But, unfortunately, for them, the UFO's aren't a joke. I say unfortunately, because to us it is becoming more and more evident that it is a grave problem — very grave. A problem intimately linked with the present crisis of our species.
—*Explain please what you mean.*
—We have discovered that there are features in the UFO phenomenon that one might describe as 'supernatural'. Unfortunately there are also 'diabolical' features in it as

well. We have the impression that there are two forces at work in the UFO phenomenon. One force which would like to help the human race, and another force which is perhaps working for our liquidation. We see the problem now under this dual aspect, but, and I emphasise this, the problem is a very serious one for our species. . . .

—*Certain sages in the East aver that the world has reached its Fourth Epoch, the Epoch of Kali Yuga, which fore-shadows the end of Mankind?*

—That is the impression which I have. And I know that, more and more, other investigators throughout the world are beginning to come to the same conclusion.

—*Is there no way of defending ourselves against these phenomena?*

—I don't think so. We are confronted with beings who know far more than we do. It would be naive to think that we are alone in the Universe. We are not alone, and we are not the masters. . . .

—*In what way are the small beings described by the eye-witnesses 'maleficent'?*—First of all, I should say that the humanoids aren't all small. There are some that are over two metres in height. In Argentina, for example, some workers at a factory saw some humanoids almost three metres high. But it is true that there are small beings. We are starting to do research into legends and into Mythology for traces of the existence of these different beings down through the centuries. This is what Jacques Vallée has done in the United States. Now, all these beings, these goblins and these giants, exist in the Western and Eastern traditions.

—*But is it true that these beings have committed serious acts, such as kidnappings or killings?*

—Quite frequently! And read the mythological traditions. You will see that there is a certain proportion of these beings who are not our friends. Especially the little ones.

—*What sort of links can be established between these beings and Mankind?*

—We have discovered that everywhere in the world there are people who have met them. Often we find that, after the encounter, the eyewitnesses suffer from amnesia. By means of hypnosis we have a partial knowledge of the experiences that these witnesses have undergone. The results are pretty frightening. It would appear that these beings have the power to influence the human brain. If they can do that with an individual, they can also do it with entire peoples and with governments. And I am certain that they are already doing just that. . . .

237

—Let us go back to the reality of the UFOs. You yourself, Mr Creighton, have seen a UFO fly over, and it was in China, wasn't it?

—Yes. It was in China, in 1941. At the time, I was First Secretary in the British Embassy there. I was walking with two friends on the banks of the Yangtze when we saw a 'flying saucer'. It was at about 2.00 p.m., and so in broad daylight. It at once made a great impression on me. I felt that it must be something from another world. . . . Three years later, in 1944, I was in the U.S.A., at New Orleans. And I used to see in the newspapers the reports about the War in Europe. What struck me was that fighter and bomber pilots were reporting that sometimes their aircraft were followed by balls of fire. It was then that I began to make my collection of newspaper clippings about the 'flying saucers'. But in 1944 they weren't called that yet; we had to wait till 1947 for that.

—Do you think that we can find accounts of UFO sightings if we look back through history?

—The more you go back in time, looking carefully, the more you find this sort of account. There are at least 40 or so references in the Roman writers. In Britain too you find, in the old records, inexplicable stories which very probably relate to UFOs.

—At this present moment, in 1974, are you getting sighting reports?

—We get them every week from all over the world. Just the same as in France. The last encounter with humanoids was in 1972.

—The present 'Wave' is affecting France, Spain, and Italy. Is it reaching England?

—No. It is obviously difficult to say why. Maybe they don't like the English climate! But of course they could very easily be flying over us without our seeing them.

—Can you draw any conclusion from it all, even if only provisional?

—I come back to my initial proposition. Our humanity is passing through the gravest crisis in its history. One may even fear that our species will disappear before very long. And I am certain that the UFO phenomenon has a connection with this situation. It is probable that, among these other beings, there are some that are extraterrestrial. But it is equally probable that there are some who live here amongst us in a space that is not three-dimensional like our own. We have a mass of reports which show that the problem is in fact a very complex one. There are several types of beings who are playing a part in the UFO phenomenon. It is very probable that among these beings there are some who are our friends, *and it is certain that there are some of them who are not.*

Aimé Michel is the French specialist on UFOs. Born in 1919, he is a graduate in Philosophy. He passed the examination for engineers in sound and acoustics and joined the French Radio and Television Service (O.R.T.F.) in 1944. At present he is working in the Research Department, which suits him very well in view of the special subject of his choice — the UFOs. He has already written two authoritative books, *Lueurs Sur Les Soucoupes Volantes* (Editions Mame, Paris, 1954) and *Mystérieux Objets Célestes* (Arthaud, Paris, 1958), both now unfortunately out of print. The original tape-recording of the interview which he was good enough to grant me also was stolen, but he has given me a second interview, and here it is:

●

—*Aimé Michel, how long have you been studying the UFOs?*
—Oh, for donkey's years. ... As you know, the history of the UFOs begins with Kenneth Arnold's sighting over the State of Washington in June 1947. Well now, even then I already had in my files all — and I emphasise, ALL the clippings from the French press on the Wave of Scandinavian sightings of 1946. I thought at the time, as everybody else did, that they were captured German machines which the Russians were trying out over the Baltic. When Keyhoe's book, *The Flying Saucers Are Real*, (the first book on flying saucers) appeared in 1950, the case was so badly presented in it that I changed my mind: I now thought that it was probably all totally untrue, a fabrication, lock stock and barrel, by bad journalists. But, shortly, after that, when I was preparing a radio broadcast on Meteorology (you see, that shows how long ago it was!) an engineer from the National Meteorological Service, Roger Clausse, showed me a file of sightings reported by the weather stations. I was most astonished to find that the file contained cases that were absolutely identical with those in Keyhoe's book. So there was something in it all. But the question was: What?

I intensified my enquiries, and made the acquaintance of Captain Clérouin, who was at that time in charge of the Intelligence Section of the Air Force, under General Chassin. Clérouin gave me a lot of help. And finally, in 1953, I found I had a sufficiently substantial documentation to write a book. What a strange stroke of fate! When the book appeared, in 1954, I had no inkling that the die was cast and the future course of my life staked. . . .

—*Staked and won?*

—Yes, won in one sense, for I have the impression, indeed the certainty, of having spent these last twenty years at the centre of a philosophical revolution such as only occurs perhaps once in a thousand years. Who knows? Maybe it is even the most important revolution in the whole of history. . . . But, on the other hand, my life was involved in a losing game too, when I think of all the loneliness and the frustration that we have known during all this time.

—*We?*

—Yes. *We*. During the weeks following upon the publication of my book, I received two letters. One was from Jean Cocteau, saying: '*When you think about it, the really astonishing thing would be if they did NOT exist.*' 'They', obviously, was the saucers. The other letter which I received was signed by an astronomer whose name is familiar to you. . . .

—*Pierre Guérin?*

—Yes. Pierre Guérin. And what he said was more or less as follows: '*Neither you nor I know whether it is true, but nothing is more important than finding out.*' He also said: '*This letter is naturally confidential. I am obliged to confide in you.*' That letter from Pierre Guérin was the start of a long friendship. I discovered that, in order to study this problem, the first thing you needed was courage. You had to have no fear either of either the methods of the Inquisition or about what sort of reputation you had. Since then, I have also established links of friendship with, I think, all the scientists throughout the world who are interested in this question. They are all very different, as you can well imagine, but they all have one thing in common: courage — and curiosity too, the desire to know.

—*The desire to know — but surely that is taken for granted in a scientist!*

—No doubt! But there are several roads to truth, and not all of them are scientific. The policeman's road isn't the scientist's — this has been said several times in the course of your broadcasts. Read the beginning of the Condon Report again. Condon there explains, right from the very first page, that scientific investigation consists in first selecting a subject in which to specialize, then studying it in depth, and then looking to see where to concentrate your main effort. This implies that all research must be conducted within a pre-existing framework, by proceeding from the known to the unknown. But where is the *known* when it comes to this matter of UFOs?

—*The fact that a sighting report exists — that is something known. The report exists, so it should be studied.*

—I agree. But in what pre-existent framework are you going to pigeonhole it? No pigeonhole, no method. And no method, then no science. This is why, only a few pages later on (right at the very start of a report almost a thousand pages long) Condon declares that the UFO problem presents no scientific interest. I think that, basically, his thinking was: '*Even if it is true, it is totally without interest*'. And, incidentally, people have often said the same thing to me, in a sort of dry tone that would brook no answer.

—*And what do you reply in such cases?*

—That depends on how much time I'm given. How long are you giving me?

—*Carry on, anyway. If it's too long, I'll have to cut it.*

—Good. Well now, let us consider some facts. In 1953, when I was trying to find some linking thread running through all the cases already known, an interesting fact struck me just as I was sorting through the cases where the witnesses had reported colour changes — by that I mean changes of colour by the UFO in the course of its manoeuvres. If I may, I will read you the passage about that question from page 159 of my first book, *Lueurs Sur Les Soucoupes Volantes*: 'the colours reported seem to be related to the speed, or rather, to the acceleration. The silvery-grey tinged with dark red corresponds to very slow movements, or to immobility. Then comes bright red.... Then with powerful accelerations come white, green, and then blue and then violet. It is remarkable that there is this agreement between the acceleration and the strength of the colour emission. Certain rapid but uniform movements go with colours that are not very strong, which seems to confirm the theory that there is a link between the colour emitted by the object and the power developed at any given moment by its engine.'. (I might add, in passing, that I would now put the word *engine* in inverted commas.)

So you see, I was advancing the hypothesis of a relationship between the energy developed by the 'engine' and the energy of the radiation given off. That was published in

1954. Well now, in the autumn of that same year, the biggest sighting wave in the history of Ufology burst upon the world. In October-November of 1954, there were at times as many as 60 reported sightings per day! I spent almost three years in collecting and analyzing merely those cases that had occurred in France, or not far from the French frontiers. The enormous file for autumn 1954 gave me the chance to verify my hypothesis and, as I hoped, to define it more clearly, and maybe to derive from it a few lessons regarding the physics of the UFOs.

But alas, I had to admit defeat! And I think it was during our discussions on this subject that Guérin enounced for the first time his famous '*Guérin's Law*' (a quip, but it expresses very neatly the troubles that are so familiar to us in Ufology). '*Guérin's Law*' says: '*In Ufology, once a law has been demonstrated, it is immediately refuted by the following sightings*'.

In fact, while the UFOs of 1954, just like their predecessors, did display their multi-coloured fireworks, and while, on the whole, the energy of the colours seemed to be perhaps correlated with that of the accelerations and decelerations, on the other hand it didn't work out, for one colour or for several colours, in many of the cases. For example, during acceleration, the blue appeared first, then the orange, and then the white. Having at least, as I thought, examined the whole question in its minutest detail, I felt obliged to admit that there were definitely far too many parameters of the problem that were eluding me, and I abandoned the idea of finding any sort of correlation until a new clue should turn up. And in the end I thought no more about it.

Now, look at this book. [Aimé Michel shows me a copy of *Ufology*, by James McCampbell, published by Jaymac, 12 Bryce Court, Belmont, California, 94002, U.S.A.]. I have just received it from the United States. The author is a physicist in California, specializing in nuclear reactors. America is an astonishing country. All ideas finally encounter the most suitable specialist, for this physicist named McCampbell read my book and said to himself: 'there is perhaps something that those Frenchmen didn't think of'. Thanks to Jacques Vallée, McCampbell accumulates a massive documentation on multicoloured UFOs, and finds his way out of the *cul-de-sac* into which I had got myself.

—*Namely?*

—Namely that, instead of classifying the increasing or decreasing energies of the light radiation, McCampbell catal-

243

ogues the ionization potentials of the gases of the atmosphere. He then finds that it is xenon that has the lowest potentials of ionization, and that consequently it is the first gas to become luminous when the exciting energy increases. And the light emitted by xenon is an intense and pure blue! So it isn't surprising that the first colour reported is often the blue. I don't know if he is right. But, in the first place, his hypothesis is clear and sound. It is expressed in the well-tried language of quantum physics. Secondly, it can be tested: all you have to do is to gather up all the thousands of eyewitness accounts and classify them. Just ask yourself whether the Papuans, or even the average Frenchman on the whole (and that's what statistics is) are capable of describing the evolutions of an imaginary machine making their visions of it fit the requirements of quantum physics and of ionization potentials of the atmospheric gases.

Thirdly, it seems that McCampbell may very well be right. Whenever it has been possible to test this ionization, at a landing site, for example, as was done recently in France, it has indeed been found that the ionization of the air around has been modified. In the case to which I refer, the engineer who went to the spot found the exact site of the landing — which was unknown to him — simply by observing the reaction of his ionometer.

—*But wait a moment — what you are here explaining is rather a proof by means of physics than a clarification of the UFOs. Can you give us one more simple proof?*

—Yes, but it's very important. In this particular case McCampbell proves that, contrary to what Condon had said, UFO study can advance within the framework of the pre-existing methods.

To begin with, of course, there are the eyewitness accounts. That's fine. But then? It's a pity, but I have this weakness that I believe the scientific spirit consists in studying things as they are, rather than waiting for them to mould themselves to our requirements. The phenomenon here is this: that there are millions of people who say they have seen UFOs (look at the Gallup Poll of November 1973.) And the problem is the problem of finding out if it is true, and if yes, then what is it that they have seen. All right — to begin with, let us distrust all these eyewitness accounts, since that's what they are. Let us file them away without pronouncing on them. If you want to have it that way — all right. It so happens that they obey the laws of quantum physics. They are the inventions of crackpots — but inventions that obey the laws of quantum physics, all the same.

But, besides, I am exaggerating, for there aren't only the eyewitness accounts. There are also the recordings and the measurements. Smith has demonstrated the complete parallel between the statistics on electricity failures, published by the American Power Commission, and the statistics of UFO flyovers published by the U.S. Air Force. And Claude Poher too has shown that the vertical component in geomagnetism is disturbed by UFOs.

—*Yes, but all the same, all those are secondary proofs; 'bits of evidence', as the English say. What precisely does all this teach us about the UFOs themselves?*

—Let us take the example of a fact reported by countless eyewitnesses, and which at first sight seems devoid of any significance: the descending movement like a dead leaf, or like a pendulum. In certain circumstances, and always the same circumstances, the object, when losing height, rocks to and fro like a dead leaf. As we have my first book here at hand, let us take an old case, reported by two officers and three enlisted men of the Royal Air Force on 19 September 1952. The sighting took place over the Dishforth Air Force Station, during the *Operation 'Mainbrace'* manoeuvres of the naval and air forces of NATO. Here is a passage from the report written by Lt. John W. Kilburn: '*While we were watching the disc, which continued on its course, we saw it reduce speed for a few seconds, and then begin to descend. When it started to lose height, it began to oscillate like a dead leaf or, if you prefer it, like a pendulum. The Meteor* [the RAF fighter which the five eyewitnesses were watching as it came in to land] *banked as it prepared to circle the field before landing. The object began to follow the plane, but stopped after several seconds. It seemed to remain suspended in the sky, revolving on its own axis like a spinning top. Then suddenly it accelerated, and shot off at a staggering speed towards the West, where it disappeared.*' Now this description, I must repeat, is typical of a very great many others, given on other dates, and in all countries, and I could go on quoting them to you for hours.

But now, let us just think for a moment. In a machine which maintains itself at an altitude, what is it that determines the vertical movements (descent, ascent, or remaining in the same place)? It is the relationship of the weight of the machine to the vertical force it develops for rising, falling, or maintaining constant height. If the vertical force is equal to the weight, it maintains its altitude; if the vertical force is greater, it rises; and if the vertical force is less, the machine descends. Let us suppose that the machine exerts this force along the axis — that is to say, perpendicularly to its own plane, then it will be understood that, in order to lose altitude, it is much simpler to keep this force constant, not modifying it, and merely to tilt the machine alternately towards the right and then towards the left. For then the force will divide alternatively into two components, one vertical and one horizontal, this latter changing direction with each oscillation, and the vertical component varying with the cosine of the angle of inclination. The analysis of this manoeuvre, which is entirely in conformity with the simplest and most standard mechanics, ends by anticipating precisely what the eyewitnesses describe. And wait! Still within the framework of this elementary mechanics, what is the simplest method for terminating this oscillation when one considers one has descended close enough to the ground? It is to start a rapid rotation, for in this way stabilization is brought about by a gyroscopic effect. Well now — this again is precisely what the eyewitnesses describe. This vertical stabilization is especially necessary before a forward movement is begun again. So a machine will be seen to be revolving while still stationary, just before it departs. Once again, this is just what the eyewitnesses have described.

Physics, or to be more accurate, mechanics, teaches us (we see it in this particular case of the pendulum movement) that the UFOs are to be regarded as material objects conforming amenably — and even right on into the most complex consequences — with certain of our own laws.

—*With certain of our laws? But not with all of them, then?*

—Oh no! Even in the case that I have just described, there are some incomprehensible details, and it is through them that we come to our second question, which is: *what do the UFOs teach us about Physics?*

—*Can you give us some examples?*

—Oh! There are plenty of examples, all right, but even here you will find no incoherency, as you will see. It is beyond us, but it is all of a piece.

First point: what is this force perpendicular to the plane of the object, and which does not have to be vertical? Our physics has only one such force in its armoury — *reaction*. In the case of an aircraft or a helicopter, the reaction of the blades of the propellor against the air. In the case of a rocket, reaction to the inertia of the gases ejected. In the case of the UFOs, we see no imaginable kind of reaction. At first sight — and I am very careful to say at first sight — it is irritating. The close encounter sightings, and often the marks left behind on the ground (for example in the case at Poncey-sur-l'Ignon in 1954) show that the space surrounding the object seems, like the UFO itself, to be enclosed in a sort of force-field. Contrary to what would happen if reaction were involved, objects — including the air — are carried along with the UFO, and are not thrown backwards. If you will reflect on what this implies, you will be led to ask yourself some questions about our most advanced physics on the nature of gravitation, on the nature of inertia, and on the hypothesis that the inertial mass and the gravitational mass are equal (which was a hypothesis proposed by Einstein.) Such reflection is full of perils, you rapidly run the risk of saying something silly, like for example, inventing perpetual motion. If it were not rather wearisome, I would show you a splendid way for solving definitively the energy crisis with hypotheses proposed by certain imprudent and, above all, ignorant theoreticians who, under the pretext that it is saucer physics, still coast along with the good old physics of the physicists — the physics that works and that is verified by experiment. The first rule to observe when speculating about the physics of the UFOs is to have at the outset a good knowledge of the physics of the scientists! Otherwise, you're doing what the British call 'kitchen physics' — making a salad of it! The second rule is to have a good detailed knowledge of all the observed facts, and to start by examining thousands of cases, under the magnifying glass as it were, and patiently comparing them all, while at the same time refraining from making too many hypotheses yourself.

Meanwhile, a number of very interesting facts are already well attested. Consider, for example, the rotation at the termination of the pendulum movement. I said a moment ago that this rotation was the best means for terminating the oscillation, by means of a gyroscopic effect. The trouble is however that, in order to start turning, the UFO would need — according to our way of thinking — to brace itself against something that was not part of its own mass; otherwise there would be no gyroscopic effect. So we ought to be able to see the clouds — for example — turning around it, or, at low altitudes, objects on the ground turning around it. We ought to see them turning in the opposite direction to the UFO (except when the rotation is slowed down by braking.) Well now, if the eyewitnesses have observed correctly, nothing of the sort is seen. It is true that the marks on the ground do often display the pattern of a rotary movement. But this seems to be always in the same direction as the UFO's rotation. Without going overmuch into detail, it seems therefore, in view of what has been observed, that the rotation presents theoretical difficulties of the same nature — vis-a-vis what we know — as the unknown method by which the craft is maintained in the air, and the unknown means of propulsion. It shows the same 'strangeness': all this behaviour would appear to be in complete violation of the principle of the equality of action and reaction.

But what is so interesting is that the UFOs apparently violate this principle in an identical and coherent fashion, which is something that the witnesses naturally would not know when they are telling their entirely unrelated stories; if these facts violate the principle in a coherent manner, what does it mean? Well, we have here something that is quite familiar to anyone who knows a little about the history of science — it is the discovery of a new and inexplicable fact, like the measurement of the black body just prior to Planck; like the experiment of Michelson just before Einstein; and, maybe, like the recent discovery of quasars. When such a fact appears, it always leads to a scientific revolution. And the mass of facts observed in connection with UFOs is beginning to be such that some physicists in America, Sturrock, and McCampbell, and others also, believe there is going to be a total overthrow of all our old ideas. There are also folk in France who have the presentiment of this coming revolution and, probably, of the whole series of revolutions in physics to which we shall be compelled by Ufology.

It is hard to put this across in front of a microphone, but I will illustrate the idea by a quite recent example, as it concerns a sighting that was made near Villeneuve-sur-Lot last March. The crucial fact in that sighting is that a UFO passed close by a diesel engine and the latter sputtered and stalled. We already had a vast mass of cases of engines stopped by the approach of a UFO, but for obvious reasons we thought that the failure in such cases was due to some interference with the ignition system, so much so indeed that up till then these cases had always been published under the heading of 'Electromagnetic Effects'.

It had been thought — and I myself have written quite a lot about it — that it was electromagnetic interference. But we were wrong. As you know, there's no electrical ignition in a diesel engine.

But now follow my reasoning: a diesel engine that stalls — this implies that the combustion of the fuel is no longer taking place, and that it is being prevented by some unknown action. Now, combustion is a chemical combination. And here we fall into a further seeming contradiction, for if the UFO prevents chemical combinations (we haven't of course

248

the remotest idea how) then the close-range eyewitnesses ought to die on the spot, since breathing, the nerve impulses, cerebral activity, and all the metabolic processes, are all chemical reactions.

Do you still follow me? I proceed then: engines stall, but living beings do not die. What difference is there between the chemical reactions inside a living being and those of a combustion engine? Doubtless there are many differences — but there is one difference that is already obvious — namely the temperatures at which the processes occur. The UFO does not generally have any effect on the chemical reactions in living beings, which occur (incidentally, we have absolutely no idea how) at low temperatures. Reflecting on this incomprehensible fact, and looking at it from all angles, I said to myself: *'let us suppose that the UFO causes all chemical reactions to break down above a certain temperature, then what else would we also expect to see?'* Well — one consequence would be to cause firearms to fail to work. And, more precisely, the bullet would leave the gun, but then misfire, 'funk out', if you will permit me to use this French artilleryman's expression. For the combustion would start at a low temperature, and then would stop as soon as the critical temperature was reached. And then I remembered the UFO case at Hopkinsville, Kentucky, where, in 1955, a family fired their guns in vain many times against 'little men' throughout the course of a whole night. I re-read the case, and imagine my excitement when I read that the two Kellys, at one moment, both fired at a 'little man' who was only about ten metres from them, and that the shots *'sounded just as though they had been fired into a bucket'*, and all the bullets did was to make the mysterious visitors 'give a little jump'.

Needless to say, nobody in this world would know how to tell of a means of preventing — at a distance — all combustion above a certain temperature. But physicists know what combustion is. It is a phenomenon which calls into play the bonding of electrons; it is an electronic phenomenon. Well now, there are hundreds and hundreds of cases of apparently electronic effects in our files.

—*So, in this case, and I imagine in a large number of others, the facts recorded by Ufology are just so many experiments in physics — but in the unknown physics of someone else.*
—Precisely. Or rather another physics, where everything that we recognize as familiar is in conformity with our own physics, but in which there are also new, unknown phenomena — other phenomena, the effects of which we do not yet

know how to reproduce ourselves. All the physicists among my friends who know about it say it is fascinating. Imagine, for example, if, in the last century, Faraday could have visited the laboratory of Alfred Kastler — it would be just like that! Condon is dead, peace to his ashes, but you must surely admit that to refuse — as he did — to visit a laboratory of the future was an act of utter stupidity. For that is precisely what he was doing when he said that Ufology presented no scientific interest. In reality, Ufology is destined to become the principal source of knowledge in the future.
—*But look now, Aimé Michel, aren't you surely exaggerating a bit?*
—Now listen, and I am most anxious that you won't cut this because I have done a lot of thinking about these matters for more than twenty years, and because I am positive of what I am saying: namely that, before a century has passed, Ufology will be our principal source of knowledge — at least in physics, and maybe in psychology, taken in the widest sense of the 'science of thought'.

But I'd like, in conclusion — and I'm afraid I have gone on at great length and still said hardly anything — I'd like to emphasise the importance of Ufology in the domain of a science that is even more important than physics and psychology. I mean in the domain of epistemology, the study of knowledge. Ufology is going to bring about a veritable earthquake, a cataclysm, in this field, by compelling our reason — our rational instrument, the sole source of all our certitudes — to face up to phenomena that are of such a nature that they surpass it totally, and to get accustomed to the idea of its own complete relativity. Yes. It is Copernicus all over again, and this time far worse. Copernicus obliged us to admit that this human body of ours is not the centre of the Universe. The UFOs are now revealing to us that our human mind isn't the centre of the Universe either.

> '*In the order of intelligible things, our intelligence possesses the same rank as our body has in the compass of Nature:*
> signed: Pascal

I have already set this thought of Pascal's at the head of my second book, back in 1958. Since then I have called it '*the Principle of Banality*'. Man is indeed the summit of terrestrial biological evolution. But the Earth is only an imperceptible speck in the immensity of the Universe. And Man occupies therein just as banal and ordinary a position as the

Earth does in the Universe. In one way, it is utterly demoralizing. But on the other hand, the discernment, the perception, that there is above us a psychomental hierarchy of life that is maybe boundless — why, this alters everything, and totally. Such is my personal belief: *Like the physical Universe, the Universe of Mind is possibly infinite too.*

(Everyone interested in UFOs and other strange phenomena is urged to write to Neville Armstrong, Flying Saucer Information, 3 Broad Oak, Groom Bridge, Near Tunbridge Wells, Kent, for details of new books and publications on the subject as they are published. Please enclose stamped addressed envelope.)

ACKNOWLEDGEMENTS

This, for the time being, at any rate, ends our Dossier on the UFOs. I think I can say that this book will be epoch-making in the annals of the subject. I am all the more able to make this assertion, since the only credit that I can take for myself in the affair is that I gave the opportunity to all the scientists throughout the world, who have long been studying this exasperating problem, to express their views about it. And I am especially anxious not to end the final page of this book without thanking them all most deeply. My thanks likewise to all those others, Pierre Kohler, Michel Carrouges, Professor Boutry, Dr Favre, and Suzanne Pierre, who should have been in the book but whose taped interviews mysteriously vanished.

The eyewitnesses who had the courage to disclose their adventures to you also obviously deserve that we should raise our hats to them. Neither must we forget all the O.R.T.F. reporters in France and elsewhere in the world who have taken part in this great international enquiry.

Finally, I would like to express my special thanks to all the private investigatory groups who have given me their help; *Lumières Dans La Nuit* and *G.E.P.A.* in France, *S.O.B.E.P.S.* in Belgium. Jean Cazeau in Canada. Rolland Vagnetti and M. Demercurio in Switzerland, Gordon Creighton in Great Britain, Jacques Vallée in the United States, and Carlos Marques in South America.

UFOs. A PARTIAL BIBLIOGRAPHY

So far as we know, no complete bibliography of writings on the UFO problem has yet been attempted. The task would be a difficult one, since several hundreds of titles already exist, principally in English and French, and there have also been a considerable number of books in Spanish and Italian, a few in German, and two or three in Dutch, in Romanian, and Croatian or Serbian.

Most of the works are long ago out of print. Many titles were in very small editions, and often poorly written. A remarkable number of books and booklets, issued mainly in the United States in the 1950s and early 1960s, contained extraordinary 'contactee' claims. Most of these were too absurd to be true — so we felt at the time. But, as Aimé Michel has pointed out, the whole UFO business is nothing but a wild festival of total absurdity, and some of the more penetrating of our researchers are now beginning to perceive that the vast majority — indeed possibly all — of the amazing 'contactee' stories from Adamski onwards are most probably true, but that they are evidence of the manipulation and brainwashing of humans by the unknown entities or powers which are responsible for the 'UFO phenomenon'. Seen in this light, the early 'contactee' stories acquire a very different character.

G.C.

Part I The Most Important Documentation

Hynek, Dr. J. Allen: *The UFO Experience.* Henry Regnery, Chicago, 1972. Abelard-Schuman, London, 1972. (Published in French edition as *Les OVNI: Mythe ou Réalité?*) (Belfond, Paris, 1974.)

Hynek, Dr. J. Allen and Vallée, Dr. Jacques: *The Edge of Reality: A Progress Report on Unidentified Flying Objects.* Henry Regnery Co., Chicago, 1975.

The National Investigations Committee on Aerial Phenomena (NICAP), (Editors Major Donald Keyhoe and Mr. Richard Hall): *The UFO Evidence.* Washington, D.C., 1964. *UFOs: A New Look.* Washington, D.C., 1969.

Symposium on Unidentified Flying Objects: Hearings before the Committee on Science and Astronautics, U.S.

House of Representatives, July 29, 1968. (U.S. Govt. Printing Office.)

Catoe, Lynn E.: *UFOs and Related Subjects: An Annotated Bibliography.* (A survey compiled by the Library of Congress, at the request of the Office of Aerospace Research, U.S. Air Force). U.S. Govt. Printing Office, Washington, D.C., 1969.

McDonald, Dr. James E.: *Unidentified Flying Objects: The Greatest Scientific Problem of our Times.* NICAP, Washington, D.C., 1968.

Condon, Dr. Edward U.: *The Condon Report: A Scientific Study of Unidentified Flying Objects.* Bantam Books, N.Y., 1969.

Saunders, Dr. David: *UFOs? Yes!: Where the Condon Committee went Wrong.* Signet Books and New English Library paperback edition, N.Y., 1970.

Maney, Professor C.A., and Hall, Richard: *The Challenge of Unidentified Flying Objects.* With a foreword by Dr. Charles P. Olivier, President, American Meteor Society, and Emeritus Professor of Astronomy, University of Pennsylvania. Published by the National Investigations Committee on Aerial Phenomena (NICAP), Washington, D.C., 1961.

Bowen, Charles (Editor): *The Humanoids: A Survey of World-Wide Reports of Landings of Unconventional Aerial Objects and their Alleged Occupants.* Flying Saucer Review Special Issue, October-November, 1966. Hardback expanded edition issued by Neville Spearman, London, 1969. Now in paperback edition by Futura Books, London. U.S. edition by Henry Regnery Co., Chicago. (Japanese, Spanish, French and Italian translations have also been issued.)

Ruppelt, Capt. Edward J.: *The Report on Unidentified Flying Objects.* Doubleday, N.Y., 1956. (In this book the author, who had formerly been in charge of the U.S. Air Force's UFO Investigations (*Project Blue Book*), admitted the reality of the phenomena and strongly hinted at an extraterrestrial source. But pressure was brought to bear upon him, and in a fresh edition of the book, he changed several chapters and the original impact of the work was nullified.) A British edition of the original version was issued in London by Victor Gollancz in 1956.

Michel, Aimé: *Mystérieux Objets Célestes.* Arthaud, Paris, 1958. (An English translation was issued by Criterion Books, N.Y., in 1958, under the title of *Flying Saucers and the Straight Line Mystery.*)

Michel, Aimé: *Lueurs sur les Soucoupes Volantes*. An English edition was issued by Robert Hale, London, as *The Truth About Flying Saucers*, 1957. Re-issued as paperback by Corgi Books, 1958, and Pyramid Books, 1967.

Vallée, Dr. Jacques, and Vallée, Janine: *Les Phénomènes Insolites de l'Espace*. La Table Ronde, Paris, 1966. (This is an expanded French version of Dr Vallée's earlier work *Challenge to Science: The UFO Enigma*, published in 1966 by Henry Regnery Co., Chicago, and Neville Spearman, London, 1967.)

Vallée, Dr. Jacques: *Anatomy of a Phenomenon: Unidentified Objects in Space — A Scientific Appraisal*. Henry Regnery Co., Chicago, 1965, and Neville Spearman, London, 1966.

Vallée, Dr. Jacques: *Passport to Magonia: From Folklore to Flying Saucers*. Henry Regnery Co., Chicago, 1969. English edition by Neville Spearman, 1970. Paperback edition by Tandem, London, 1975.

Vallée, Dr. Jacques: *Le Collège Invisible*. Editions Albin Michel, Paris, 1975. English translation, *The Invisible College*, by Dutton, N.Y., 1975.

Lagarde, F., Michel, Aimé, Vallée, Jacques, and colleagues: *Mystérieuses Soucoupes Volantes*. Published by Lumières Dans La Nuit, Le Chambon-sur-Lignon, France, 1974.

Blum, Ralph, and Blum, Judy: *Beyond Earth: Man's Contact with UFOs*. Bantam paperback, N.Y., 1974. British edition by Corgi paperbacks, 1974.

Sagan, Dr. Carl: *The Cosmic Connection: An Extraterrestrial Perspective*. N.Y., 1973. British edition by Hodder & Stoughton (Coronet Paperbacks), 1974.

Sagan, Dr. Carl, and Page, Thornton: *UFOs: A Scientific Debate*. N.Y., 1973.

Shklovskiy, I.S., and Sagan, C.: *Intelligent Life in the Universe*. N.Y.

Jung, Dr. Carl G.: *Flying Saucers: A Modern Myth of Things Seen in the Skies*. Translated from the German original edition, and published by Routledge and Kegan Paul, London, 1959. (An important book. The public has not understood that Jung uses the term "myth" not in the modern, popular sense, but in the old Greek sense of something *"more than real"*, or *archetypal*.)

Ballester-Olmos, J.-V.: *A Catalogue of 200 Type-1 UFO Events over Spain and Portugal*. Published by Dr

Hynek's Center for UFO Studies, Evanston, Illinois, 1976.

Chapman, Robert (Science Correspondent, *Sunday Express*): *Unidentified Flying Objects*. Arthur Barker, London, 1969. Re-issued as paperback, *UFO: Flying Saucers Over Britain?*, Mayflower Books, 1969.

Clark, Jerome, and Coleman, Loren: *The Unidentified*. Warner Books, N.Y., 1976.

Goddard, Air Vice-Marshal Sir Victor: *Flight Towards Reality*. Turnstone Books, London, 1976.

Zigel', Yuri F.: *UFO Observations in the USSR*. (In Russian.) 1974.

Jacobs, Dr. David: *The UFO Controversy in America*. Indiana University Press, 1975.

James, Trevor (pseudonym of Trevor James Constable): *They Live in the Sky!: Invisible, Incredible UFO around us*. New Age Publishing Co., Los Angeles, 1958.

Constable, Trevor James: *The Cosmic Pulse of Life: The Revolutionary Biological Power Behind UFOs*. Merlin Press, Santa Ana, Calif., 1976. (British edition to be published by Neville Spearman, 1977.)

Puharich, Dr. Andrija, M.D.: *URI: The Original and Authorized Biography of Uri Geller — the Man who baffles the Scientists*. Lab Nine Ltd., U.S.A., 1974. British edition by W.H. Allen, London, 1974.

Geller, Uri: *My Story*. Robson Books Ltd., London, 1975.

Salisbury, Dr. Frank B.: *The Utah UFO Display: A Biologist's Report*. Devin-Adair Co., Greenwich, Conn., 1974.

Creighton, Gordon: *A New Catalogue: the Effects of UFOs on Animals, Birds, and Smaller Creatures*. (219 cases, from all over the world, up to year 1968.) In *Flying Saucer Review*, Vol. 16, No. 1, to Vol. 18, No. 3.

Part II   A Selection of the Principal Background and
Investigatory Books
(In alphabetical order of authors)

Arnold, Kenneth, and Palmer, Ray: *The Coming of the Saucers*. Published Palmer, U.S.A., 1952.

Barker, Gray: *They Knew Too Much About Flying Saucers*. Tower Books, N.Y., 1967.

Barker, Gray: *The Silver Bridge*. Gray Barker Publications, Clarksburg, W. Virginia, 1970.

Bender, Albert K.: *Flying Saucers and the Three Men*. N.Y. U.K. edition by Neville Spearman, London, 1963.

Cade, C. Maxwell: *Other Worlds than Ours*. Museum Press, London, 1966.

Cramp, Leonard: *Space, Gravity and the Flying Saucer*. Werner Laurie, London, 1954.

Cramp, Leonard: *Piece for a Jig-Saw*. Somerton Publishing Co., 1966.

Eden, Jerome: *Orgone Energy: The Answer to Atomic Suicide*. Exposition Press, N.Y., 1972.

Eden, Jerome: *Planet in Trouble; The UFO Assault on Earth*. Exposition Press, N.Y., 1973.

Edwards, Frank: *Flying Saucers: Serious Business*. Lyle Stuart, N.Y., 1966. Paperback edition, Bantam Books, N.Y., 1966.

Edwards, Frank: *Flying Saucers — Here and Now!*. Lyle Stuart, N.Y., 1967. Paperback edition, Bantam Books, N.Y., 1968. (British paperback editions also appeared.)

Fowler, Raymond E.: *UFOs: Interplanetary Visitors*. Exposition Press, N.Y., 1975.

Fuller, John G.: *The Interrupted Journey*. Dial Press, N.Y., 1966.

Fuller, John G.: *Incident at Exeter*. Putnam, N.Y.

Heard, Gerald: *The Riddle of the Flying Saucers*. Carrol & Nicholson, London, 1950.

Hervey, Michael: *UFOs over the Southern Hemisphere*. Robert Hale, London, 1975.

Girvan, Waveney: *Flying Saucers and Commonsense*. Frederick Muller, London, 1955. (A useful little "classic", long out 'of print, by the first Editor of *Flying Saucer Review*.)

Jessup, Dr. M.K.: *The Case for the UFO*. Citadel Press, N.Y. U.K. edition by Arco Publications, London.

Jessup, Dr. M.K.: *The Expanding Case for the UFO*. U.K. edition by Arco, 1957.

Jessup, Dr. M.K.: *UFO Yearbook for 1956*. N.Y. U.K. edition by Arco Publications, 1957.

Jessup, Dr. M.K.: *UFOs and the Bible*. Citadel Press, N.Y., 1956.

Barker, Gray: *The Strange Case of M.K. Jessup*. (The "suicide" of Dr. Jessup in 1959 may — like certain other deaths — possibly not have been contrived by the victim.)

Keel, John: *UFOs. Operation Trojan Horse*. Putnam, N.Y., 1970. Souvenir Press, London, under title *Operation Trojan Horse*, 1971.

Keel, John: *Strange Creatures from Time and Space*. Fawcett Gold Medal paperbacks, N.Y., 1970. Neville Spearman, London, 1975 (hardback). Sphere Books, London (paperback), 1975.

Keel, John: *Our Haunted Planet.* N.Y., 1971. U.K. edition by Neville Spearman (hardback), 1971.

Keel, John: *The Mothman Prophecies.* Dutton, N.Y., 1975.

Keel, John: *The Eighth Tower.* Dutton, N.Y., 1975.

Keyhoe, Major Donald E.: *Flying Saucers From Outer Space.* Henry Holt, 1953. British paperback editions by Hutchinson (Arrow Books), 1954, and Universal-Tandem Books, 1970, 1973, 1974.

Keyhoe, Major Donald E.: *The Flying Saucer Conspiracy.* U.S. edition (Doubleday?), 1957. Hutchinson, London, 1957.

Keyhoe, Major Donald E.: *Flying Saucers: Top Secret.* Putnam, N.Y., 1960. (An important book, seemingly never reprinted?)

Keyhoe, Major Donald E.: *Aliens From Space ... The Real Story of Unidentified Flying Objects.* Doubleday, N.Y., 1973. Panther paperback edition, London, 1975.

Lane, Meade: *The Coming of the Guardians.* Published 1958 by the Borderland Sciences Research Associates (BSRA), San Diego, California.

Leslie, Desmond, and Adamski, George: *Flying Saucers Have Landed.* Original edition by Werner Laurie, London, 1953. Revised and enlarged edition by Desmond Leslie, published by Neville Spearman, London, 1970. (An important book, though intensely controversial, because it contains the first widely reported claim of "contact" with "other beings." In the early years it was generally dismissed as a fabrication. More thoughtful students of the subject perceive today however that Adamski may not have been the hoaxer at all, but himself the victim of hoax and deception practised by nonhumans.)

Lorenzen, Coral: *Flying Saucers: The Startling Evidence for the Invasion from Outer Space.* Paperback, Signet Books, N.Y., 1966. (Originally published in U.S.A. in hardback edition as *The Great Flying Saucer Hoax.*)

Lorenzen, Coral and Jim: *Flying Saucer Occupants.* Signet Books, N.Y., 1967.

Lorenzen, Coral and Jim: *UFOs Over the Americas.* Signet Books, N.Y., 1968.

Lorenzen, Coral and Jim: *UFOs: The Whole Story.* Signet Books, N.Y., 1969.

Michell, John: *The Flying Saucer Vision.* Sidgwick & Jackson, London, 1967.

Sanderson, Dr. Ivan T.: *Uninvited Visitors.* Cowles Book Co., N.Y., 1968. Neville Spearman, London, 1969.

Sanderson, Dr. Ivan T.: *Invisible Residents.* World Publishing Co., U.S.A., 1970. Paperback by Tandem Books, London, 1970.

Sanderson, Dr. Ivan T.: *Things.* Paperback, U.S.A.

Sanderson, Dr. Ivan T.: *More Things.* Paperback, U.S.A.

Sanderson, Dr. Ivan T.: *Investigating the Unexplained.* Prentice-Hall, N.Y., 1972.

Scully, Frank: *Behind the Flying Saucers.* One of the earliest UFO books. First published in the U.S.A. in 1950. British edition by Victor Gollancz in 1950, re-issued in 1955. Most folk seem satisfied nowadays that the main story, about two saucers alleged to have crash-landed in the American south-west, each with sixteen small dead men aboard, is entirely fraudulent. There are however many reasons why the book is still well worth reading. Much of the other material in it is unquestionably authentic (and very early).

Steiger, Brad: *Strange Disappearances.* (Paperback, U.S.A.).

Steiger, Brad, and Roberts, August C.: *Enemies from Outer Space: The Flying Saucer Menace.* Award Books, paperback, N.Y., 1967.

Steiger, Brad, and Whritenour, Joan: *Flying Saucers Are Hostile.* Paperback, N.Y., 1968. Tandem Books, London, 1968.

Steiger, Brad, and Whritenour, Joan: *Strangers From the Skies.* Paperback, N.Y. Tandem Books, London, 1968.

Steiger, Brad, and Whritenour, Joan: *UFO Breakthrough.* Award Books, N.Y. Tandem Books, London, 1968.

Trench, Hon. Brinsley le Poer: *The Sky People.* Neville Spearman, London, 1960.

Trench, Hon. Brinsley le Poer: *Men Among Mankind.* Neville Spearman, London, 1963.

Trench, Hon. Brinsley le Poer: *Forgotten Heritage.* Neville Spearman, London, 1965.

Trench, Hon. Brinsley le Poer: *The Flying Saucer Story.* Neville Spearman, London, 1966 and Tandem paperback, 1973.

Trench, Hon. Brinsley le Poer: *Operation Earth.* Neville Spearman, London, 1969.

Wilkins, Harold T.: *Flying Saucers on the Moon.* Peter

Owen, London, 1954. (Published in U.S.A. as *Flying Saucers on the Attack*.)

Wilkins, Harold T.: *Flying Saucers Uncensored*. Arco, London, 1956.

Part III   Some Background Reading

Blatty, William Peter: *The Exorcist*. 1971. Corgi Books, London, 1972.

Blavatsky, Helena Petrovna: *Isis Unveiled*. London, 1877.

Blavatsky, Helena Petrovna: *The Secret Doctrine*. London, 1888.

Briggs, K.M.: *The Fairies in Tradition and Literature*. Routledge, Kegan Paul, London, 1967.

Evans-Wentz, Dr. W.Y.: *The Fairy Faith in Celtic Countries*, 1911. Reprinted by University Books, N.Y., 1966.

Fairfax, Edward: *Daemonologia: A Discourse on Witchcraft*. c.1621. (Not published until 1859. Republished by Ackrill in 1882. Facsimile reprint by Frederick Muller, London, 1971.)

Fort, Charles: *The Books of: (The Book of the Damned; Lo!; New Lands; Wild Talents*.) Henry Holt & Co., N.Y., 1941.

Kirk, Robert: *The Secret Commonwealth of Elves, Fauns and Fairies*. 1691. Pub. with comment by Andrew Lang, 1893. Reprinted by Eneas Mackay, Stirling, Scotland, 1933.

Michelet, J.: *Satanism and Witchcraft*. Citadel Press, N.Y., 1939.

Oesterreich, Prof. T.K.: *Possession, Demoniacal and Other*. Paul, Trench and Trubner, London, 1930.

Rawcliffe, D.H.: *Illusions and Delusions of the Supernatural and the Occult*. Dover Publications, N.Y., 1959.

Sargent, William. *Battle for the Mind*. Heinemann, London, 1957.

Scot, R.: *The Discoverie of Witchcraft*. 1584. Reprinted by Rodker, London, 1930.

Spence, Lewis: *The Fairy Tradition in Britain*. Rider, London, 1948.

Summers, Rev. Montagu: *The History of Witchcraft and Demonology*. Routledge, Kegan Paul, London, 1926.

Summers, Rev. Montagu: *Witchcraft and Black Magic*. Rider, London, 1946.

Summers, Rev. Montagu: Translation of *Malleus Maleficarium*, (15th century handbook for witch-hunters). Pushkin Press, London, 1928.

Thurston, Rev. Herbert, S.J.: *The Physical Phenomena of Mysticism.* Watkins, London, 1951.

Homer: *The Iliad.*

The Rāmāyana.

The Mahābharata.

The Koran, and *Islamic texts of Sufism.*

Mahayana Buddhism. Chinese and Tibetan texts.

Popol Vuh: The Sacred Book of the Quiché Maya. Adrian Recinos. English translation by Delia Goetz and Sylvanus G. Morley. Wm. Hodge & Co., London, 1951.

Mythology of Greece and Rome.

Mythology of the Celts.

Mythology of the Norsemen.

Mythology of the Hindus.

Mythology of the Chinese.

Mythology of the Tibetans.

Mythology of the Japanese.

Mythology of the Aztecs and Mayas.

Mythology of the American Indians.

The Bible.

(Everyone interested in UFOs and other strange phenomena is urged to write to Neville Armstrong, Flying Saucer Information, 3 Broad Oak, Groom Bridge, Near Tunbridge Wells, Kent, for details of new books and publications on the subject as they are published. Please enclose stamped addressed envelope.)